# Also by Vincent Schiavelli

# Vincent Schiavelli

ILLUSTRATIONS BY SANTO LIPANI

SIMON & SCHUSTER

NEW YORK   LONDON   TORONTO   SYDNEY   SINGAPORE

# Many Beautiful Things

### Stories and Recipes
### from Polizzi Generosa

SIMON & SCHUSTER
Rockefeller Center
1230 Avenue of the Americas
New York, NY 10020

SIMON & SCHUSTER and colophon are registered trademarks
of Simon & Schuster, Inc.

For information regarding special discounts for bulk purchases,
please contact Simon & Schuster Special Sales at 1-800-456-6798
or business@simonandschuster.com

Designed by Karolina Harris

Manufactured in the United States of America

10  9  8  7  6  5  4  3  2  1

Library of Congress Cataloging-in-Publication Data
Schiavelli, Vincent.
    Many beautiful things : stories and recipes from Polizzi Generosa / [Vincent Schiavelli ; illustrations by
Santo Lipani].
        p.   cm.
    Includes index.
        1. Cookery, Italian.  2. Cookery—Polizzi Generosa (Italy)  3. Polizzi Generosa (Italy)—Social life and
customs.  I. Title.
TX723 .S364      2002
641.59458—dc21          2002075512

ISBN 0-7432-1528-1

*For Carol,*

*my angel*

# Contents

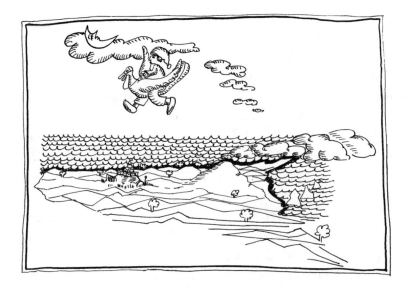

As we grow, there is a point in childhood when our vision of the world widens. We begin to understand, in a very rudimentary way, that we are part of something larger than the boundaries of home and family. For example, learning our last names, addresses, and telephone numbers helps place us in this big new world.

Among my earlier recollections of learning these details—Schiavelli, 1264 Myrtle Avenue, Glenmore 2-2543, Brooklyn, America—there is another place-name as deep and as old in my memory: Polizzi Generosa.

My grandparents Carolina (Vilardi) and Andrea Coco had separately emigrated from this small city in the Madonie Mountains of Sicily at the turn of the twentieth century. She had been a schoolteacher and he a master chef, a *monzù*. I grew up in their household, learning Sicilian as a close second language to English.

After school, I would sit at one end of the kitchen table and do my home-work as my grandfather stood at the other end preparing dinner. The *monzù* chose to share all his culinary secrets with me, secrets guarded over a lifetime. While Papa Andrea worked, both he and my grandmother told me endless, wondrous stories about Polizzi Generosa; stories about a magical land where prickly pears and figs abounded, watermelons were round, and artichokes could be eaten whole.

They told me about their own childhoods and of their grandparents. Sometimes the stories had lessons, but always they were a look at a world far different from mine, although people there lived by the same rules as they did in our urban Sicilian-American neighborhood.

I listened to these stories over and over, always hearing them as if for the first time, even though the words and phrasing never varied. As I grew older, I understood them as part of my heritage.

My grandmother died in 1960. In 1968, when I was twenty, my grandfa-ther died at ninety-six, but their stories of nineteenth-century Polizzi Generosa are still vivid in my mind and heart. And the great gift of food Papa Andrea gave me is still alive at my table.

As years passed, Polizzi Generosa became to me more mythic than real. I could never find it on any map. College, relationships, working as an actor in Los Angeles, and all the other joys and responsibilities of life served to post-pone a Sicilian quest. It wasn't until I was nearly forty that I made my first trip to Polizzi. What I found there in 1988, and what I continue to discover on each return, is far more extraordinary than I ever could have imagined: the "once upon a time" of my childhood.

The beautiful city of Polizzi Generosa is perched three thousand feet above sea level, nestled at the edge of a pristine mountain national park. Un-touched by fire, flood, or war for centuries, Polizzi looks virtually the same as it did in the eighteenth century, and more recently in my grandparents' day. Carolina's and Andrea's descriptions of churches, convents, palazzi, even spe-cific streets and balconies are accurate even today.

Although the population of Polizzi sadly dwindles each year, the people diligently maintain their culture and traditions, like an eternal flame to an an-cient goddess. Their integrity, pride, intelligence, grace, and generosity have been nurtured by a unique history.

In the seventh century B.C.E., the ancient Greeks invaded and colonized

Trinacria, the Mediterranean island known today as Sicily. The Greeks introduced the olive tree to this fertile land, and Sicily soon became their major source of olive oil. Although the specific origins of Polizzi remain in archeological debate, all agree that the colony was established during this period. Most scholars believe a Grecian cult devoted to the Egyptian goddess Isis came to Sicily, seeking freedom from religious persecution. Its members established an outpost in the mountains of northwestern Sicily, far from the major Greek settlements of the eastern and southern regions. They named it *Polis Isis*, the City of Isis. At its center they built a temple to their goddess.

The Romans, during their later occupation, built roads, aqueducts, fortifications, and country villas in and around Polizzi. The mountain forests were clear-cut to provide timber for Roman warships. Agriculture was intensified, and all of Sicily became known as "the granary of Rome."

The oldest surviving written record of Polizzi is dated 880, from the Byzantine period; a fortress built a century earlier is referenced in this document. The ruins of this fortress still grace the cityscape.

In 882, Polizzi was conquered by the Saracens. People still live in the low, connected, stucco-covered houses remaining from that time. The streets of this section of town twist and turn like an ancient casbah. At its center, a minaret reaches toward heaven, reconsecrated almost a millennium ago as the bell tower of a Roman Catholic church.

North African rule, although lasting for only two centuries more than a thousand years ago, has made an indelible mark on Polizzani culture and cuisine. Incomparable hospitality, the traditional code of propriety between men and women, even the rigid concepts of respect and vendetta—all of these embody a worldview that is more Levantine than European.

The Saracens brought pasta, almonds, and the spices of the East, such as saffron and cinnamon, to the table. They were the first to refine sugar and to explore the art of confectionery and pastry-making. Most important, however, the culturally advanced North Africans introduced Polizzi to the very notion of cuisine.

At that time, and in most of Europe for centuries to follow, rich and poor ate the same fare; the only difference was that the rich ate more of it. The Saracens, however, followed a grand tradition of dining rather than of feeding. Refined cooking techniques, meals served in courses, and the use of exotic golden spices, all new concepts for the Sicilians, were quickly embraced.

• • •

A generation before the Norman conquest of England in 1066, a powerful coalition of Greeks and Byzantines formed to hire the Norman army to expel the Arabs from Sicily. When the Normans saw the wonders of Sicily, they decided to break their mercenary agreement and take the island for themselves.

The "other" Norman conquest was accomplished by 1080. By 1071, Polizzi and the region of the Madonie Mountains was under Norman occupation. Within a hundred years, the island would lose its place as the geographic center of the Arab world, as a link between North Africa and the Middle East. Ever after, Sicily has been considered a southern outpost of Europe, always occupied but, as the Polizzani say, "never conquered." Some maintain that Sicily is still occupied — by the Italians.

Holy Roman Emperor Federico II was the grandson of the Swabian ruler Barbarossa. His mother was Norman, and through her line he became the hereditary King of Sicily. While Federico was still a boy, his father died. His "uncles," German nobles, usurped the kingdom and kept the boy-king and his mother, the queen, captive in the royal castle at Palermo. When the boy reached his majority, the queen found a way of escape and Federico was crowned Holy Roman Emperor.

In 1234, Federico II was in the midst of a fourteen-year military campaign. His objective was to regain control of his island. The long campaign was not going well, and the Emperor was not having a good time. He longed for the magnificent pleasures of his court, which included a seraglio. The lavish oriental style Federico maintained in Palermo had prompted the Pope to sarcastically dub him "The Baptized Sultan."

Federico needed to furlough his battle-weary troops and to rest himself. The mountaintop town of Polizzi, easily secured because of its geographic position, seemed like a good stopping place. He fully expected to find its populace, at the very least, indifferent to his condition, but to his surprise, Federico and his army were received with open arms.

So moved was he by the generous hospitality he encountered during his time there, Federico decreed henceforth the place would be called Polizzi *la Generosa*. In a second, more important, decree, he gave Polizzi the status of *città demaniale*, a city of the dominion. This meant that Polizzi would have a seat in the Sicilian parliament of the day and be under the direct rule of the king. The city would be free to make its own civic decisions without the intrusion of barons or other feudal lords. Until the unification of Italy six hundred years later, this status was reconfirmed by succeeding rulers of Sicily.

The city was granted its own coat of arms. In it is pictured the crowned imperial eagle, standing against a gold background. A shield on his chest contains the image of seven roses, representing the seven sections of the city. Caught in his talons is a banner that reads *Politium Generosa Civitas*, the City of Polizzi Generosa.

Polizzi Generosa flourished and prospered over the next seven centuries, growing to become the educational, cultural, and social center of the region. To this day, the Polizzani show an enlightened, free spirit unlike the populations of other nearby towns with less independent pasts.

Local lore hints that the ensuing improvement in the fortunes of Federico II was attributable to the clear mountain air, the serene setting, and the delicious, wholesome food he enjoyed during his sojourn in Polizzi Generosa. And perhaps this footnote to history is responsible, indeed, for turning Federico II into the preeminent ruler of the age, known to this day as *Stupor Mundi*, the Wonder of the World.

The anchor for this book is food. Over the centuries, Polizzi has developed a cuisine as unique as its history and as striking as its bucolic mountain setting. Millennia of occupation can be traced through the Polizzani cupboard. Olives from ancient Greece; almonds, spices, and sugar from North Africa; and tomatoes, potatoes, squashes, beans, peppers, and prickly pears from the Western Hemisphere by way of Spain are a few examples of the many imports that fill this cornucopia of edible culture.

What people eat and when they eat it is determined by seasonal availability, tradition, and good planning. Since the Middle Ages, homemade liquers have been popular in Polizzi. Through a simple process of maceration, fruits, herbs, and nuts are transformed into delicious, brilliantly colored cordials and after-dinner drinks. Canning, preserving, and sun-drying all play an important role in bringing the sweetness of summer to the winter's table. In Polizzi Generosa, a family's true wealth is calculated according to the cleverness with which these tasks have been accomplished and by the bounty of its cupboard.

This simple, frankly rustic cuisine, still enjoyed today, also has an enchanting playfulness about it. Literal translations of recipe titles produce such whimsical phrases as "Drowned Lettuce Soup," "Cauliflower Under Siege," and "Almond Love Bites."

The wisdom and skill of many people, both home cooks and professionals, are included in these recipes. In Polizzi, culinary expertise is divided into two categories: those who cook and eat, and those who don't cook but still eat heartily, knowing every recipe in minute (sometimes tedious) detail.

Many of the recipes that follow were shared by friends and relatives. In 1987, the *Associazione Culturale Naftolia*, the local Polizzani cultural organization, published a community cookbook. Charmingly titled *Polizzi, Generosa Anche a Tavola (Polizzi, Generous Also at the Table)*, the book contains recipes authored by men and women of the city. A number of the recipes in this book are from that source.

As originally offered, orally or written, all of these recipes were intended for an audience that already knows them. Quantities were given in "handfuls of this" or "ladlefuls of that." A more enigmatic measurement used for everything from salt to tomato sauce is *q.b., quanta basta,* "whatever is enough."

I have translated and adapted these recipes to a format more suitable for the American cook. When necessary, ingredient substitutions have been noted, but happily, most of the traditional ones can easily be found in this country.

The key to Polizzani cuisine is utter simplicity. The actual taste of the main ingredient is always spotlighted, and changing one ingredient can produce an entirely different-tasting result. Centuries of refinement provide the counterpoint and complexity of flavor. There is an old Sicilian saying, easily adopted for the Polizzani table:

> *Quannu i Polizzani si fannu i casi,*
> *Pensanu c'annu a campari pi mill'anni.*
> *Ma quannu mancianu,*
> *Pensanu c'annu a muriri u nnumani.*

When the Polizzani build their houses,
They think they're going to live for a thousand years.
But when they eat,
They think they're going to die tomorrow.

I welcome you to this place of delicious imagination. I hope that the following pages will provide a panorama of the people, culture, and food of this ancient jewel of the Madonie. I hope that the so many beautiful things of Polizzi Generosa will find a place in your heart, and at your table, as they have for me.

# Many Beautiful Things

# One

# My First Visit

*F*irst impressions are often accurate. They may not provide the whole story about a person or a place, but the insight they offer becomes a lasting reference point. My first visit to Polizzi Generosa, a place familiar through my grandparents' stories yet physically unknown to me, falls into exactly this category.

The weeks before my first trip to Sicily in 1988 were an exciting time in my life, a time of renewal and beginnings. I had spent September working on a film in France for the first time. At the beginning of October, I met an American harpist, Carol Mukhalian, who was living and working in Paris. As destiny would have it, it was love at first sight.

I had planned to go to Sicily after the Paris trip. I wondered if anyone named Vilardi, my grandmother's family name, was still alive. Since the emigration of my grandparents' generation nearly a hundred years ago, contact with the Sicilian part of the family had virtually ceased.

The only clue I had was from Angelina, one of my grandmother's first cousins. She had told me that we have a cousin who plays the tuba in the Police Band of Rome. But that was twenty years ago, and beyond that, I knew nothing of my Sicilian relatives. Having never found Polizzi Generosa on any map, it would be a true journey of discovery. When I told Carol of my plans, she agreed to join me.

We thought it best to travel as husband and wife. We had a hard enough time explaining to ourselves what was happening between us; a more traditional culture, we were certain, would not understand at all. Carol always wore an antique diamond and sapphire band on her right hand. She asked me if I would place it on the fourth finger of her left hand, and when I stopped shaking, we were on our way from Paris to Palermo.

The connecting flight from Milano to Palermo was impossibly delayed. I had managed to phone our hotel, the Grande Albergo della Palme (the Grand Hotel of the Palms), from Milano and asked to have a cold supper placed in our room for our midnight arrival.

When we finally arrived, we could see that the Grand Hotel must have been truly grand once, but time and neglect had taken their toll. Even the palms showed the wear of war and occupation. A diffident, aged bellman ceremoniously led us into a miniature modern elevator, and then down an endless twenty-foot-wide corridor to our room. Upon opening the door, I noticed first of all a hat rack. I always wear a hat and have observed that the modern world offers few places to hang one.

In a corner of the ample, high-ceilinged room was a small table set with two places. Under the protection of starched white linen napkins was laid the cold supper: chicken baked with garlic, herbs, and orange juice, green bean salad in a vinegary dressing, and potato salad with olive oil, capers, and onions. There was a chilled bottle of Sicilian white wine from the Regaliali winery and one of mineral water.

Dessert was a bowl of perfectly ripe fresh fruit. The pears seemed to cry when we peeled them, their flavor sweet and perfumy with an ever-so-slight astringency. Without doubt we were in Sicily. The thrill of our being there together kept us up until dawn.

The next afternoon, we bought a road map. For the first time I saw the name "Polizzi Generosa" printed on a map. My eyes filled at the reality: This place of childhood myth really does exist.

We rented a car, a Renault Cinque with Milano license plates. It took only the four-block drive from rental office to hotel to understand that in Palermo, to relinquish the right of way holds the same social status as being cuckolded. There are fewer traffic lights than Americans are used to, and their signals are mostly ignored anyway. To traverse an intersection, one must simply pull out into the chaos, leaving oneself in the hands of fate. Being in a small French car with continental plates gave us no primacy whatsoever in this madness.

Our destination, Polizzi Generosa, lay about seventy miles southeast of

Palermo. The last quarter of the trip was on a two-lane state road that turns off the main coastal highway just past the city of Termini Imerese. When we reached this junction, it was dusk. Above us in the distance were the lights of Polizzi. As we wound our way up and around the mountain, the city would disappear, then reappear larger, closer, like a series of stop-motion photographs. Sooner than seemed possible, after a perilous set of switchbacks, a large sign proclaimed *Welcome to Polizzi Generosa* in several languages.

Our arrival, while momentous for Carol and me, was hardly noticed by the men at their work on the outskirts of town. I asked a garage mechanic, in my best Sicilian, if he knew of a hotel in town. He graciously answered with great formality that unfortunately there wasn't a hotel in town, but there was one in the countryside below, the Villa Cariddi.

We wound our way back down the mountain and, following his directions, turned through an open gate into a courtyard. Before us was a charming little villa. In one room near the window, a grandmother sat crocheting. We had obviously turned into the wrong driveway, since the woman pretended not to notice us. We probably could have stayed parked in her courtyard all night. After all, this was Sicily, and what these strangers were doing in her courtyard was certainly none of her business.

I tapped on her window. She opened it. I respectfully apologized for the intrusion and said that I believed I'd made a mistake. With a warm, pleasant smile, she said, "Perhaps. But if you are looking for the Villa Cariddi, it is the next house up the road."

The Villa Cariddi was a strangely austere Sicilian baroque structure. The windows were shuttered, the grounds overgrown. The property was filled with howling cats in heat. At first impression it seemed abandoned, but wisps of light seeping through the cracks in the shutters, and the wonderful aroma of cooking, implied otherwise.

Carol waited in the car as I walked up to the massive door and knocked. I expected it would be opened by a kindly grandfather not unlike my own. The door swung open wide, filling the courtyard with light and noise from a bustling room. The porter was not a sage old man in a well-worn cardigan at all, but a young man wearing a Brooks Brothers–like button-down shirt and a crew-neck sweater.

He rudely asked, "What do *you* want?" Thrown by his greeting, I mustered enough Sicilian to explain that we were looking for board and lodging.

With flat indifference, he answered, "We are full," and slammed the door, leaving us in the darkness with the cats.

I looked to Carol for encouragement and knocked again. He opened. I asked if there were any other places he could recommend. He said, "To tell the truth, there are other places, but they are difficult to find, there are no telephones, and only I know where they are."

I knew what he was getting at, but his manner was rather disappointing. Instead of crossing his palm with silver, I quipped, "So, if you please, tell me something: How do they find clients?" He laughed coldly, slamming the door in my face once more. I turned and walked back to the car. Without understanding a word, Carol knew what had happened. She suggested that we go back to town for another look around.

We returned up the perilous route to Polizzi. Around the bend from the mechanics, we found a pizzeria. We stopped for a coffee and to regroup. The place was named *Il Pioniere,* The Pioneer, and was oddly decorated with large original paintings of the American Old West. In the center of the large room, well-worn rustic tables and benches made of split logs completed the theme. Near the bar, at small café tables and chairs, sat a group of old men drinking coffee. We stood at the bar and drank ours. The room rumbled with the same kind of silence as in a western movie when the stranger walks into the saloon.

I asked the man behind the bar if he knew of any hotels. He sang out, "The Villa Cariddi." I told him that we had already been there and that it was full. I asked if there were any others. He nervously answered, "I don't know. I don't know." Suddenly, one of the old men stood up and declaimed in a loud voice, "You know what you should do?" And then to the crowd, "You know what they should do?" Everyone held his breath. He continued, "You should go to the *Università della Muratori."* I translated for Carol, explaining that he said we should go to the "University of the Bricklayers." She rolled her eyes. I, uncertain of his meaning, asked if this was a hotel. "Yes," he said. "It has an odd name but it is comfortable, with very good food. The owner is named Santo Lipani. Be sure to tell him that the *Distribbuturu Agip* sent you." At first I thought this was some grand municipal title, but soon realized that this gentleman was the distributor or owner of an Agip-brand gasoline station.

As the kind gentleman was giving us directions, the barman magically remembered that he had, behind the bar, a stack of brochures for the place. Carol and I exchanged a glance but said nothing.

After the business of hotel directions was settled, I mentioned that my grandmother was Polizzani. The distributor said, "I know that. I can hear it in your accent." All of the old men now smiled and nodded at us.

I realized that everyone we had come in contact with knew exactly why I had come to Polizzi Generosa. Their code of respect prevented them from speaking to the issue; they would not invade my privacy. But now that I had brought it up, they were free to ask my family's name.

"Vi-lar-di," the distributor pronounced carefully. He said it again almost in a whisper, building the drama of the moment. He became lost in great brow-knitting thought. Finally he said, "There is a barber here with that name who has a brother who plays tuba in the Police Band of Rome."

"My God!" I almost shouted, "that's my cousin!"

With a fatherly attitude, the gentleman told me to calm down. "It's late now," he said. "Go to the hotel, have a nice dinner, rest, and tomorrow come back to town and you'll find your cousin Giuseppe Vilardi." I thanked him and we finally shook hands. As we left, all of the old men came to the door to see us off.

Soon we were down the mountain again and turning onto the dirt road leading to the University of the Bricklayers. The night was cold, foggy, and dark, the road muddy and rutted. A light, barely visible in the distance, encouraged our progress. When we grew closer, the outline of a square, rustic two-story building could be seen.

I parked the Renault in the courtyard and we entered a warm room, over-lit by fluorescent lights and cozy from the fire in an enormous hearth. At the far corner sat two men eating *pasta fasoli,* macaroni and beans. They were shocked to see these two strangers on their threshold. I asked for Signur Santo Lipani and one of them came forward. He was in his mid-thirties, squarely built with fair skin, reddish hair, and a large blond mustache. The other man, of similar age but thin and dark, introduced himself as Domenico.

There was a room available; in fact the place was empty. He asked if we were hungry. He showed us to our room and said dinner would be ready in twenty minutes. I thanked him, using the old Sicilian formal pronoun, *vossia.* He said, "We are in the country here. It is very peaceful, serene. There is no need to be formal, no reason to call each other *vossia.* We can use *tu.*"

The room was charming. A good bed, covered in a brightly colored quilt, filled most of the tiled floor. The tile continued past a door into the bath. The casement windows had beautifully carpentered shutters with hand-forged wrought-iron latches. The room was cold and had that sweet smell rooms acquire deep in the country. Although not yet eight o'clock, the peacefulness of the night was broken only by the wind and an occasional barking dog.

We lugged in our bags (I always carry too much and so, it turns out, does Carol), washed up, and returned to the main room. A table close to the fire had been laid with a crisp oilcloth and set for two. The dinner began slowly, with a modest antipasto of salami, olives, and bread. The flavors, however, were rich with country Sicilian robustness.

We "oohed" gleefully at the incredible flavor of the salami. Santo explained that this salami was made locally from pigs raised in the traditional way—herded, not penned. The animals forage the hillsides, eating chestnuts before the time of their slaughter. The meat has a delicate sweetness and a richness, while at the same time having little fat.

The olives were rich and oily; black-brown, they were slightly larger than calamatas. They were skewered on toothpicks and toasted over an open fire. We learned that this was a style of preparation unique to Polizzi.

The bread, yellow with a firm crust, was made of durum wheat flour. Santo had baked it in a large wood-burning brick oven that stood on the patio outside the kitchen door. *Pani 'i casa*, as it is called, is the traditional bread of Sicily. Breaking bread here, in the land of my roots, stirred an ancient part of my soul.

Our pig-squeals of delight over the antipasto inspired Santo to prepare the first course. The antipasto, I realized later, was a sort of test to measure our appreciation of what would follow. Had our response been cooler, Santo would not have prepared the magnificent first course that soon came from the kitchen. Placing it on the table, he announced, *"Taggiarini chi funci sarvaggi."* I translated for Carol, "Homemade pasta with wild mushrooms."

Santo had foraged the mushrooms that very morning. *Funci 'i ferla*, as he called them, they look somewhat like our cultivated portabella, but there is little comparison in flavor. They have a deep, musty quality, enhanced by their preparation with parsley and the perfume of garlic.

Next came coils of thin sausage, made from the same pork as the salami. Sea salt and a pinch of black pepper were the only flavorings added to the ground meat. The sausages were pan-cooked, finished with red wine, and accompanied by a green tomato salad dressed with a wonderfully fruity extra-virgin olive oil and dried oregano. Santo said that the tomatoes were green because in these Sicilian mountains the growing season is relatively short. All of the tomatoes that turn red by the beginning of September are cooked into sauce and canned, or sun-dried into paste for the winter.

The wine was local, very fruity and very young, about two weeks old. It looked like unfiltered apple juice. Santo tapped it from a small barrel into a beautiful majolica pitcher. Despite its youthful flavor, it was strong. Carol and I became giddy as we toasted our arrival in Polizzi and the mutual pleasure of our company. I caught Santo and Domenico smiling in our direction. I could see in their eyes that they knew, "wedding ring" aside, we had just met.

On the table next to the wine was a glass carafe filled with the water of Polizzi, of which my grandfather had often spoken. I was thrilled to see it still as clear as the finest ground-glass lens, still as pure and sweet as the first flower of spring. I had now drunk the sweet water of Polizzi Generosa, and I felt as if the thirst of every cell of genetic memory was quenched by it. I think that I shall remember always my first meal in Polizzi Generosa, on October 30, 1988. My grandfather would have been 116 on that day.

After dinner we asked Santo and his colleague Domenico to join us. We sat around the table cracking hazelnuts and talking. The dark night was growing colder, and the fireplace provided great comfort against it.

The first thing they wanted to know was how we had found their place. I told them the story of our rude experience at the Villa Cariddi and how the *Distribbuturu Agip* had told us about the University of the Bricklayers. They were amazed to learn that we were told about the place in town. Domenico nervously laughed and remarked, "It is the mafia." This word Carol understood without translation. Her face registered alarm. Santo explained as I translated for her: "Domenico doesn't mean what you think. You are not from here, and perhaps your sense of the mafia is like it is in *The Godfather*, with gangsters and guns. But it's different here; it's about respect."

He cracked a nut for emphasis. "Let's say, for example, an important, well-respected man opens a hotel in the countryside. By and by, a stranger comes to town asking for a hotel. There are sixteen hotels around Polizzi, but the townspeople will give directions to just that one place, out of deference to the man of respect. Of course, tourists can stay wherever they wish, but a different hotel might be hard for them to find." He took a sip of wine.

"You see, it is much more profound than the American idea of mafia. It is something more difficult to grasp, this ancient culture of respect." For final punctuation, Santo put the nut-meat in his mouth and crunched it hard between his molars.

Domenico dissolved the sobriety of the moment by quickly changing the subject to America. "I lived there once for nine months, in *Bruculinu*," he gleefully announced. The section of Brooklyn he described was, not surprisingly, my old neighborhood. "What a place! People always running, and for what? After a while I couldn't take it, so I returned to Polizzi. I'm very happy about that."

Santo had never been to the United States, but he had spent time in Nicaragua, teaching farming techniques to the native people. "We were in the jungle," he said, "showing the people how to grow tomatoes and potatoes, the two most important foods originally from that part of the world, and they'd never seen them before. It was very strange."

I asked him why he called his hotel the University of the Bricklayers. "I have been building it on and off for ten years," he said, "and for me it has been a university." The walls were hung with a collection of paintings. Their style was a kind of modern realism, and the subjects ranged from historical battles to portraits that looked a bit like Sicilian Botero. Santo modestly acknowledged that the work was his. Domenico went on to say, less modestly, that Santo's paintings have been exhibited in Palermo, Catania, and Rome, as well as in galleries in other major cities throughout Italy. "Santo Lipani is not only a chef and a bricklayer," boasted Domenico, "but also a famous artist." Santo blushed.

They asked us how we had heard of Polizzi. I told them about my family. Santo said, "I know. I hear it in your accent."

It now being official that we were sort of *paisani*, Domenico brought out a bottle of homemade hazelnut liqueur. We toasted, first to my "wife," and then to our arrival. We toasted the dinner, and Polizzi, and the universe, and the mind of God.

Santo drew something on a small piece of paper and handed it to me. It was a caricature of me. At first it seemed very funny, but the information held in its image showed otherwise. On my shoulder flew two flags: the *trinacria* of ancient Sicily and Old Glory. Above my head were the words

I DO NONT REMEMBER SICILY.

Santo understood why I had come to Polizzi Generosa.

We drank and laughed and talked well into the small hours of the morning, our actions punctuated by the howling wind and the fire's crackle.

Back in our room, there was not the benefit of a fireplace, but the warmth produced by the liqueur held long enough for Carol and me to undress and climb into bed. Reviewing the day's events by the dim yellow light of a small candle, it was hard to remember that only the previous afternoon Polizzi Generosa had been just a red dot at the end of a squiggly blue line on a road map.

As we talked, lying on our sides facing each other, we inched closer. We could see our breath in the candlelight as we whispered "I love you" over and over to each other for the first time. The breath that formed these words surrounded us in a great protective dome, as we dreamily drifted asleep in each other's arms.

All at once, we were frightened awake by the sound of many feet in the gravel outside the window at the head of our bed. The candle had burned out, leaving us in complete darkness. There was the hushed voice of someone giving orders. We wondered what could be causing the disturbance, our imaginations certain of the worst. Could it be that we were to be targeted for staying in the unapproved hotel? We realized that we knew very little of Santo or Domenico or of Polizzi. How easy it would be for two people like us to disappear here without a trace.

Hearts pounding, we finally found the muscles needed to untangle ourselves. With all the courage we could muster, we quietly rose to wobbling knees on the unsteady bed and listened at the shuttered window. I could understand nothing of what was being said, and trying to convince us both that it probably was none of our business, I suggested that we return to bed. I dove for the safety of the covers.

Carol's curiosity, however, could not be postponed. Slowly she unlatched the shutters and peeked out the window. She whispered, "Oh Vince, you have to see this." I looked up to see the dawn's light illuminating the nude form of a beautiful woman kneeling on the bed beside me. Joining her at the window was beginning to seem like a pretty good idea.

What we saw outside was a man trying to negotiate his cow away from

under our window. He pulled and tugged at the collar to no avail. His pleading turned to anger. He cursed the cow and all her kind in a colorful stream of epithets. The window was high and we remained unnoticed. At his final moment of desperation, the stubborn cow graciously complied and she led the farmer away.

Still on our knees, heads framed by the window, we felt embarrassed by our foolish assumption of mafia assassins. Our eyes followed the trail of man and beast. As our heads tilted up, we sighted for the first time the incredible splendor of where we were. Before us lay a mountain pasture, dotted with olive trees. In the distance, on a hill covered with broom, sheep grazed. We threw open the casement. The room filled with the clear, cold morning air. It was scented with wild fennel, and bay laurel, and earth—rich, fertile earth. There was no machine noise, only the sounds of bleating sheep, and cowbells, and the chime of someone tinkering.

I thought of my grandfather sitting at our kitchen window in Brooklyn. Looking out over that bleak landscape through a tangle of clotheslines, could the remembrance of this splendor have caused the sparkle that ran across his eyes? What determination to find a better life must have driven him, must have driven all of them, to trade these pristine Sicilian mountains for Brooklyn's tenements.

The cold air made us shiver and we scurried to find our clothes. While stamping our feet and flapping our arms, we dressed quickly and went out into the light of the new day. Hand in hand, wandering the narrow dirt roads near the hotel, we found the morning alive with the activity of a rural life. Shepherds were moving their flocks to graze, and farmers were carrying implements on their shoulders to the fields. One man was riding a donkey, hurriedly traveling somewhere.

We smiled and bid *boniornu* to everyone we passed. Their eyes shared with us the pleasure of our being in love. They knew we had come from far away, and were honored and pleased by our obvious joy at being there. It was as if we had traveled all this way just to see them. They returned our *boniorni* and smiled back at us with gracious pride.

An hour later, we flew into the hotel, excited and invigorated by the walk. A barely awake Santo was preparing coffee. He scooped a generous amount of finely ground espresso into a pot of boiling water. He let it return to the boil, removed the pot from the heat, and added a trickle of cold water to settle the grinds. Then he strained it through a small fine-mesh strainer. I remember my grandmother preparing coffee this way every morning of my childhood.

First Santo served the strong brew black, in small cups, as a kind of eye-opener. Then we had it in coffee bowls with hot milk, accompanied by toast and jam. Santo turned to face me and, looking squarely into my eyes, asked, "*Now* do you remember Sicily?"

After breakfast, we drove up to Polizzi to find my cousin Giuseppe Vilardi, the barber. It was Sunday morning, and the center of the city was closed to vehicular traffic. In traditional Sicilian fashion, the women were on their way to church and the men were filling the piazzas and cafés. Some were engaging in the Sunday ritual of *passíu*, strolling back and forth along the main street. Their pace was almost processional. Even though we were obvious strangers, everyone ignored our presence.

We found a barber shop. I stood in the doorway, but before I could speak, the barber informed me that we wanted a different barber shop, pointing us in the right direction. Clearly, he knew who we were.

Finding it, we stood outside the opened doorway and looked inside. It was an old shop. The chairs were white porcelain with green leather cushions. A client reclined in one of them with his eyes closed. A portable sink of shiny copper was in place under his head. The barber, who had his back to us, was wetting the man's hair with a kind of copper watering can and giving it a shampooing.

"Excuse me," I said, "I am looking for a barber named Giuseppe Vilardi." The barber turned, his hands full of soap, "I am Giuseppe Vilardi."

"I think we're cousins," I said.

With that, the man in the chair turned in our direction, opening one eye to give us the once-over. Remembering this was none of his business, he turned back and closed his eye.

Giuseppe was stunned with excitement. He moved toward me, his arms extended. We half shook hands and half embraced, the soap on his hands making it awkward. "But where did you come from?" he asked. I told him that we were from America, and about Cousin Angelina's information about his brother the tuba player. Although his portrayal of surprise was impeccable, I was sure he already knew all that. I also was now certain that the news of our arrival in Polizzi was all over town.

A genealogical review determined that we were, indeed, cousins. Although he was twenty years my senior, our great-grandfathers had been brothers. We were third cousins, not a distant relationship in a Sicilian family. Had we known each other during my childhood, I would be calling him Zù, (uncle) out of respect.

The shop was filling up with clients. Some of them spoke to me, happy at the reunion, pretending to be hearing of it for the first time. I did not want to further interrupt Giuseppe at his work, and said as much. He very apologetically said that Sunday morning was his busiest time. We made a plan to meet later in the day. He invited us to his home, to meet his wife and children. We embraced good-bye, *sans* soap, until later. Amazing! I could barely comprehend the ease with which I had found family six thousand miles away and ninety years later. I think Guiseppe took it more in stride. After all, family is family.

The city was becoming busier with the activities of Sunday morning. We stopped in a café to drink cappuccino and eat horn-shaped pastry filled with cream. Carol and I stood very close to each other at the bar, pastry cream running down our mouths. Carol moved to lick away a particularly luscious glob from the corner of my mouth when her eye caught a stern look from the barman. I turned to see what had stopped her. We moved a little apart to maintain propriety. The barman's acerbity changed to a smile, but still he scolded us with a shaking finger.

We finished our snack like proper Sicilian ladies and gentlemen and then left the café to find a place to steal a kiss, easier said than done. Our quest for an isolated spot took us on a grand tour through the beautiful winding streets of Polizzi Generosa.

We found ourselves in an ancient part of town with narrow winding streets walled by small two-story houses. At the center of this section rose what was, obviously, at one time a minaret. Clotheslines laden with brightly colored laundry, waving in the warming sun, bridged the streets. As Carol and I passed underneath, I felt as if these banners were placed there to herald our arrival.

It was near noon when we returned to the center of town. The strollers were now walking faster, on their way to Sunday dinner, carrying cake boxes or loaves of bread. From out of nowhere, an old lady in black appeared in front of us. She was uncommonly pale, with wispy white hair and a mouth full of misplaced teeth.

She spoke in a loud, exasperated, craggy voice. "Are you Vilardi?" she croaked. I half-nodded in the affirmative, and clasping her hands to heaven, she said, "Thank God! I found you! I *felt* you were here." In Sicily one would never betray a confidence by saying, "So and so *told* me you were here."

She fell in between us and, grabbing our arms in a vise-like grip, led us, silently, at breakneck speed through a maze of winding streets. We came to a halt in front of a small house. She nudged us inside to a large dark kitchen. In it were three men, the two older men sitting at an oilcloth-covered table. It was illuminated by the light from a giant television set, on which a soccer match was in progress. The youngest man was stirring a large pot of tomato sauce on the dimly lit stove. Without looking up, he bellowed gleefully, "You found them?" "Of course," she said nonchalantly. She now turned to us with a big smile. Her teeth sparkled like a drunken jeweler's fantasy. "Now," she said, "I can embrace you. On the street, what would people think." She clasped each of our heads, in turn, in her strong hands, planting firm kisses on our cheeks.

We introduced ourselves. Her name was Pasqualina Vilardi. Her youngest son, Peppe, came forward with his right hand extended and the wooden sauce spoon in the left. He pumped ours with great enthusiasm. His kisses on our cheeks were just as earnest. The two older sons, Moffu and Franco, were slightly less effusive. After all, cousins from America are one thing, but it *was* the crucial moment of the game.

In a jump-cut we were at the table enjoying a dish of macaroni. The sauce was a hearty tomato-meat ragù with rich, sharp pecorino grated on top. The second course was a veal shoulder roast, flavored with onion and Marsala. The meat was accompanied by a potato gratin made with olive oil and pecorino, perfumed with the woodsy mountain flavor of fresh bay leaves. There was also *cicoria*, a wild field green that is similar to dandelion, only shorter and more bitter. The *cicoria* was cooked and dressed with olive oil and lemon.

Pasqualina, whom I called Zà (aunt) out of respect, sat next to me at dinner. She stared at me the whole time, smiling with watery eyes. She thanked the Lord, the Virgin Mary, and all the saints in heaven for "bringing my cousin safely back to me." We figured out that her late husband was descended in some way from my great-great-grandfather. She kept taking my face in her hands and kissing my cheeks. This made it difficult to eat, but after all, the event wasn't about food.

The soccer match ended unfavorably for the favorite team. Immediately relegating the loss to the remote past, the sons spoke of how different Los Angeles must be from Polizzi. (More, I knew, than they could ever imagine.) Carol was sitting on the other side of me and I endeavored to keep her abreast of the conversation. They all watched with great interest the attention I was paying to my "wife."

Conversation drew to a slow stop. We sat around, sort of smiling and nodding at each other. There seemed to be one common thought: "Who are these people? What if we're *not* related?" Peppe ran to another room and returned with a photo album. Zà Pasqualina opened it and, pointing at a picture, said, "This is your grandmother." The battle-ax to whom she was pointing bore no resemblance to my delicate, beautiful grandmother.

She tried again: "This is your cousin Philip." I feigned memory loss. She turned pages in silence, pointing at photos, hopefully trying to coax some recognition from me. It was to no avail. All of these people were total strangers to me. Taking the book from her, I started to turn pages myself, frantically looking for a familiar face. At last, there she was. "Ah!" I said in victory, "Zà Angelina!" The photo was of the woman who had told me about the tuba player. The whole room sighed in relief. Then we ate hazelnuts. I looked up from nut-cracking and noticed that the Vilardis were not using nutcrackers to open these hard shells. They accomplished this strenuous task with their teeth.

All at once, the room filled with more than twenty people. They were Zà Pasqualina's other children and grandchildren and their families. It was a party. We toasted and were toasted with homemade hazelnut liqueur. I grew lax in my simultaneous translation. Carol had to tap me on the shoulder and ask, "What's going on?" A "Don't you know?" with a giggle was all I could manage.

Loosened a bit by the liqueur, the eldest daughter, Vincenzina, a no-nonsense woman, asked questions about this alleged marriage between Carol and myself. When I told her that we had been married for only three months, she said, "Well, that explains the attention. You're newlyweds."

The other daughter, Anna, and her family kept a large kitchen garden. The end of October is prickly pear season, and Anna's husband, Giovanni, had brought a bushel basket of the fruit. *Fucurinnia*, as the Sicilians call them, comes from the Italian *fichi d'India*, Indian figs. The Spaniards planted this cactus, indigenous to the American Southwest and Mexico, at a time when Europeans still believed that the Western Hemisphere was part of India.

Over the centuries, the Sicilians have come to believe that the prickly pear is theirs. The sweet deep red fruit found beneath the dangerously spiny skin could be a metaphor for the contradictions of Sicilian life itself. As befits their ironic sense of humor, Sicilians love to make jokes about prickly pears. Somehow the punch lines always have to do with someone sitting on the spiny fruit. The family howled as they told their favorite prickly pear stories, some of which were so old—and so widely known—that I had heard them from my grandfather as a boy.

Giovanni carefully peeled the prickly pears, presenting them to us whole at the end of a fork. While we were lost in ecstasy eating these rubies, someone asked what Carol and I were doing later. I said we were going to see Giuseppe the barber. The room went suddenly and profoundly silent. Vincenzina said, "We don't speak to Giuseppe the barber." It was an awkward moment. I did not wish to be thrown into the middle of a family feud.

It seems that the rift had something to do with money sent by their mutual great-grandfather from America. Although intended for the whole family, the story goes that Giuseppe's grandfather kept it all for himself. "It's not for the money," Anna insisted, "it's for the principle of the thing." All of the original players in this melodrama were long dead, but that hadn't changed this "principle."

Moffu, the eldest son, stood. Everyone turned to hear his opinion. "You know," he said, "you have come from far away. It is the right thing for you to do, to see Giuseppe the barber. After all, he's family too." Everyone agreed, pleased to have found a way out, and the party continued.

A short while later we left. There was much hugging and kissing all around. I took the opportunity to kiss Carol. Everyone chuckled at the playfulness of the "newlyweds." Zà Pasqualina came to the door and waved, slowly and solemnly, long after, I am certain, we had turned the corner and were out of sight.

We were to meet Giuseppe at his barbershop, and as we approached, he was strolling up the street toward us. When we met, he greeted us with a warm open smile and much hand-pumping. He probably knew about the dinner with Zà Pasqualina and her family, but I didn't mention it. Although in Sicily only a short time, I was beginning "to remember," as Santo might have put it.

We were now walking through a section of town Carol and I had not as yet seen. From behind high walls could be glimpsed the grand palazzi of the titled rich. Their terra-cotta roofs unified a mélange of architectural styles, built over centuries. I wondered in which one of these cold stone palazzi my grandfather had cooked for the Baron Rampolla.

The modest two-story house in which Giuseppe and his family lived faced a small piazza with a fountain. Francesca, his wife, came down to greet us from the upper floor. She was an ample, attractive, primly dressed woman in her mid-fifties. "At last, cousin," she cooed, "you've finally arrived," as if she had been expecting me for months. "And who is this beautiful lady?" I introduced Carol, "my wife," and we waited for the usual flicker of disbelief. Francesca did not disappoint us. Quickly changing the subject, she said, "But why are we standing here in the doorway? Please, come inside."

The hallway was under major renovation, with temporary stairs and railings. "Excuse the construction," Francesca chirped, "but there is an unsettled question about it with our downstairs neighbor; for twenty years it has been unsettled."

The apartment was beautifully decorated. The floors were made of colored marble laid in geometric patterns. The furnishings were antique, family treasures. Everything was immaculate and in its place.

We perched on a settee. Francesca offered pastries and coffee. The pastries were arranged on a silver tray covered with a crocheted doily. They all looked, somehow, like little breasts. The coffee was espresso, served in ornate china demitasse cups with silvered rims and handles. The coffee was excellent, with a sure layer of gold, *'a crema*, on top. I complimented her, asking what brand of home espresso machine she used to prepare such wonderful coffee. She blushed and giggled like a schoolgirl. "Oh," she said, "I don't use a machine. You see, I take a little of the coffee and beat it with a little sugar. With a little spoon, I put a little on the top of each cupful. And that's my little secret."

We were joined by their son, Antonio, and their daughter, Maria. Antonio was handsome and fit, in his early twenties. He lived in Palermo, where he was a policeman. Maria was a girl of sixteen. She was shy and innocent, in the flower of her adolescence. She would be going to college next year in Rome. Giuseppe assured me that she would be living under the protective eye of her uncle, the tuba player. She rolled her eyes at this prospect.

We spoke of the family in America and made small talk. Both Antonio and Maria laughed at my Sicilian. To them, as to most young educated people from Sicily, the dialect is considered low-class and provincial. Perhaps one day they will see it for the strong expression of the refined ancient culture that it is.

Giuseppe wished there were some modern industry in Polizzi to hold the youth. I nodded agreement, but I knew that work was not their only reason for leaving. For them the past has not yet concluded, and they struggle in the present to find a Sicilian image for the future.

As if in response to my unspoken thoughts, Giuseppe stated his case. "Cousin," he said, "I know that there are other places in the world. But here I have my work. I go home for lunch. My family is nearby, all around me. My life is peaceful, contented, serene. You know World War II? We didn't have it here."

Dusk was gathering. It was time to go. The whole family accompanied us to the street. There were good-bye hugs and kisses, with reminders to send best regards to the unknown family in America. Giuseppe grabbed both my hands and squeezed them hard. Allowing me to look deep into his eyes, he wished me the old Sicilian farewell with slow, special emphasis: *Tanti beddi cosi*, so many beautiful things.

Carol and I strolled arm in arm to our car, parked early that morning. We reviewed the day's events to plant them, in every detail, deep in our memories. As we approached the overlook, the hazelnut and olive trees below were silhouetted by the setting sun. The echo of our voices and the sound of our footsteps on the cobbles were soon the only ones we heard. All of the townspeople had gone home. At long last, we were alone. Our eyes met, and we kissed and kissed and kissed as darkness fell.

Capunata 'i Cacuocciuli

# Artichoke Caponata

In northern Italy, caponata is a relish, usually composed of peppers and tomato. Sicilian caponata, however, is a dish of one or more vegetables cooked separately and joined together by a sauce. In Polizzi, this sauce always has a sweet-and-sour flavor.

This delicious caponata joins artichoke hearts, celery, and olives with a reduced tomato sauce, and is flavored with capers and vinegar.

The type of artichokes to use are called baby, or cocktail, artichokes. Although tiny, they are fully mature. Every artichoke plant produces a number of these on its outermost stalks. Except at the end of their season in early summer, these tiny artichokes do not produce a choke and their hearts are very tender.

This dish is best served at room temperature, as part of an antipasto or as an accompaniment to simply grilled meats or fish.

*For 6 servings*

**For the tomato sauce**

One 35-ounce can peeled whole Italian plum tomatoes, drained

2   cloves garlic, peeled

¼   cup extra-virgin olive oil

2   teaspoons sugar

Sea salt

Black pepper

½   teaspoon dried basil

**For the vegetables**

6   ounces (about 20) large green olives

3   lemons

2   pounds (about 20) baby or cocktail artichokes, about 2½ inches long and 1½ inches in diameter

⅓   cup extra-virgin olive oil

Sea salt

4   ribs celery

2   tablespoons capers, rinsed

¼   cup red wine vinegar

Black pepper

Prepare the tomato sauce: Put the drained tomatoes into a bowl and crush them with your hand.

Put the garlic and oil in a heavy 1½-quart saucepan. Sauté the garlic over low heat until it is lightly cooked on all sides; remove and discard it.

Add the tomatoes, sugar, salt, black pepper, and basil. Cook, uncovered, stirring with the back of a wooden spoon, until a creamy consistency is reached. Then raise the heat to medium and let the sauce boil gently for 15 to 20 minutes, until it is reduced to a thick pulp. Stir from time to time to keep the sauce from burning. If the sauce is ready before the artichokes, take the pan off the heat and set aside until needed.

Prepare the vegetables: Smash each olive with a meat pounder or kitchen mallet and remove the pits. To greatly reduce the saltiness of the olives, soak the pieces in cold water for the remainder of the preparation time, changing the water three times.

Pour cold water into a medium-sized bowl. Juice 2 of the lemons and add the juice and rinds to the water.

Working with 1 artichoke at a time, cut off about ½ inch from the top of the artichoke. If the stem is long enough to trim and peel, do so; if not, cut off and discard the stem. (To help prevent the artichokes from turning black, pass the knife through the third lemon prior to each cut.) Remove the outer leaves to the place where the leaves are thin and pale green. Cut the artichoke into quarters and place the pieces in the lemon water.

Pour the olive oil into a heavy 9-inch skillet and place it over medium-high heat. When the oil is hot, drain and add the artichokes. Sauté for 2 minutes to sear them. Add salt to taste. Reduce the heat to low, and continue to sauté until cooked but still crunchy, 15 to 20 minutes. Turn the artichokes with a spatula from time to time to prevent burning.

While the artichokes cook, blanch the celery in boiling water, uncovered, for 2 minutes. Drain it in a colander and rinse it under cold running water to quickly cool it. Thinly slice the celery, and reserve until needed.

When the artichokes are ready, raise the heat to medium-high and gently fold in the drained olives, the celery, and the capers. When these additions are hot, add the vinegar. Let the aroma rise for about a minute; then add the tomato sauce and continue to cook for 5 minutes, stirring to let the flavors amalgamate.

Turn the caponata onto a serving platter, and sprinkle with a few grindings of black pepper. Serve at room temperature.

Carni Cuotta ca Marsala

## *Veal Shoulder Roast with Marsala*

Adding butter to Marsala imbues its flavor with a subtle richness. Mixed with onions and peppercorns, it becomes an exquisite marinade for this veal shoulder. Slow-cooking the meat in this mixture gives it a soft, melting quality. In the end, this cooking liquid is transformed into a delicious gravy with which to sauce the veal.

*For 6 servings*

1¼ cups dry Marsala wine
1   medium-sized yellow onion, coarsely chopped
½   cup (1 stick) unsalted butter, in small pieces
22  whole black peppercorns
2   bay leaves
3   pounds boned veal shoulder roast, tied or netted, about 4 inches in
    diameter
    Sea salt

The day before the veal is to be served, put the Marsala, onion, butter, peppercorns, and bay leaves in a small saucepan. Cook over low heat, stirring, just until the butter melts. Transfer to a bowl and cool to almost room temperature.

Meanwhile, put the veal in a bowl and salt it on all sides. When the marinade has cooled, pour it over the veal, cover well, and marinate in the refrigerator for 24 hours. During this time, turn the meat several times.

About 3 hours before the veal is to be served, preheat the oven to 350°F, with a rack positioned in the center.

Put the veal in a heavy round or oval 4- to 5-quart pot with a tight-fitting lid. Pour the marinade, including the solidified butter pieces, over the meat, and bake for about 2¼ hours, until it reaches an internal temperature of 160°F. Turn the meat every 30 minutes.

Transfer the meat to a platter and let it rest in a warm place for 20 minutes before slicing. Discard the bay leaves and pour the remaining liquid, with the onions and peppercorns, into a small saucepan. Let it settle for a minute or two, and then skim off the fat (this will be about half the contents). Add ¼ cup water and bring to a boil. Reduce the heat to very low, cover, and simmer gently while you are cutting the meat.

Cut off the strings or netting and thinly slice the meat. Arrange the slices on a warmed oval platter. Spoon on the onion and peppercorn gravy, and serve.

## Patati chi Addauru

# Potato Gratin with Bay Leaves

This dish captures like no other the perfume of the clear mountain air of Polizzi Generosa. Whenever I cook these potatoes, I imagine that that glorious breeze has traveled 6,000 miles to visit me in my kitchen.

In Polizzi, the gratin is made with fresh bay leaves, but dried ones may be substituted. Just remember that bay leaves are inedible.

*For 6 servings*

2¼ pounds Yukon Gold, Yellow Finn, or russet potatoes
1½ medium-sized yellow onions
    Extra-virgin olive oil for greasing and drizzling
    Sea salt
    Black pepper
6   bay leaves
1   cup grated imported pecorino cheese, preferably Locatelli brand

Preheat the oven to 375°F, with a rack positioned in the center.

Peel the potatoes and cut them into lengthwise slices about ⅛ inch thick. Peel the onions, slice them, and separate the rings.

Using a small amount of olive oil, grease the bottom of a gratin pan that is just large enough to accommodate the potatoes in three layers. Put a layer of sliced potatoes in the pan. Lightly salt them, and sprinkle generously with black pepper. Cover with one third of the pecorino and onion, a light drizzle of oil, and 2 bay leaves. Arrange the second and third layers in the same way.

Bake for 1 hour, and serve hot.

# Two

# Viva Gannuarfu!

n Good Friday 1996, Nino Gianfisco, a close friend in Polizzi Generosa, phoned me in Los Angeles. "Hold the line," he said. "The mayor wants to speak to you." The mayor, Giuseppe Lo Verde, introduced himself and said that he had recently been to America and had seen my first cookbook, *Papa Andrea's Sicilian Table*. He was thrilled to have discovered an English-language cookbook that mentioned his city.

He went on to say that it would be a great honor for Polizzi if I would come, as its guest, to present my book to the city and to receive an award for my work in films. I responded in my best Sicilian, "The honor would certainly be all mine." He burst into mighty laughter, sizzling the phone line. He asked me when I would like to come. I said perhaps in May or June. He thought that would be too soon; he needed time to prepare. He suggested that I come in September for the festival of the city's patron saint, St. Gandolfo. "You would be," he said rhapsodically, "the Godfather of the Festival!"

As it has been for the last 682 years, the festival of St. Gandolfo is held on the third weekend in September, falling that year from September 13th to the 17th. I know Sicilians well enough to understand that the mayor had decided the time for my arrival, down to the finest detail, long before he phoned. Even his rhapsody had been carefully rehearsed. Nonetheless, when we "agreed" on the date, I said, "This date is now written in my appointment book with an ink that can never be erased." Amused by my quaint, old-fashioned Sicilian, the mayor again burst into a mighty torrent of laughter which surely flashed up to the satellite that transmitted our voices, sealing the date in heaven.

• • •

St. Gandolfo, or San Gannuarfu (gan-wa-foo), as my grandmother called him, was well known in our household in Brooklyn. I remember her sending a yearly donation for the maintenance of his church in Polizzi when I was a boy. Throughout the neighborhood, as in Polizzi, many people bore the name Gandolfo or Gondolfa, the feminine version. Nicknames are Moffu or Moffa, respectively, and Momó for either gender. Grandma told me the saint's story many times over.

In the early part of the thirteenth century, there lived a Franciscan monk and mystic named Gandolfo. Following the revelation of a dream, he walked from his home town of Binasco, in northern Italy, to Polizzi, at the time a journey of many months. On the very day he arrived, Gandolfo saw a boy jumping and gesturing wildly on a riverbank. A closer look made the monk realize that the boy was deaf-mute, and also showed the reason for his excitement. A mule had fallen into the river and was about to drown in the strong current. Quickly, Gandolfo placed his hands on the boy's head, saying, "Speak in the name of the Lord!" The boy's mouth and ears were opened, and he yelled out, "Papa! The mule is here!"

To an agricultural-pastoral culture, the importance of this event is easily understood: The loss of a mule means the loss of livelihood. The people of Polizzi became convinced that Gandolfo was truly a man of God. He stayed, living there as a hermit, in deep meditation, isolated in the countryside near the river. As the years passed, the people looked after him, and he employed his powers to counsel and aid them.

The task of bringing the saintly man his daily meal was always assigned to young novitiates from a nearby convent. One pair of young girls given the task wondered what Gandolfo did all day, alone in his hermitage. In an effort to find out, one spring day, they attempted to sneak up on him. Giggling and trying to be quiet, they tripped on a vine and fell. The bowl of food crashed to the ground, and the bowl broke in two.

Pretending to be aroused by the commotion, Gandolfo emerged from his hut to find the girls frightened and crying at the prospect of the Mother Superior's anger. Gandolfo quieted the girls and, to their astonishment, repaired the bowl so perfectly that it looked like new. The grateful girls ran back to the convent and reported the story to Mother Superior. Seeing the bowl, the Reverend Mother accused the girls of lying, beat them, and confined them to their cells.

The next day, an older nun brought Gandolfo his food. When he asked about the two young novitiates, she told him of their sinful behavior. After eating his meal, Gandolfo himself broke the bowl in two on a rock. He repaired it as seamlessly as before, but this time, he made it whole with the pieces flipped, so that the surface was joined top to bottom. He then ordered the old nun to take *that* to Mother Superior. The bowl was presented to her without a word. Upon seeing it, she asked the young girls' forgiveness and God's absolution for her own sinful assumptions.

On Holy Saturday, April 3, 1260, Gandolfo died. His body was laid out on the altar of a small church, San Nicolò de Franchis, resting on a bed of cut jasmine branches. The whole city mourned the death of their benefactor. When the church was opened the next morning, Easter Sunday, the air was filled with a sweet perfume—the jasmine branches had miraculously flowered in the night. The event remains a fitting image for the sweetness of the life of this gentle man.

Before his death, Gandolfo prophesied that Polizzi Generosa would never be touched by fire, flood, or war. Cynics might say that a stone city on top of a mountain needs never worry about fire or flood. They might add that the minor strategic significance of Polizzi could never warrant the attention of a military campaign. Nevertheless, Gandolfo's prophecy has remained true to this day, and since 1320 he has been the city's Patron Saint Protector.

For me, each visit to Polizzi had been an adventure, revealing more of the magic of Sicily each time. I wondered what magic this trip would hold.

After a long day of flying, I finally arrived in Palermo and was met at the airport by Santo Lipani and Nino Gianfisco. Over the years since my first visit, Santo and I had become good friends, calling each other *frati* (brother). We all embraced over the low fence that separated us, under the watchful eyes of somber customs officials and the noses of a free-roaming pack of drug-sniffing dogs. In short order I cleared customs, and my caravan of baggage, which included copies of my book and a half-dozen bottles of homemade green-walnut liqueur, was packed into Santo's Lancia station wagon.

An hour later, at dusk, we turned off the highway onto the winding mountain road that leads up to Polizzi. Before reaching the city, we turned off the road into an area known as *'i Mulini*, The Mills. In it stand a group of ten water-powered grain mills, built between 1177 and 1382. Some of these mills remained in operation until the 1960s.

We stopped in front of the oldest, beautiful stone mill house. Its owner, Francesco Ficile, met us at the door. Francesco is a taciturn, melancholic intellectual, always surrounded by a cloud of cigarette smoke. He is an official of the city government and the proprietor of a popular café-restaurant. He welcomed me with great cordiality, his facial muscles unaccustomed to the broad smile he couldn't suppress.

We passed through the massive oak door into the eight-hundred-year-old structure. The great mill wheel, with its wooden housing and hopper, was the centerpiece of the main room. Francesco told me that he had restored the entire mechanism to operating condition. He had tried to use it once, and it functioned well, but flour flew into every crevice of the room. It took days to clean up the mess. "In the twelfth century," he concluded, "millers had a different sense of housekeeping than we do today."

In addition to restoring the mill, Francesco had added three bedrooms and two baths, new construction built in stone, in the same style as the old mill. This magnificent, ancient dwelling was where the city had arranged for me to stay.

The stillness of the evening was broken by only our voices and the gentle sound of the millstream. This mountain stream provides water for the house—that sweet, crystal-clear water of Polizzi. After a long day of airplanes, I wished only to rest in this pristine bucolic setting, but there was a schedule to keep. With barely enough time to wash my face, I was whisked out the door and up to Polizzi to Santo's new restaurant for dinner. I could sleep later.

The restaurant is called *Orto dei Cappuccini*, The Kitchen Garden of the Capuchins. Santo told me that actually the walled terraced garden and the stone building in its center once formed the kitchen garden of a Franciscan monastery built in the fourteenth century. "But since it is on the Via dei Cappuccini," Santo added with a wry smile, "I named it Orto dei *Cappuccini* to avoid confusion."

When Santo bought it two years ago, the ruined building was filled with five feet of dirt. Now the garden has been replanted along its ancient rows and the building has been excavated, expanded, and reroofed in a magnificent restoration, all of the work done by Santo himself.

As usual, Santo's food was exquisite and plentiful. Some of the dishes were new to me, but delicious as always, created and named with his unique sense of humor. My favorite that evening was one that Santo placed on the table with great flourish: *Calamari 'i Muntanga*, Mountain Calamari. The battered and fried little rings he set down certainly looked like calamari, but in the end I realized that the closest thing to seafood any mountain could yield was onion rings.

Another dish from the antipasto was sweet-and-sour meatballs, small veal meatballs cooked with tomato paste, then coated with finely chopped almonds. The subtle sweet-and-sour taste is created with vinegar and a bit of sugar. Santo said that this dish evolved from one introduced by Saracen invaders twelve hundred years ago. Nino leaned in to me and whispered, "That's why we call him *Santu 'i 'a Cucina*, The Saint of the Kitchen."

We ate, and talked, and laughed for hours. It was after 1 a.m. when I returned to the mill. I had been awake now for a day and a half, and as soon as my head hit the pillow, I drifted off to sleep, floating down the millstream.

My appointment to meet the mayor for the first time was at eight-thirty the next morning. As I was getting ready, I heard the ear-piercing siren of a police car. I looked out an ancient casement just as a little white four-wheel-drive Fiat arrived with its disproportionately large blue dome light flashing. The driver and captain of the three-person police force, Epifanio (Epiphany—his birthday is January 6), found this display endlessly amusing.

Polizzi was bustling with activity by the time we arrived. Preparations for the Festival of St. Gandolfo were in progress. Tall poles supporting arrangements of lights were being set in place. Beneath them, traveling merchants were unloading their wares. The goods included everything from pots and pans to farm implements. A thirteenth-century imperial decree, designed to stimulate trade, proclaimed that every city and town in Sicily was to have an annual fair. For the past 682 years in Polizzi, the fair has been combined with the festival of the Patron Saint Protector.

Mayor Giuseppe Lo Verde was waiting for me in his office. Upon seeing me, his round handsome face burst into a huge smile. He rose from behind his massive desk, a short, exceedingly corpulent man in his late thirties. He strode toward me with his right hand extended, his booming voice bouncing off the stone and marble surfaces. He grabbed my hand, shaking it vigorously. "It is a pleasure to meet you! How was your trip? How is the mill? How long will you stay?" He added his other hand for increased support in the pumping. Before I could answer, he added, "Let's go have a coffee."

On the short walk to the café run by Francesco and his parents, he treated all as if he were running for re-election. There was much handshaking, and backslapping, and laughing. He even kissed a baby or two. At times he was approached by someone with serious business, and the mayor would drop his joviality for a more businesslike attitude. Overall, the *cittadini*, the city-folk, were very proud of their mayor and his fine mayoral appearance and demeanor.

We drank cappuccino and ate horn-shaped pastries filled with pastry cream, the same kind and in the same place Carol and I had eaten them on that first visit, eight years before. As we dabbed away the cream from the corners of our mouths, the mayor announced to me that at six o'clock that evening, in the city hall, I was to present my cookbook and to be honored by the city. "Don't be late," he added, punctuating this with a mighty handshake. He turned, and his short legs windmilled his round torso with great velocity up the street.

I strolled to the nearby barbershop of my cousin Giuseppe Vilardi. "Ah! You are here now," he said as a form of greeting. The waiting customers, too, bid me good morning. Many men in Polizzi do not shave themselves, but visit a barber two or more times a week. Today everyone wanted to look especially sharp for the festival.

Aware that my *ommaggiu*, homage, was to be that evening, Giuseppe took one look at me, snapped his chair cloth for emphasis, and offered me a shave and a haircut. I was to spend the remainder of the morning there, for good grooming was Giuseppe's life. When it was my turn, I climbed into the antique porcelain and leather barber's chair (more like a throne). A lever was pulled, the chair reclined, and Giuseppe lathered my face with a soap redolent of almonds. The straight razor flashed over my face, guided by Giuseppe's sure hand.

The chair snapped back to a sitting position, and a meticulous hair cutting followed. Organizing my unruly, thinning curls presented no challenge for the master. Giuseppe used the long nail on the pinkie of his scissors hand as a pointer to keep his rows straight.

The chair was snapped down again for an unexpected shampooing, also scented with almonds. After a brisk towel-drying, my head was anointed with almond hair tonic and my hair combed to astounding neatness. Giuseppe did good work. I left feeling renewed, refreshed, and a bit like a marzipan pastry.

Some friends and I went to Francesco's family's café for lunch. We were greeted by Francesco's father, Don Ciccio, a man in his late seventies. He asked for my wife with a smile that remembered our first visit.

The name of the café is DA . . . DA . . . CI . . . CCIO. When Don Ciccio was a young man, he had a severe stutter. This good-natured man had the sign made to put all at ease about his difficulty in pronouncing his name. When he reached the age of forty, his stutter vanished, for no earthly reason. But he keeps the café's name, for continuity.

The bill of fare was *casalingu*, home cooking, typical and honest. Already on the table were bread, wine, olives, and preserved artichoke hearts, put up by Francesco's mother, Zà Rosa. She holds the distinguished honor of having been officially named the best home-style cook in the entire region.

After our appetites had been properly stimulated by these vinegary flavors, *pani cunzatu*, adorned bread, was brought to the table. Durum wheat bread, warm from the oven, was split and "adorned" with *sarde salate*, salted sardines, a sprinkle of local pecorino, a drizzle of the best extra-virgin olive oil, and pinches of dried oregano and black pepper.

Next came the first course, *taggiarini cu sugu*, homemade pasta with a pork tomato sauce. It was flavored with onion, celery, carrot, potatoes, and peas and had the subtle, unlikely, but delightful aftertaste of cinnamon. Local pecorino was grated on top, as the final layer of these complex flavors.

The second course was baked sausages with wild mushrooms. The mushrooms, *funci 'i ferla (Pleurotus ferulae)*, were the same rich- and earthy-flavored variety Santo had used on my first visit. Available in the autumn, they have thick stems like porcini and crowns that resemble our cultivated portabella, sometimes as large as a foot across. Incredibly, this variety of wild mushroom originated in the Gobi Desert, evidence of the far-reaching scope of the ancient Arab trader.

The sausage dish was accompanied by a salad of lettuce, onion, and green tomato, dressed in vinegar and olive oil. The meal ended with a cornucopia of fruit. We peeled and ate sugary-sweet figs and prickly pears, and popped fleshy grapes the size of plums into our mouths.

In Polizzi before lunch, one says *boniornu*; immediately after lunch, it is already time to say *bona sera*. With a bit less exuberance, the police escort transported me back to the mill *pi ripusari*, to repose, as siesta is called here. Afterwards, I prepared for the big night. Catching myself in the mirror, I admired, once again, my cousin the barber's good work.

The city council chamber is a long, narrow room with a high ceiling. In the central part of the room is a large U-shaped table, at which sit the mayor and the council members. At one end, on a raised platform, the president of the council and the assessor are enthroned. At the other end is a small gallery for spectators. Although the city hall has moved over the centuries, the layout of the city council chamber has not changed in more than seven hundred years.

The mayor escorted me to the chair next to his. From this vantage point, I could see the gallery filled to overflowing, with still others craning their necks around the doorway. Front row center sat my cousin Zà Pasqualina, looking very proud.

The session was called to order. After some brief city business, the president of the city council made a speech welcoming and honoring me as a returning native son. He turned the floor over to the council members, who, each in turn, made similar speeches of welcome and praise. The mayor took the floor last, adding, "Although American-born, Vincent Schiavelli is so truly Polizzani that he doesn't even speak Italian, only Polizzani! We honor him today not because he is an actor, or because he is a writer of Sicilian cookbooks, but because he is ours." The room burst into thunderous applause. The mayor turned to me and whispered, "Now it's your turn."

I rose to my unsteady feet, trying to see my notes through the tears welling up in my eyes. I had prepared a speech in Sicilian. I steadied myself and began.

Excuse me if I don't speak Sicilian so well. It is not my first language, and I never learned even Italian in school. But the Sicilian language is strong, frank, and courteous. It is the language of an island always occupied, never conquered. Sicilian is truly the language of my heart.

From when I was a very small boy, my grandmother Carolina, born Vilardi, and my grandfather, Andrea Coco, always spoke of the beauty of Polizzi Generosa and the fineness of its people. I never forgot the stories they told me. Thoughts of Polizzi were always with me. I believe that it's a thing of genetic memory, a thing of roots, a thing of blood.

When I finally saw Polizzi for the first time, I filled with emotion. I thought of my grandfather sitting at the window in Brooklyn. When he looked out at that ugly cityscape, perhaps it was the memory of this beautiful city that brought the light to his eyes. I know this is true, because when I think of Polizzi, and of my family, and of my friends, the same light comes to my eyes.

It is not possible for me to put into words what a great honor Polizzi bestows upon me tonight. But I must tell you, there is a bit of a scandal here. This cookbook is not mine. In reality, the true authors are my grandfather, Andrea Coco, and my great-grandfather, Calogero Vilardi. They were master chefs, *monzù*, for the nobility of Polizzi a hundred years ago.

I grew up in my grandfather's house, and the lessons of cooking and life he taught me one could never find in school. I can see him here, tonight, close to me. With his high-waisted trousers, his handsome, con-genial face, his clear eyes full of life, and also of the devil, with his large white mustache, all smiles, very happy for me. He looks at this assembly and he fills with pride.

But at one moment he takes me aside and looks me in the eye, very seriously. Half to avoid hubris and half joking, he says, "Ne'er-do-well! So it's come to this!"

With great pleasure, I graciously present my cookbook to the city of Polizzi Generosa. There are seven copies, one for every rose in the an-cient coat of arms of the city.

Ten thousand thanks to the mayor, the city council, and the people of Polizzi for this great honor. I will never forget this day.

After my speech the room was silent for what seemed like an eternity. Then they broke into loud, sincere applause; some yelled *bravu*, others rose to their feet. When order was restored, the mayor, with tears in his eyes, pre-sented me with a silver plaque in a beautiful handmade leather-covered box.

*The City of Polizzi Generosa*

*to*

*Vincent Schiavelli*

PRESTIGIOUS ACTOR OF CELEBRATED FILMS

IN WHOSE SIGNIFICANT EMERGING SPIRIT

IS ALWAYS PRESENT HIS POLIZZANI ROOTS

AND THE HOT TONES OF THE MEDITERRANEAN

13 SEPTEMBER 1996　　　　GIUSEPPE LO VERDE, MAYOR

The moment touched me deeply. My grandparents had left this place poor and oppressed by an ancient social code that afforded them no options. They went to America, the great freedom across the sea, with the hope of change. Perhaps the streets in their new land weren't paved with gold, but the options they could provide for their children and for their grandchildren al-lowed me to become an actor and a writer, and to return in a position that closed the circle of their emigration.

•　•　•

The next day, the festival was in full swing. Merchants had set up their booths and were doing a brisk business. Dressed in their Sunday best, the Polizzani strolled the main street, greeting relatives, friends, and neighbors.

In the mid-afternoon, a lone drummer boy marched through the streets reminding everyone that the procession was soon to begin. I was standing with Francesco as the drummer passed. I said, "This is a very sacred event, isn't it?" Francesco took a particularly deep drag on his cigarette as he considered his response. "Yes," he said, tentatively, "but sacred and profane at the same moment." I puzzled at his response.

At five, a large group of men gathered in front of the city hall. A caravan of cars assembled to transport us two miles outside the city, to the Church of St. Gandolfo, built on the site of his hermitage. The sacred procession would begin there. The vehicles were filled with the men of the saint's fraternal society and of the many societies of other saints. Originally these organizations were craft guilds, and so the men wore aprons or tunics displaying a representation of that fact. I rode in the lead car with the mayor and the president of the St. Gandolfo Society.

At the church, we were ushered up worn steep stairs to a long, narrow upper room. A long table was laid with a modest meal designed to fortify us for the walk ahead. Each man in the jammed, low-ceilinged room was given a fork. With arms extended toward platters of succulent sausages, we'd spear one, chomping on it off the end of the fork in one hand, alternating with a piece of bread in the other. Salty black olives and sweet wine accompanied the meal.

Shortly it was time to begin. A life-sized statue of St. Gandolfo had been taken out of the church, placed on a litter, and loaded onto a well-used red pickup truck. Beside the statue stood a drummer and a young boy, representing the boy of the first miracle. A Franciscan priest sat in the cab adjusting a bullhorn. When all was ready, the cars fell in to formation behind the truck. We rolled slowly up the winding mountain road toward Polizzi. The priest chanted a song of praise to St. Gandolfo, alternating with the drummer's stately processional tattoo:

> *Long live Gandolfo! Gandolfo is living!*
> *Long live Gandolfo, and those who praise him!*

About half a mile below the city, we reached a small shrine to the saint. The statue and its litter were off-loaded and long poles were attached. Twelve strong young men hoisted this heavy load, weighing nearly eight hundred pounds, atop their shoulders. Led by the priest chanting over his bullhorn, and followed by the mayor, the city council, myself, and the rest, the procession began. We walked with our hands clasped behind us at a slow, stately pace. No one smiled; this was serious business.

A large crowd met us at the entrance to the city. They greeted the yearly visit of the statue of their protector with solemn, enthusiastic applause. A band played with great brio, albeit slightly sharp. The priest then led a prayer of thanks and blessed the crowd, punctuated by a lone trumpet playing the shrillest *Te Adoramus* I have ever heard. It seemed to pierce heaven; I'm sure the angels sang in response.

Our procession re-formed, with the band and the townspeople now behind us. The band accompanied our strolling gait with *sicilianae*, cymbals crashing to mark the slow Moorish rhythm.

The parade route, unchanged for centuries, wound its way through the narrow cobbled streets of the seven sections of the city. The saint-protector bobbed his way, carefully navigated around protruding baroque balconies and power lines. Everyone, from leathery-faced old men to innocent young girls, crossed themselves and blew kisses at the passing statue. The route took us past the house in which my grandmother was born and lived until she left for America. I imagined her beautiful face witnessing this spectacle from her balcony.

It was dark now. We paused in front of each church, their bells ringing at a frenzied speed to welcome the saint. The priest chanted St. Gandolfo's hymn over his bullhorn; the band played; the sky exploded with fireworks. At one point during the march, I turned around to see the whole town in procession, glutting the narrow street as in a Brueghel painting.

At the Chiesa Madre, the main church, the statue was carried up the steps, into the church, and installed at a side altar. The townspeople passed in single file around the statue and kissed its feet. They then proceeded, as if still in procession, to the overlook, where a temporary stage had been erected. In front of a blasting rock group danced three young, sexy women from Palermo in tight, short mini-skirts—as Francesco said, the sacred and the profane.

• • •

The next night's procession was even more spectacular than the first. This time, a solid silver bust of St. Gandolfo mounted on an ornate silver box containing his bones was carried through the streets. The massive statue weighs twice that of the wooden one, nearly sixteen hundred pounds.

This reliquary is the centerpiece of a side altar in the Chiesa Madre. The statue can be viewed only at the commemoration of the saint's death in April and at his festival in September. The rest of the time it is obscured from view behind thick velvet draperies. The entire altar is locked behind an impressive gilded-bronze gate.

With great ceremony, the gate was unlocked. At the moment the draperies were pulled open, the crowd gasped at seeing the beauty and opulence of the statue. It took the arms and backs of many men to lift it off its resting place and onto its poled litter. For this purpose, a special group of young men was selected. The honor of having been chosen for this mighty task is somewhat diminished by the muscle strain that is sure to follow for the next weeks.

The procession assembled similarly as the night before, although now the front ranks contained wives and daughters, sisters and mothers. The solemnity was broken with a bit of gaiety, but in contrast, the drumbeat was more somber and the parade route longer. An army of older women marched behind the initial group. Fulfilling their promise of thanks to St. Gandolfo for answering their prayers, many of them took the cobblestoned route barefooted in self-mortification. The fervent murmuration of their prayerful chant haunted the narrow, winding streets.

That night, at dinner, the mayor complimented me on the Sicilian I had used in my book's recipe titles. "It is important that you have written these recipes, for many of them have been lost to us over the years."

"I will cook them for you," I responded. "Tomorrow night?" he half-asked, half-demanded with anticipation. Santo nodded in agreement, so the date was set for the next night in Santo's restaurant.

Early the next morning, I went marketing. This task, which would have taken the better part of the day in Los Angeles, was accomplished in twenty minutes. I first visited the butcher to buy a pork loin for the second course. The pigs around Polizzi are herded, not penned, and subsist largely on a diet of acorns and chestnuts. Although smaller than American pigs, they develop a

thicker fat coat as protection against the cold winter. Most of them are pink-skinned, but there are a number of black-skinned ones in the small herds. Over the centuries, a variety of domesticated pigs have mixed with wild boar to produce this indigenous breed. The pigs are slaughtered at eight months to a year old, twice the age of ours. All of these factors produce a meat that is succulent and sweet, with a slightly wild flavor.

The loin the butcher proudly presented to me was boneless, weighing about seven pounds. It was deep pink in color and had a soft, melting texture even when raw. After we discussed its magnificence for several minutes, he slipped it into a net, lovingly wrapped it in butcher paper, and tied the bundle with string.

The cheese store was dark and cool, its air filled with humid, earthy aromas. I asked the proprietress for pecorino for grating. She led me to the back of the shop, where stood stacks of sixteen-inch round, thick wheels of cheese. The rind was a deep brown color, the cheese itself snowy white. She gave me a small taste of the creamiest, deepest-flavored pecorino I have ever tasted, moist but at the same time a good consistency for grating. I asked her where it came from, and she replied proudly, "It is ours." Her husband and her sons tended the flock and made the cheese in the nearby countryside.

Crates of fruits and vegetables spilled out into the street where I shopped for produce. My purchases included white mushrooms for stuffing, crisp deep green lettuces and pungent fennel for salad, and broad flat green beans that were so fresh they popped like champagne corks when snapped. Parsley, of course, was on the house. The old proprietor and his daughter were very helpful, and when I left he presented me with a bottle of his homemade wine. "It is very good this year," he said, "but don't worry, it isn't too strong."

The first course of the evening's meal was *tumala*. It is my grandfather's adaptation of a rice bombe conceived by a tenth-century emir of Sicily, Ibn-al-Tumnah. In my grandfather's version, a shell of rice, mixed with grated cheese and eggs, is filled with pasta, sauced with the ground meat from a ragù, and dotted with peas. The result is surprisingly light, with delicate, refined layers of flavor.

The rice must be prepared at least six hours before the *tumala* is put together, to permit proper absorption of the eggs and cheese. When I arrived at Santo's with my bundles, I discovered that he was off on other business. Time was growing short for this preparation, so Francesco and Zà Rosa were quick to provide me with a kitchen and all that I needed. After cooking the rice and mixing it with the eggs and cheese, I carried the platter of cooling rice, covered with a dishcloth, through the streets to Santo's restaurant.

Santo arrived just past noon, and as the afternoon progressed, I prepared the dinner. There I was in Polizzi Generosa, in a four-hundred-year-old kitchen, preparing *tumala* for the mayor. My thoughts turned to my grandfather, who had cooked in a similar kitchen a hundred years before. Surely he must have made *tumala* for important dinners in the baron's house, even, perhaps, ones at which the then mayor of Polizzi was in attendance. The sense of this continuity pleased me, and I glided through the cooking as if guided by another pair of hands.

The guests arrived early. I had invited eight, but twenty appeared. Fortunately I had cooked generously for twelve, and Santo filled in the gaps by quickly preparing additional antipasto.

I had prepared a mountain of mushrooms stuffed with bread crumbs and grated cheese, bathed with Marsala. The green beans, called *fasoli a badda*, were steamed and served at room temperature, with lots of vinegar and a bit of olive oil. The prosciutto and *cascavaddu* were from Santo's stores. He added baked green cauliflowers with wild mushrooms. The cauliflower was first blanched whole and then covered with chopped mushrooms. The center of each cauliflower was covered with a circle of deep red tomato sauce, perfumed with garlic, melted anchovy, and red pepper. Beautifully arranged on a platter, looking like exotic flowers from an ancient Mediterranean garden, the simple vegetable was baked to perfection.

Another of the antipasto dishes I prepared was sweet-and-sour onions. I couldn't decide whether or not these onions, stewed in honey boiled to the candy thread stage, and then mixed with the flavors of vinegar and black pepper, would be too strange for my guests, but I decided to give it a try. Surprisingly, they devoured every last morsel, scooping up the sauce with their forks.

The presentation of the *tumala* was greeted with wide eyes of wonder and delight. Upon seeing its interior, the wonder turned to applause. As they ate it, the room grew silent with the kind of reverence reserved for church. The mayor said that he had never tasted or seen anything like it. He should know, obviously being a man who enjoys his food—*na bona furchetta*, "a good fork," as the Sicilians say.

I had crusted the pork loin with black pepper and chopped onions, as my grandfather did, and surrounded it with golden potatoes. But never before had it tasted like this—his simple preparation was perfectly complementary to that incredible pork loin. Everyone marveled at the simplicity of its goodness, sopping up the *jus* created with a basting of white wine and the burnt onion.

I took as a great tribute everyone's enjoyment of my salad dressing. The simple artistry of its preparation was taught to me by my grandfather when I was a boy. The salad was followed by fruit. All began to speak again, their faces filled with the sort of contentment that can only be produced by a good meal.

The best pastry in all Sicily came next, sent with the compliments of Pino Agliata. After espresso, I served my homemade green-walnut liqueur, carried all the way from Los Angeles. Now I was in potentially dangerous territory, for *nucina virda* is a matter of great pride for every Polizzani family who makes it. The guests examined it carefully, tilting their glasses to see if the nearly black liqueur would yield green around the edge. Having passed that test, they tentatively touched the liquid to their lips. They liked it. They liked it very much. Francesco emerged from his smoke cloud to make the final pronouncement: "The walnuts in America are different from ours, but they are also very good."

We toasted and drank, and laughed at bawdy Sicilian jokes. At one quiet moment, Santo said that he had a very important toast to make: "To Papa Andrea Coco, who this night finally returned to Polizzi to put this feast on our table." First mine, than everyone's eyes filled as we all rose, raising our glasses to heaven.

Tuesday was the last day of the festival. In the evening, the statue of St. Gandolfo was again placed on the red pickup and transported down the mountain to his church. Many were in attendance to get one last look at the saint's kindly face. Up above, a large, silent, motionless crowd pressed against the railings of the overlook to make certain that their protector was properly settled in again at his altar.

The next morning, the air had turned cold and damp. I bid farewells to family and friends. As we wound our way back down the mountain in Santo's Lancia, it rained.

## Pani Cunzatu

# *Adorned Bread*

The basis for this delicious treat is semolina bread, the bread of Polizzi, found in every home and restaurant. Some households still bake it in large batches for the week, although it is usually purchased from the baker. When it is to be eaten hot and "adorned," baking is planned to coincide with lunch or snack time.

The bread is made with a finely ground hard, yellow wheat flour. It is often called durum wheat flour, so as to distinguish it from the coarser-ground semolina or pasta flour. The proper grind can be found at some Italian groceries and health food stores in the United States. Depending on the area in which you live, however, you may need to use mail-order sources.

To emulate the crust produced by the brick ovens of Polizzi, it is advisable to bake this bread on a baking or pizza stone. Place the stone in a cold oven and allow it a good 30 minutes of preheating before use. Do not attempt to remove it until it has cooled, as a rapid change in temperature may cause it to crack.

Although only one loaf is needed for adorned bread, this recipe will make two. Allow the second loaf to cool, and enjoy it with meals. When it grows stale, it makes excellent breakfast toast with butter and jam.

*For 9 servings adorned bread, plus 1 loaf plain bread*

**For the bread**
1½ teaspoons sugar
1   tablespoon active dry yeast
2½ to 3 cups hot water (105° to 115°F)
5   cups durum wheat flour, plus additional for dusting
1   cup semolina (pasta flour), plus additional for dusting
1½ teaspoons sea salt
3   tablespoons extra-virgin olive oil

**For the adornment**
¼   cup extra-virgin olive oil
3¾ ounces (1 small tin) sardines packed in olive oil or spring water,
      or 4 salted sardines *(sarde salate)*
      Pinch of dried oregano
1   tablespoon grated imported pecorino cheese, preferably Locatelli brand
      Black pepper

**Prepare the bread:** Mix the sugar and yeast together in a tall warmed glass. Add ½ cup of the hot water and mix with a wooden spoon. Let stand for 7 to 10 minutes, until the yeast is foamy.

Meanwhile, mix the 5 cups durum flour, 1 cup semolina, and the salt together in a large warmed bowl. When the yeast is foaming, mix it in. Then mix in the oil and 2 cups of the hot water. Continue mixing until it forms a ball. If the dough is too sticky, add a bit more flour; if it is too dry, add more water. Turn it out onto a floured surface and knead until the dough is smooth, about 10 minutes.

Lightly sprinkle durum flour on the inside of a warmed bowl that is large enough to hold the dough when it has doubled in size. Put the dough in the bowl, cut a ½-inch-deep cross on top with a sharp knife, and dust the top with durum flour. Cover with a dish towel and set it in a warm place for 2 to 3 hours, until the dough has doubled in bulk.

Gently punch down the dough. Dust a work surface with durum flour. Roll and stretch the dough into a cylinder 2 feet long. Cut it into two equal-sized loaves with squared ends. Cover the loaves with a dish towel and let them rise for 40 to 50 minutes, until almost doubled in height.

At least 30 minutes before you bake the bread, place a baking stone on the center rack of a cold oven and preheat the oven to 450°F.

When the loaves have completed their second rise, brush the surface of each one with warm water to enhance the crust. Using the point of a sharp knife, cut a 1-inch-deep incision in the center of the top of each loaf.

Dust a paddle or a piece of stiff cardboard with semolina, and slip a loaf onto it. Make sure there is enough semolina on the paddle to allow the loaf to move easily. Gently slide it into the oven, placing the loaf as far back on the stone as possible. Slide the second loaf in front of it.

Bake for 45 minutes to 1 hour, or until the crust is a deep rich gold and the loaves sound hollow when thumped with a knuckle.

**Adorn the bread:** A minute or two after the bread comes out of the oven, split one of the loaves in half horizontally with a serrated bread knife. It will be very hot, so use an oven mitt to hold it against the cutting surface.

Drizzle the inside of each half with 2 tablespoons of the olive oil. Split the sardines and distribute the pieces evenly over the bottom half of the loaf. Sprinkle with the oregano, grated cheese, and grindings of black pepper to taste. Put the top half back in place.

Cut the loaf into 9 slices and serve while still hot.

# Purpetti cu l'Auruduci

## *Sweet-and-Sour Meatballs*

This dish is delicious when served with an assortment of olives. The meatballs taste best when slightly chilled. If you make them in advance, remove the meatballs from the refrigerator 45 minutes before serving and let them warm, uncovered, at room temperature. Leftovers make a great snack.

*For 6 to 8 servings*

4   ounces (¾ cup) shelled whole raw almonds
1   pound ground veal
2   eggs
¾   cup grated pecorino cheese, preferably Locatelli brand
2   tablespoons unflavored bread crumbs
⅓   cup finely chopped Italian parsley
    Black pepper
¼   cup extra-virgin olive oil
1   tablespoon tomato paste dissolved in ⅔ cup water
    Sea salt
½   cup red wine vinegar
1   teaspoon sugar

Preheat the oven to 450°F.

Toast the almonds on a baking sheet in the oven for 10 minutes, being careful they don't burn. When they are cool enough to handle, grind them in a food processor or with a mortar and pestle into a fine meal. Reserve until needed.

Put the veal, eggs, grated cheese, bread crumbs, parsley, and a few grindings of black pepper in a bowl. Knead together by hand, squeezing the mixture through your fingers. Gently form the mixture into 30 round meatballs, about 1¼ inches in diameter, placing them on a waxed paper–lined sheet pan until needed.

Pour the oil into a heavy 9-inch skillet and place it over medium-high heat. When it is very hot, sear the meatballs on all sides, about 3 minutes. Gently shake the pan to prevent sticking and to ensure that the outer surface does not become dark and hard.

Reduce the heat to medium-low, add the thinned tomato paste, and salt lightly. Turn the meatballs in the liquid, cover, and cook at a gentle simmer for about 8 minutes, until they are cooked through. Turn them once during this time.

Using a slotted spoon, remove the meatballs from the skillet. Pour all the liquid out of the pan and discard it. Place the skillet back on the stove over medium heat. Return the meatballs to the pan and cook for a minute or so until they are hot. Sprinkle in the almond meal. Turn the meatballs in the meal to coat them well.

In a small bowl, whisk together the vinegar and sugar, and slowly pour it into the pan, distributing it evenly. Add several grindings of black pepper. Turn the meatballs in the liquid and let it boil for 1 minute. Immediately turn the meatballs out onto a platter on which they will fit comfortably in one layer.

Cool, uncovered, to room temperature. Cover with plastic wrap, and chill for at least 1 hour. Serve slightly chilled.

# *Meat Sauce*

*Sucu* is the progenitor of the hearty tomato meat sauce that some Sicilian- and Italian-Americans call "gravy." In this version, pieces of pork shoulder and sausages are cooked in a tomato sauce with a base of onion and celery. Carrots, peas, and potato are added for flavor, along with a perfume of cinnamon.

Traditionally the sauce is served over homemade pasta, *taggiarini*, or a smaller type of rigatoni called *sedani*, and the meats are eaten as a separate course out of the same bowl.

*For 8 to 10 servings*

3½ pounds pork shoulder

Three 28-ounce cans peeled whole Italian plum tomatoes, undrained

1    medium-sized yellow onion

2    ribs celery and their leaves

2    large carrots

1¼ pounds plain, thin, sweet (mild) Italian sausage, cut into 5-inch lengths, or 8 thick Italian sausages

2    tablespoons extra-virgin olive oil

2    tablespoons tomato paste dissolved in 1 cup dry white wine

Sea salt

Black pepper

1    tablespoon sugar

Pinch of cinnamon

1¼ pounds Yukon Gold or white potatoes

½    cup chopped Italian parsley

2    pounds *sedani* (a small rigatoni, about 1¼ inches long and ¾ inch in diameter)

2    cups fresh peas (2 pounds in the pod)

1    cup grated imported pecorino cheese, preferably Locatelli brand

Trim the pork shoulder roast as explained in the sidebar. You should have about 2 pounds. Set the cubes aside until needed.

Fit a food mill with the disk with the smallest holes (1 millimeter), and place it over a bowl. Pour the tomatoes and their liquid into the mill in two batches. Puree the tomatoes to remove the seeds, which can make the sauce

A note about cutting and trimming the pork shoulder: Purchase a 3½-pound pork shoulder roast. This cut of meat tends to be very fatty; trim off all the outer fat. (In Polizzi, home cooks would render this into lard.) Separate the meat along the interior veins of fat, and then cut it into 2-inch cubes. Trim off all the surface fat from the pieces. Prepared in this fashion, the 3½-pound roast will yield about 2 pounds of meat.

bitter. Scrape the pulp from underneath the mill into the bowl. Set aside until needed.

Peel and finely chop the onion. Clean the celery and remove the leaves. Chop the ribs and leaves separately, and reserve in separate piles. Scrape the carrots, and cut them on the diagonal into ¼-inch-thick rounds. Put aside until needed.

Place a heavy 6-quart pot over medium-high heat. When it is hot, sear the pork pieces on all sides, about 8 minutes. Remove the pork from the pot.

Lightly brown the sausages, about 6 minutes, and remove them from the pot.

Remove the pot from the heat, and pour off all the fat. Add the olive oil, onion, and celery ribs. Return the pot to medium-low heat, and sauté until golden, about 7 minutes. During this time, scrape the bottom of the pot with a wooden spatula to loosen any brown bits.

Return the pork pieces and sausages to the pot, turn up the heat a bit, and when the meats are hot, pour the tomato paste mixture over them. Let the alcohol evaporate for a couple of minutes while completely deglazing the pot by scraping it with a wooden spatula.

Pour in the milled tomatoes, and stir well. Add the carrots. Season with salt, and add a few grindings of black pepper, the sugar, the cinnamon, and the celery leaves.

Cook, uncovered, at a lively simmer for 1½ to 2 hours, until the pork is tender. Stir from time to time to prevent the bottom from burning.

During this time, peel the potatoes and cut them into ¾-inch cubes. Place the potatoes in a bowl of lightly salted cold water. When the meat mixture has cooked for 1 hour, drain the potatoes and add them to the pot.

Fill a large pot with 6 quarts water, add 2 tablespoons salt, and bring it to a boil over high heat.

When the meat sauce is ready, stir in the parsley. Keep the sauce simmering over low heat. Meanwhile, cook the pasta and peas together in the boiling water for about 10 minutes, until the pasta is al dente.

When the pasta is cooked, remove the sauce from the heat and allow it to settle. Drain the pasta and peas very well, and divide them among individual pasta bowls. Dress with the sauce, including the potatoes and carrots but setting the meat aside. Serve with pecorino to sprinkle on top. Serve the meat as a separate course after the pasta.

## Sucu Fintu

# *Bogus Meat Sauce*

In Sicilian, *pasta cu sucu* means pasta with a hearty meat-tomato sauce. In times past, this luxury was not available to poor farmers very often. To compensate the palate, they devised their own *fintu* (false) version.

This tomato sauce looks as if it has big pieces of meat in it, but in reality the chunks are hard-boiled eggs. They are halved, coated in a mixture of eggs and grated cheese, and then fried before being left to simmer in the sauce.

In traditional style, eat the pasta as a first course, then the eggs out of the same bowl as a *secondo*.

*For 4 to 6 servings*

11   eggs
    One 35-ounce can peeled whole Italian plum tomatoes, undrained
½   medium-sized yellow onion, finely chopped
2   tablespoons extra-virgin olive oil
1   tablespoon tomato paste dissolved in ⅓ cup water
    Sea salt
    Black pepper
2   teaspoons sugar
¾   cup grated imported pecorino cheese, preferably Locatelli brand, plus additional for serving
1   cup pure olive oil
4   sprigs Italian parsley, chopped
1   pound linguine

Pierce the large end of 8 of the eggs with a pin (to prevent cracking). Put the eggs in a pot, cover with cold water, and cook for 10 minutes after the water comes to a boil. Drain the eggs and run them under cold water to stop the cooking and loosen the shells. Peel the eggs and set them aside until needed.

Meanwhile, fit a food mill with the disk with the smallest holes (1 millimeter), and place it over a bowl. Pour the tomatoes and their liquid into the mill. Puree the tomatoes to remove the seeds, which can make the sauce bitter. Scrape the pulp from underneath the mill into the bowl. Set aside until needed.

Put the onion and the extra-virgin olive oil in a heavy 4-quart pot over medium heat, and sauté the onion until it turns translucent, about 4 minutes. Stir in the thinned tomato paste. Cook for about 1 minute, and then add the milled tomatoes. Season with salt, grindings of black pepper, and the sugar. Reduce the heat to low and simmer the sauce, uncovered, stirring from time to time, for the remainder of the preparation time.

Fill a large pot with 6 quarts water, add 2 tablespoons salt, and bring it to a boil over high heat.

While waiting for the water to boil, beat the remaining 3 raw eggs with the ¾ cup grated pecorino in a shallow bowl. Cut each hard-boiled egg in half. Heat the pure olive oil in a heavy 9-inch skillet over medium-high heat. When it is hot, quickly but thoroughly coat 8 hard-boiled egg halves with the egg-and-cheese mixture, and using a spoon, gently slide the pieces into the oil, one at a time. When the pan is full, give each piece a gentle shove with a spatula to prevent sticking. Fry until golden, about 2½ minutes on each side.

Remove the egg halves with a slotted spoon, and roll them on brown paper or paper towels to drain the excess grease. Prepare and fry the remaining 8 halves in the same way. When all the eggs are fried and drained, lower them into the sauce and simmer for 10 minutes. Add the parsley.

Cook the pasta in the boiling water until al dente, about 10 minutes. As soon as the pasta is cooked, remove the sauce from the heat and let it settle.

Drain the pasta thoroughly, divide it among individual pasta bowls, and top it with some of the tomato sauce. Serve it with grated cheese to sprinkle on top. Serve the eggs separately, as a second course, with a bit of sauce.

## Sosizza a' Furnu chi Funci

# Baked Sausages with Mushrooms

The sausages in Polizzi are thin because they use lamb instead of pig intestines for the casings. They are made from pork butt, usually seasoned only with salt, and formed in a continuous rope. Such sausages can be found here in Italian specialty shops. Thick mild (sweet) Italian pork sausages can be substituted, provided they do not contain extra flavorings. It is preferable to use ones without fennel seeds.

In this recipe, I have substituted the wild mushrooms, *funci 'i ferla (Pleurotus ferulae)* used at DA . . . DA . . . CI . . . CCIO with large cultivated portabella mushrooms.

*For 4 servings*

8   ounces large portabella mushrooms
2¼ pounds thick or thin mild Italian sausages (see headnote)
2   tablespoons tomato paste dissolved in ⅔ cup water
    Sea salt
½  cup dry white wine
¼  cup chopped Italian parsley

Preheat the oven to 450°F, with a rack positioned in the center.

Clean the mushrooms with a soft brush or a damp cloth, using as little water as possible. Slice them ¼ inch thick and 1½ inches long. Save until needed.

Coil the sausages in a round ovenproof baking pan or skillet. To facilitate removing the sausages from the pan when they are cooked, fix the coil with two bamboo skewers.

Bake for 35 to 45 minutes total, depending on the thickness of the sausage.

After 15 minutes (25 minutes for thick sausages) of baking, pour the thinned tomato paste over the sausages. Distribute the mushrooms on top, season with salt, and bake for another 15 minutes. Then pour the wine over the mushrooms and continue to bake until the sausage is cooked, about 5 minutes.

Lift the sausages and mushrooms out of the pan and place them on a deep serving platter. Mix the parsley into the pan juices and pour the juices over the top. Serve hot.

# Three

# *The Baron and the Shepherd*

*hepherds* and their flocks have dotted the mountains of Sicily since before history was written. The *Odyssey* establishes the first literary reference to a Sicilian shepherd in the story of the Cyclops: Homer writes that when Odysseus first spied the ogre Polyphemus, he was sitting among his sheep eating fresh ewes'-milk ricotta from a straw basket. Polyphemus's flock is the mythological ancestor of present-day Sicilian sheep, and Sicilian shepherds still make the same cheese using the same ancient method.

The life of a Sicilian shepherd is a lonely one. His days are spent milking, making cheese, and leading his flock from one mountain pasture to another. He passes the night alone in the mountains, guarding his vulnerable animals against accidents and the dangers of attack by wild boar. If he is lucky, the pasture will have a *pagghiaru*, a conical-shaped straw hut of prehistoric design, to shelter him; if not, he will sleep exposed to the elements with one eye open. The words of an old Sicilian folk song are still true today.

> *I spent last night in a yellow pasture,*
> *But soon my blanket will be snow.*
> *Such is the life of a shepherd.*

As is often the case in Sicily, however, things are not as they seem. Beneath the surface of this seemingly simple existence, there is a sharply different aspect to the shepherd's personality.

Traditionally, farmland in Sicily was divided into large baronial estates called *latifondi*. Peasant farmers, *cuntadini*, worked these lands for their powerful masters. This feudal system remained virtually intact until the great land reforms following World War II.

Throughout this long history of servitude, however, shepherds were never brought under the heel of any barony. The wandering nature of their lives, leading their flocks from pasture to pasture in search of food, made it difficult to determine under whose baronial jurisdiction they belonged. The shepherds became a fiercely independent group. If laws and decrees were unjust or taxes harsh (as was usually the case), the shepherds simply ignored them.

At the same time, they maintained a strict code of honor and morality among themselves. For example, the *pagghiaru*, made of straw, could not be locked. These structures were regarded as communal property and any supplies used were replaced for the next occupant. These straw huts became the drop-off point for secret communications among the leaders of popular uprisings and resistance movements as recent as World War II. At times, the leaders of these causes used them as their own hiding places, secure that betrayal would never come from a shepherd.

Over time, stories and legends about the shepherds' independence, cunning, and ingenuity became part of Sicily's folklore. Following in this tradition is the story of the baron and the shepherd.

In 1997 I had the good fortune to spend the month of August in Polizzi Generosa. The principal summertime social activity there is to pass the evening strolling back and forth along the Via Garibaldi, the main street, between the principal piazza and the overlook, a distance of a few city blocks. The entire population puts in an appearance at one time or another during the course of an evening. On Sundays or holidays, the Polizzani pursue the same activity dressed in their finery.

One evening, as I was about to stop at Bar Cristallo for a coffee, I saw my friend Nino Gianfisco striding down the street toward me. Nino, an electrician by trade, is of cherubic build. His dark, almond-shaped eyes hold the luster of some ancient Levantine forebear. His long tangle of black curly hair, often tied in place at the back, was straining at its tether. Nino's smile, a rare jewel, sparkled as he entered the bar. Speaking in Sicilian with a quiet, low voice, he said that he had made arrangements for us to visit a *pagghiaru* the next morning and to eat hot ricotta with the shepherd. My excitement at the prospect of this outing gave him great pleasure, and his smile grew even brighter.

The next morning at six-thirty, I walked from the house I was staying at on the Via Roma through the barely awake town to our meeting place. The streets were still quiet as the brilliant morning sunlight touched the ancient buildings. I passed rows of narrow, balconied three-story houses, which gave way to more imposing structures, like the ruins of a Byzantine fortress built in 780. Nowadays, the only invaders storming its ramparts are blades of grass, forcing their way between the granite blocks, these final conquerors rallying in the sun.

At one point the narrow street opened to reveal the Chiesa Madre, perched at an angle on its surrounding pedestal steps. Farther along, after the main piazza, I turned onto the Via Garibaldi and soon climbed the massive stairway that leads to the palazzo of the Baron Gagliardo di Carpinello, seat of the city's oldest and most powerful aristocratic family. The huge compound encompasses four city blocks, and the adjoining baroque buildings contain an astounding 365 rooms, one for each day of the year. The massive stone portal is carved in exquisite baroque style. Above the substantial wooden doors, a marble slab is carved with a simple sundial and moon-dial, representing the family's temporal power.

Nino was waiting at our meeting spot under the palms of the square in front of the palazzo. He carried a pink pastry box tied with string. As he had told me, it is tradition when visiting the *pagghiaru* to bring the shepherd ricotta-filled pastry. The shepherd rarely gets to town to sample sweets. Besides, the pastry gives him an opportunity to take pride in the delicious city ways in which his ricotta is put to use.

Nino and I went back down the steps and into Bar Cristallo for a cappuccino and a custard-filled horn-shaped pastry, the favorite Polizzani breakfast. Santo Lipani, who would be taking a few hours off before beginning morning preparations at Orto dei Cappuccini, and his sister Mimma would be joining us on the expedition. In a moment, they, too, entered the café.

Although born of the same parents, Mimma and Santo bear little physical resemblance to each other. She is the exact opposite of her fair-skinned, squarely built brother, who so clearly has the blood of Viking or Swabian conquerors in his veins that we jokingly call him Ulrich. Petite, with dark hair,

Mimma has large, shining brown eyes that are filled with laughter and a glint of mischief. She was home for vacation from Pisa, where she works as an executive assistant in a shoe factory. By now, in mid-August, her olive complexion had been well bronzed by the Sicilian sun. With a knowing smile, Mimma opened her knapsack to show a freshly baked round loaf of semolina bread. "What?" she said incredulously, with arched eyebrows and emphatic hand gestures. "Were you going to eat ricotta without bread?"

After breakfast, our little band climbed into Nino's red Fiat. We wound our way down the state road from Polizzi, turned onto a dirt road, and in five minutes were deep into the countryside. The summer wheat harvest was over, and the hilly landscape was a palette of gold and sand. Occasionally there was a patch of black where fire had been used to clear a field, a time-honored method used to keep this land fertile.

After some discussion as to which upcoming unmarked dirt road would lead us closest to the *pagghiaru*, and several failed attempts, Nino declaimed that we were finally on the right course. We others were doubtful but respectfully silent. When this road dead-ended in an empty, sun-parched pasture, we remained doubtful but followed his lead on foot anyway.

Ten minutes of walking, and silent thoughts of mutiny, led us to a walled sixteenth-century farm estate, a *massaria*. These buildings had belonged to an aristocratic family, stabling farm animals and housing generations of tenant farmers in cramped living quarters. Above the main entrance was emblazoned the sun- and moon-dials of the Baron Gagliardo di Carpinello's coat of arms.

Fifty sheep were penned in a nearby pasture, guarded by canine sentries. Just outside the far wall of the baron's compound was the *pagghiaru*. Through spaces between the boards of the door, we could see a fire burning inside. Ricotta preparation had begun.

This was the first *pagghiaru* I had ever seen, except in photos or drawings. It was surprisingly large, its stacked stone base twenty feet in diameter. Above it, a conical skeleton of cane poles thatched with straw rose to about the same height. The symmetry and proportion of its design were strangely reminiscent of the Great Pyramid, I thought.

We called out a greeting, and the door opened slowly to reveal the slight figure of a man shadowed by the ancient darkness. He stooped to pass into the light, and I saw his face framed by the straw of the *pagghiaru*.

It was oval, with a somewhat pointed chin; a long, straight nose divided it exactly in half. Even though his complexion was weather-beaten from years of working outdoors, and it showed him to be a man past seventy, his cheeks were a brilliant, childlike pink. His eyes, thick-lidded and nearly hidden by his bushy brows, held the most kind, most docile expression I have ever seen. A salt-and-pepper mustache adorned his upper lip, and the rest of his face was covered in snowy white stubble. His ears stuck out a bit from his head. The sum of his countenance made the shepherd look remarkably like a sheep.

Nino introduced us to the shepherd, Mastru (maestro, an elder title of respect) Stefanu Gugliuzza. While shaking hands all around, Nino discreetly presented the shepherd with the pastry. Lowering his face to hide the blush that came to his already bright cheeks, Mastru Stefanu accepted the offering with both hands.

He quickly invited us inside and closed the door, explaining that the draft was diminishing the fire. The light of the small fire did little to dispel the darkness inside the *pagghiaru*, but the darkness sharpened our noses to the sweet smells of straw, and milk, and fresh cheese. Our eyes adjusting, we saw the shepherd removing the morning's first cheese from tubs filled with whey and placing it in straw baskets.

Near to the fire sat a large copper cauldron. It was blackened on the outside from years of use on an open flame, but its tinned interior was immaculately clean. Mastru Stefanu asked if we would help him set it on the fire. He poured in the whey, salted water, and whole ewes milk, and we waited for the ricotta to come to the top.

The process of ricotta-making is a simple but arduous one. While the milk in pails is still warm from the ewe, most of it is poured into tubs and mixed with rennet (*quagghiu* in Sicilian), a preparation made from the stomach lining membrane of lambs or calves that is used in practically all the world's cheese-making. In Sicily, rennet is always made from lambs. It clabbers the milk, turning it to curds and whey.

The curds, called *'a quagghiata*, are broken up with a wooden pounding tool, a *ruottula*, and quickly form again. This first cheese is called *tuma*. The word derives from the Greek *tomos*, meaning section; the English word *tome*, meaning a large book, comes from the same root. An amount of *tuma* is sold fresh, unsalted, for use in both savory and sweet dishes. Most of it, however, is salted in brine. After ten days, it becomes *primusali* (first-salt); after two months, *purmintiu* (tender pecorino, like the first green of spring); and after four months, *tumazzu*, known outside Sicily as pecorino-Siciliano, a hard cheese for grating.

After the first cheese is formed, the whey is placed in a cauldron, mixed with an amount of fresh ewe's milk and some salt dissolved in water, and re-cooked (which is what *ri-cotta* means). As the mixture heats, *schuma*, a white froth of residue and fat, rises to the surface. This is removed with a copper skimmer and fed to the dogs.

As the mixture reaches scalding temperature, the ricotta, as if by magic, rises to the top. It is lifted out of the liquid and transfered to straw baskets or slatted wooden containers, placed on a high wooden rack covered with straw, and left to drain. The remaining liquid, called *sieru*, is poured into tubs and the first cheese replaced in it for five hours to complete its formation. Ricotta not sold within a day is salted in brine and pressed into hard ricotta, *ricotta dura*, used as grating cheese for soups and pasta dishes. It is the whey-cheese version of *tumazzu*.

It takes an astonishing amount of ewes' milk to even start this process: Ten liters of milk is required to make *one* kilo of cheese. At each milking, a ewe gives a mere half liter (about two cups) of milk, meaning that the milk of ten ewes is needed to produce a single pound of cheese! Unlike cows, ewes must be milked twice a day, morning and evening.

I asked Mastru Stefanu if he had any help with this task. He proudly told me that two of his sons were also shepherds. He added, with a note of sadness, that his third son, "the one who studied," never comes to the *pagghiaru*.

Mastru Stefanu presented the hot ricotta and *sieru* to us in a copper bowl. With a humble bow, he returned to the task of skimming off the rest of the morning's ricotta. We set the bowl atop a five-gallon milk can in front of the *pagghiaru*, in the glorious morning sun. On Mimma's cue, Santo cut crusted slices from the circumference of the bread, hollowing them out into spoons.

We crouched around the milk can and filled our bread spoons with hot ricotta, blew over it to cool it off, then slid the fluffy hot cheese into our mouths. Our senses filled with a delicate, slightly smoky flavor. Between swallows, our ears tuned in to the buzzing of insects and the nearby bleating of sheep and barking of dogs, all carried on a Polizzani still-early-morning summer breeze. Our little band smiled and laughed, taking as much pleasure in watching each other eat this ancient, simple food as in eating it ourselves.

At one point, Santo cut bread into chunks and dropped them into the *sieru* to soak. Mimma smiled. We ate that as well, fishing it out with our fingers and slurping up every last bite. Mastru Stefanu came outside with a shy, pleased expression and a container of drained ricotta for us to take back to town. We thanked the gracious shepherd for his hospitality, and after several go-rounds of well-wishes and hand-shaking, we bade him farewell. Reaching the little red Fiat, I turned around to find that the *pagghiaru*, the small flock, and the baron's compound had disappeared back into the landscape.

Nino, Santo, Mimma, and I rode back to town in contented silence. Speaking as if joining an ongoing conversation, Nino said, "You know, the life of this shepherd is not as poor and lonely as one might think."

It seems that Mastru Stefanu and his sons have a flock of 700 sheep, producing about 130 pounds of cheese a day. Although the work is demanding, and his sons (two of them, at least) do spend lonely nights with the flock in distant pastures, Stefanu returns to his bed in Polizzi every night. And what a bed it is!

Twenty years ago, the Baron Gagliardo di Carpinello could no longer manage the taxes and upkeep on his 500-year-old, 365-room palazzo. For a mere $50,000, the largest, most prestigious residence in Polizzi was sold to a partnership of local businessmen. It was partitioned into apartments and sold off as cooperative units.

Mastru Stefanu, the humble shepherd, and his wife bought one of these units. It not only includes the baron's bedroom, but also the baron's bed, a massive baroque artifact complete with eight-foot-high bedposts and full canopy.

Every night, the fortunate shepherd sleeps in the baron's bed and dreams the baron's dreams. But in the morning, his animals waiting to be milked call him to the *pagghiaru*, and he is the shepherd again. A small victory, perhaps, for the humble over the haughty, but a modern conclusion to the age-old strife between the baron and the shepherd.

Practically all of the ricotta made in this country is from cows' milk, rather than ewes' milk. Polizzani ricotta is thicker and dryer than most of the commercial product found in this country. Good-quality whole cows'-milk ricotta, however, can now be found in many places. It is made by smaller producers, and it is white, thick, and fluffy, never yellowish, grainy, or watery.

One way to increase your odds of getting good ricotta is to read the labels. The best ricottas are made with whole milk and are set with rennet (sometimes labeled "enzymes"). Less authentic ricotta is made with skim milk and is set with an acid, usually lemon juice or vinegar.

Pressed ewes'-milk ricotta is imported into this country. It is sometimes called hard ricotta, *ricotta salata*, or *ricotta dura*. There is also a Greek variety called *myzithra*. All are available in several textures. The softer ones are creamier and less salty, closer to the Polizzani type.

Purchase *ricotta salata* in small quantities, as it has a tendency to oxidize and turn brown. If the oxidation layer is thin, it may be pared away and the remainder of the cheese can be used.

Grate *ricotta salata* into small slivers on the large holes of a box grater. Prepare just as much as is needed, because it will dry out if grated in advance.

Pasta ca Ricotta

## Pasta with Ricotta

The delicate, subtle flavor of this dish depends entirely on the quality of the ricotta. The sheer simplicity of *Pasta ca Ricotta* has nourished and nurtured many generations of Polizzani, shepherds and aristocrats alike.

*For 4 servings*

2  tablespoons extra-virgin olive oil
2  tablespoons sea salt, plus additional as needed
1  pound linguine or spaghetti
¾  pound ricotta

Fill a large pot with 6 quarts water, and add the olive oil and the 2 tablespoons salt. Bring it to a boil over high heat, add the pasta, and cook until al dente, about 10 minutes.

Meanwhile, heat a serving bowl with hot tap water. Dry it, place the ricotta in the bowl, and mash it with a fork. Mix in ¾ cup of the starchy pasta water to loosen it.

When the pasta is cooked and drained, toss it with the ricotta. Check the salt, and serve immediately.

## Ricotta Fritta cu l'Ova

# *Fried Ricotta Omelet*

If the best-quality ricotta cannot be found, lesser-quality ricotta can be used for this dish with a bit of preparation. Take a 1-pound plastic container of ricotta, and poke numerous holes in the sides and bottom with a small knife. Set the container in a bowl, and let it drain for at least 2 hours. Push the ricotta down with a soupspoon to squeeze out as much liquid as possible; then remove the ricotta from the container as from a mold. Dry the surface of the ricotta with paper towels. The ricotta will now be dry enough to slice and fry.

*For 4 servings*

16 oil-cured black olives
12 ounces ricotta (or 1 pound prepared as described above)
3 eggs
  Sea salt
¼ cup extra-virgin olive oil
  Black pepper

Pit the olives by squeezing out the pits. Slice the ricotta into roughly 3-inch triangles or circles, about 1 inch thick. Break the eggs into a bowl, add a little salt, and beat until fluffy.

Pour the oil into a heavy, well-cured ovenproof skillet that is large enough to accommodate the ricotta in one layer. Heat it over medium heat until hot. Slip the ricotta and olives into the skillet and fry for 5 minutes.

Turn the ricotta over with a spatula. It will not have taken on much color, but it will be firm and easy to handle. Roll the olives to fry them on a different side. Fry this side of the ricotta for only 2 minutes (it will continue to brown after the eggs are added).

Pour the beaten eggs over the ricotta and olives. Evenly distribute them with a fork. Be sure that there are no olives at the very edge.

Turn down the heat to medium-low, cover the skillet, and cook for about 8 minutes, until the underside is a rich golden brown. This can be checked by gently lifting an edge with a spatula.

Meanwhile, preheat the broiler.

Remove the cover and place the skillet under the broiler, as close to the flame as possible. (Leave the handle sticking out if it is not flame proof.) Cook for about 2 minutes, until golden.

Carefully turn the omelet onto a plate. Use pieces of brown paper or paper towel to absorb any excess oil. Add a few coarse grindings of black pepper, slice, and serve.

## Minestra 'i Qualazzi

### *Rapini Soup*

*Qualazzi* are wild rapini. They grow in the countryside around Polizzi, from after the rains in early autumn until the first frost. This wild variety is thin-stemmed, mostly leaves with very few broccoli-like buds per stalk. Their flavor is more intense than the cultivated variety. Even so, cultivated rapini, sometimes called broccoli rabe, has the characteristic bitter, pungent flavor of the field variety and is a fine substitute.

For this recipe, the greens are cooked until quite soft in the same pot as the pasta, and their flavor enhances the pasta. Simple to prepare, this rustic soup is a wonderfully warming dish. As with many of the *minestre* from Polizzi Generosa, it is served with hard ricotta to grate on top.

*For 6 servings*

1    bunch (about 1 pound) rapini (broccoli rabe)
2    tablespoons plus ¼ cup extra-virgin olive oil
2    tablespoons sea salt
1    pound *ditali* or *ditalini* (small tube macaroni about ¼ inch in diameter and ½ inch long)
2    cloves garlic, peeled
     One 28-ounce can peeled whole Italian plum tomatoes, drained
1    teaspoon sugar
     Black pepper
4    ounces *ricotta salata* (salted pressed ricotta), in 1 piece
     Crushed red pepper

Clean the greens and cut away 1 to 2 inches of the thick, fibrous ends. Cut the greens into 1½-inch lengths.

Pour the 2 tablespoons olive oil into a pasta pot and place it over medium heat. When the oil is hot, add the greens. Turn them in the oil and immediately add 5 quarts water. Stir in the salt, cover, raise the heat, and bring to a boil. Then turn down the heat and simmer gently, covered, for 10 minutes or until quite soft.

Uncover the pot and turn up the heat to high. When the water returns to a boil, cook the pasta until al dente, about 10 minutes.

Meanwhile, place the remaining ¼ cup olive oil and the garlic in a heavy

6-quart pot. Sauté over medium-low heat until the garlic is a light golden color on all sides, about 5 minutes.

Crush the tomatoes with your hand and stir them well into the oil. Stir in the sugar and black pepper (no salt). Reduce the heat and simmer gently for the remainder of the pasta cooking time. Remove and discard the garlic cloves.

When the pasta is cooked, add 7 cups of the pasta water to the tomato sauce. Drain the pasta and greens, allowing some of the liquid to cling, and toss them in the pot with the sauce. Allow the flavors to mingle for 3 minutes, uncovered, over low heat.

Serve very hot, using the cooking pot as a tureen. Sprinkle each bowl with grated *ricotta salata* and crushed red pepper to taste.

# Italieddi ca Lattuca Affucata

## *Ditali with Drowned Lettuce*

In Sicilian or Italian culinary terms, *affucata* means poached. Literally translated, it means drowned. In the process of poaching, liquid is poured over the food, effectively drowning it.

Cooked lettuce, not very common in this country, is found in dishes of many European countries, and especially in the various cuisines of the Far East. As the lettuce's liquid content is reduced through cooking, its flavor is intensified. In this soupy pasta dish, the flavor is enriched with pancetta (Italian bacon) and chunks of pecorino cheese.

*For 6 servings*

Sea salt
1   or 2 heads romaine lettuce (about 1½ pounds total)
4   ounces imported pecorino cheese, preferably Locatelli brand, in 1 piece
1   small yellow onion, finely chopped
¼   cup extra-virgin olive oil
    One ⅜-inch-thick slice pancetta (about 2 ounces), diced
2   small cloves garlic, peeled and finely chopped
1   teaspoon tomato paste
    Black pepper
6   cups spring water, hot
1   pound *ditali* or *ditalini* (small tube macaroni about ¼ inch in diameter
    and ½ inch long)
⅓   cup finely chopped fresh basil
    Crushed red pepper

Fill a large pot with 6 quarts water. Add 2 tablespoons salt and bring it to a boil over high heat.

Meanwhile, wash and dry the lettuce. Cut it into 2-inch lengths and put them in a bowl until needed.

Grate ½ cup of the cheese. Cut the remainder into ½-inch dice. Reserve until needed.

Prepare all the other ingredients, keeping them separate.

Put the onion and olive oil in a heavy 6-quart pot. Sauté over low heat until the onion is a rich golden color, about 7 minutes.

Raise the heat to medium-high and add the pancetta and garlic. Sauté for 2 minutes or until the pancetta turns clear. Stir in the tomato paste and add the lettuce, mixing it well with the other ingredients. Season with salt and grindings of black pepper. Reduce the heat to medium-low, cover, and cook for 8 minutes or until the lettuce is well wilted.

Add the diced pecorino, mixing it in well. Then "drown" the lettuce with the hot spring water. Stir, raise the heat, cover, and cook at a gentle simmer for about 10 minutes. Stir occasionally to prevent the cheese from sticking.

During this time, cook the pasta in the boiling water until al dente, about 10 minutes.

Drain the pasta, allowing some of the liquid to cling, and toss it in the pot with the lettuce. Stir in the basil, and check for salt.

Serve very hot, using the cooking pot as a tureen. Sprinkle each bowl with grated pecorino and crushed red pepper to taste.

Maccaruna ca Carni Sfilacciata

# Handmade Macaroni with Lamb Ragoût

Making macaroni by hand is an extraordinary process dating back hundreds of years. A small piece of dough is threaded onto a thin rush and rubbed against a board to form the small tube. The result is an artisanal wonder, bursting with hearty flavor.

Nowadays, even in Polizzi, a knitting needle often substitutes for the rush. Use a number 6 (4.25 mm) needle, 14 inches long. Wooden needles are best, because the ends can be easily chopped or sawed off and the wooden surface helps the macaroni to slip off more easily.

Making macaroni for six, one piece at a time, may seem like an endless task, but it actually goes quite quickly. Preparation time is only about 45 minutes.

The flour used in the macaroni is durum wheat flour—not the more coarsely ground semolina we usually use for pasta-making, but rather a finely ground product generally used for making bread.

This ragoût is thick and flavorful, more like a shredded lamb stew than a sauce. The eggplant gives the dish a surprising lightness. Baking it in a covered pan gives it a wonderfully hearty quality, making it a good choice for a one-course meal.

*For 6 servings*

**For the macaroni**
3   cups durum wheat flour, plus additional for dusting
1   teaspoon plus 2 tablespoons sea salt
    Extra-virgin olive oil, for greasing the knitting needle

**For the ragoût**
2   eggplants (2½ pounds total)
    Sea salt
    Two 35-ounce cans whole peeled Italian plum tomatoes, undrained
1   medium-sized yellow onion
2   tablespoons extra-virgin olive oil
2¾ pounds leg of lamb, boned (see sidebar)
1   cup dry white wine
1   tablespoon sugar

A note on purchasing and trimming the lamb: Buy a piece of lamb from the sirloin end of the leg, weighing 2¾ pounds. Bone it and remove every bit of fat from both sides. The trimmed meat can end up being in two pieces and should weigh about 1½ pounds. Use the bone in the ragoût for added flavor.

Black pepper
1½ cups pure olive oil, for frying
¾  cup grated imported pecorino cheese, preferably Locatelli brand

Prepare the macaroni: In a large bowl, mix together the 3 cups durum wheat flour and the 1 teaspoon salt. Using a stand mixer fitted with the dough hook, or by hand, slowly add up to 1¼ cups water to form a ball. If it is crumbly, add more water; if sticky, add more flour. Knead the dough (by hand or machine) for 5 to 7 minutes to produce a smooth, elastic dough.

Dust both a work surface and a sheet pan with flour. Take a piece of dough about the size of a lemon and dust it. Roll it between your hands or against the work surface to form a cylinder ⅜ inch in diameter. Cut it into pieces ⅜ inch long.

Grease a knitting needle with a paper towel dipped in olive oil. Put a piece of dough on the needle and roll it against the work surface with your hand to form a macaroni about 2½ inches long. Gently grasp the macaroni within your fist and pull out the needle with the other hand. Place the macaroni on the sheet pan. Continue with the remaining dough.

It may be necessary to regrease the needle between the first few macaroni to prevent sticking. After that, no further greasing will be necessary and the rest of the macaroni will slide off quite easily. As the sheet pan fills, shake it to make sure the macaroni is not sticking together or to the pan. Redust the pan as needed. When all the macaroni is made, sprinkle it with flour and let it dry, uncovered, for the remainder of the preparation time.

Prepare the ragoût: Peel the eggplant and cut them lengthwise into ½-inch-thick slices. Salt the slices on both sides and arrange them in two stacks of equal height in a large shallow bowl. Place an upside-down plate on top. Press the eggplant under a light weight, such as a can of tomatoes or a container of salt, for 2 hours to express the bitter liquid.

Meanwhile, fit a food mill with the disk with the smallest holes (1 millimeter), and place it over a bowl. Pour the tomatoes and their liquid into the mill. Puree the tomatoes to remove the seeds, which can make the sauce bitter. Scrape the pulp from underneath the mill into the bowl.

Peel the onion, cut it in half, and thinly slice it. Put the extra-virgin olive oil and the onion in a heavy 5- or 6-quart pot. Sauté over medium heat until the onions turn translucent, 2 to 3 minutes. Raise the heat to high and add the lamb and the bone. Lightly brown the meat on all sides for about 7 minutes.

Remove the pot from the heat and pour in the wine. Deglaze the pot, scraping up any bits that may have stuck during browning. Turn the heat back to medium, and let the wine bubble for about 2 minutes, turning the meat and onion in the wine.

Slowly, to avoid splattering, add the milled tomatoes, salt to taste, the sugar, and several grindings of black pepper. Raise the heat to medium-high and bring the liquid to a boil, uncovered. Stir to prevent the onions from sticking.

Reduce the heat, partially cover, and cook at a simmer for 1½ to 2 hours, until the meat shreds when tweaked with a fork. Stir occasionally. If the lamb is not completely submerged in the sauce, turn it every 30 minutes.

When the eggplant has been pressed for 2 hours, rinse it under a trickle of cold running water to remove the excess salt. Pat the slices dry with paper towels, and put them on a platter with two sheets of paper towels between the layers.

In a heavy 9-inch skillet, heat the oil over medium heat until very hot. Fry the eggplant in batches for 2 to 3 minutes on each side, until they are a rich golden color and cooked through. Drain on brown paper or paper towels.

When the eggplant has cooled to room temperature, cut it into pieces about 1 inch wide and 2 inches long. Spread the pieces on fresh brown paper or paper towels to further drain any grease, and set aside until needed.

Meanwhile, fill a large pot with 6 quarts water, add 2 tablespoons salt, and bring it to a boil over high heat.

When the lamb is cooked, turn off the heat, leaving the pot on the stove, uncovered. Take out and discard the bone. Remove the meat, thinly slice it, and then shred it. Skim off all the grease from the sauce and stir the shredded lamb back into the sauce. Keep the ragoût on the stove with the burner off, uncovered, until needed.

Preheat the oven to 375°F, with a rack positioned in the center.

Gently put the macaroni in the boiling water, leaving behind as much of the loose flour as possible. Stir it to prevent sticking, and cook it until it is al dente and not gummy, 12 to 14 minutes. Run cold water into the pot to stop the cooking process, and drain the macaroni thoroughly. Put it in a bowl and toss it with about ⅔ cup of the ragoût.

Spoon about one third of the remaining ragoût into a 12- by 8-inch baking pan. Add the macaroni in an even layer. Evenly distribute the eggplant over the macaroni, and cover with the remaining ragoût. Sprinkle with the grated cheese.

Cover the pan with aluminum foil and bake for 30 minutes, until the cheese has melted and the dish is piping hot. Serve in pasta bowls.

*Four*

# A Question of Culture

*he* unique cultural identity of Polizzi is based on a jumble of historical fact, apocryphal myth, and just plain fantasy. These elements are maintained by its small, somewhat isolated location and the ancient family clans with which Polizzi is populated.

For people from great cities, like New York or Los Angeles, or even from suburban America, the relationships small-town folks have with each other may be difficult to grasp. When I'm in Polizzi, strolling in the evening with my friend Nino, he stops to chat or nods hello to just about everyone we pass. After one such encounter, I asked, "Who's that?"

"He's the son of the fruit seller on the Piazza Barone. He goes to university in Palermo" was the answer.

"Who's she?" I asked of someone else.

"She's the niece of Pino, and that woman is her aunt."

"And him?"

"That's Mario. We were in the same class in school. His brother is standing right there, but they had an argument four years ago and don't speak."

"And them?"

"The cousins of the pharmacist. They live in Milano now, but come back every summer. The husband is German, and the children are bilingual."

"And who's that man?"

"He's not from here."

Precise knowledge of every member of each Polizzani family is reinforced by the universal use of family nicknames, or *'ngiuria* (injuries). These some-

71

what insulting, often vulgar, monikers are better recognized than people's actual surnames. But they remain a secret identity code, not shared with outsiders. Sicily's long history of foreign occupation and resistance has given everyone a ready secret identity, in some cases *noms de guerre*.

A family's *'ngiuria* might reflect the occupation of a renowned forebear, or a family's traditional trade might be the inspiration, as for the families known as *Zalidda* (Grapevine) and *Scorcia Vuoi* (Bull-Skinner). The family known as *Ting-a-tong* operates the organ bellows in church. One family is simply called *Merda*: they are chicken farmers.

An ancestor's physical trait or a common family one might be at the root. *Rapparina* is the nickname of a family with rosy cheeks; *Casciatiddu*, of one whose family members are short and barrel-like. The particularly muscular individuals of one family have given all its members the name *Valatunni* (Strong Stone). All the animals are also represented through *'njuria*. My favorite is the one my Polizzani cousins are known by: *Canazzu* (Bulldog) for their jowly, fierce faces.

Handicapped predecessors are well remembered by some *'ngiurii*. The family *Ngung-gù* got its nickname because four generations ago, a deaf-mute relative went about town making that sound. The mentally challenged great-great-grandfather of one family has forever burdened it with *Sceccureddu* (Little Donkey).

The most interesting *'ngiurii* immortalize a moment that struck a particularly deep resonance with the neighbors. For example, the "Five Favas Family," *Cinqui Favi*, is so called because a farmer great-grandfather planted five fava beans in each hole instead of one.

The inspiration for *'nguiria* can be ambiguous. The "Big Leaf Family," *Pampinazza*, may have had a member so adept at farming that even the leaves of his crops were enormous, or, perhaps, refers to the size of his "fig leaf."

"The procession is one minute late," or "The city council meeting should have started already," one citizen would always lament, consulting his pocket watch. Nothing was ever timely enough for him. For this, the family is now known as *Ruggiu Pricisu* (Precise Watch).

Sometimes the moment is lost to time but the injuries remain, in their most colorful form. Fanciful examples include *Pisca u Purtusu* (Pees-in-a-Hole), *Cca-cca Ligna* (Wood-shitter), and *Minchia 'i Puci* (Flea-penis), naming but a few of the more than three-hundred *'ngiurii* still in use. The normally refined Polizzani are not disturbed by the language of any of them. After all, they're someone's name.

In a few cases, the *'ngiuria* itself has no meaning, as in the Bafù Family. They arrived a hundred years ago, no one knows from where. Coarse, dirty, lazy, and uneducated, they are held up to children as a negative example. A child exhibiting sloppy table manners elicits parental disapproval with phrases like "What is this? Eating *Bafù*-style?" or "I'm going to send you to live with the *Bafù!*"

Some say the *Bafù* are descended from the Arab-Sicilian aristocracy, using it as the ultimate example of blue-blooded decay. This idea seemed to me a socialist revision. But when a friend from the other side of Sicily told me his town also had *Bafù*, with the same social traits as ours, I endeavored to learn more about this mysterious family.

Polizzi has a remarkable library, the core of which was bequeathed to the city by Duke Federico Lancia di Brolo in 1893. It contains several hundred printed volumes from the sixteenth century and a rare collection of earlier illuminated manuscripts. Today the library houses a collection of over forty thousand volumes, making it the second most important library in Sicily.

In its research section, I found a book on the derivation of Polizzani *'ngiurii*. This book revealed the surname of the *Bafù* to be Spagnolo, and shows its coat of arms to be filled with noble heraldry, supporting the local legend.

Sicilian historians are meticulous in their research. Each minute detail is confirmed, as is the responsibility of social scientists. The Polizzani oral tradition, however, paints history in much broader strokes, adding the alchemical elements of humanity and personality.

It is widely believed that the Chiesa Madre, the main church of Polizzi, stands on the site of an ancient Greek temple dedicated to Isis, the original patroness of the city. Eighteenth century drawings of a four-foot statue, dating from antiquity, show the form of a woman with three faces. The central face was of a beautiful woman with long thick hair and a flower on her forehead, centered in a triangular medallion. The face on the right side of the head was of an old sage; on the left, of an innocent boy. In her right hand she held a globe, and in her left were two serpents. The faces of the statue clearly represent Isis, Osiris, and Horus.

When the Chiesa Madre was built in the thirteenth century, the statue was used as the pedestal for the baptismal font. For centuries, generations of Polizzani would be baptized over the ancient statue of the original patroness of the city.

In 1775 a major renovation of the Chiesa Madre was completed. The bishop of Cefalù, the diocesan seat, was invited to the festivities. He was taken on a grand tour of the church and proudly shown the details of its art and architecture. Upon seeing the statue holding up the baptismal font, his face grew wild with excitement. He declared that it was truly profanity to have a pagan statue in a Catholic church. He ordered that the statue be removed at once, brought to the Capuchin monastery, and smashed to bits. His orders, unfortunately, were dutifully carried out.

As word spread of the bishop's idiotic actions, the townspeople's anger grew. The city council convened in emergency session to write a formal protest of the bishop's idiocy, sending it to the Church and the State. A copy of this document shows the signature of every prominent citizen of Polizzi of the day, aristocrat and bourgeois alike.

Many who tell the story point out that the broken pieces were too small to recognize; it has become more and more the belief in Polizzi that the statue was never broken. The agitated look on the bishop's face, they say, was not caused by righteous anger but by avarice: He wanted that priceless piece of art for his own. Santo Lipani made a painting portraying the bishop in a secluded garden, kneeling in greedy, lustful adoration of the statue.

Sometimes tales recount heroic events that may never have happened. Yet they supply the Polizzani with glorious archetypes, as all heroic epics do. One such story, not found in history books, tells of a long, brutal ninth-century Saracen siege. The people, cut off from fields and pastures for months, were on the verge of starvation and the town was about to capitulate.

In an extraordinary effort to save Polizzi, women turned away from their nursing infants and, dolefully ignoring their hungry babies' wails, made cheese out of their own milk. Smiling, they tossed the precious cheese over the walls to the enemy, giving the illusion that there was still plenty to eat inside. The invading force, certain their siege was futile, negotiated peace, and Polizzi was saved from destruction.

•   •   •

The Polizzani are great storytellers. Often the recounter of legends will begin with an offhand remark, such as "Some people believe . . ." or "Once everyone thought . . ." I have learned that in spite of these disclaimers, what follows is sure to be commonly accepted truth. Such is the case with the legend of the mountain of gold. The words and actual events may change from storyteller to storyteller, but the object lessons remain the same. Following is my translation based on a written account developed by Carlo Borgese, a modern Polizzani historian and culturalist.

Once, long, long ago, in a time not connected to the common era, there lived in these parts a wicked, miserly king. Through cruel taxes and heartless rule, he amassed a vast fortune of gold. As this king neared the end of his life, he realized his heirs would inherit the fortune. Obsessed by greed, the king endeavored to find a way to prevent anyone from ever obtaining his gold, even after his death.

The avaricious king decided to hide the gold in the mountains above Polizzi. He chose a cave in an area still called today *u manicu da padedda*, the panhandle. This ravine and the round canyon above it give the appearance of a frying pan on the face of the mountain.

The cave he chose had seven rooms, and the king filled them to overflowing with seven piles of gold coins. In these same mountains lived a mysterious giant monk. The king cast him under a spell, gave him a mighty hammer, and stationed him as guardian. Having done this, the spiteful king closed the entrance to the cave with an impenetrable wooden door. Using magic, he instantly covered it with thick, verdant growth, shielding it from view. A short time later, the miser died, taking to the grave the location of the secret hiding place.

They say that the gold is still in the mountain, and that the mysterious monk, known as Santu Cuonu, remains on duty with his mighty hammer. According to ancient legend, the fortified wooden door of the treasure trove opens once every seven years, on Good Friday. It remains open for the exact length of time of the Passion of Christ service at the Chiesa Madre in Polizzi. Only during this time does Santu Cuonu put down his hammer to pray. When the church service is over, the door closes, and any mortal still inside must remain in the dark, airless cave for seven years, facing a certain, horrible death.

The mountain itself has its own ways of protecting its treasure from pillage, for it too is still under the enchantment of the evil king. At the moment the service begins, the mountain engulfs itself in a thick fog. The uncommon darkness can cause even the most experienced woodsman to lose his way and fill even the stoutest heart with terror. If he is lucky enough to find the door, he might be too disoriented and fearful to find the courage to move the hammer away from Santu Cuonu. Obsessed with the desire for gold, he might lose track of the time and end up locked in the cave forever. But over the centuries, all these deadly perils have had no effect on some men's dreams of countless riches.

Years and years ago, a man of the earth, virtuous and courageous, went searching for the treasure. He prayed to heaven for guidance in his quest. One Good Friday, he arrived on the mountain with seven mules to carry away the treasure. The mystical fog could not obstruct his purpose, and after some short time, he found the door. It was open, and he realized that the hour was right for him to become rich. He entered the cave and saw the awesome giant in prayer, the mighty hammer on the ground beside him. While bowing in respect to Santu Cuonu, the brave man snatched up the hammer. At that very moment he heard the distant cries of many people and the clatter of dragging chains. He understood these sounds to be from the souls of the many who had been enchanted by the treasure and lost.

Redoubling his courage, he began to fill sacks with gold coins and to carry them outside. The mules were burdened with the fortune of gold, which barely made a dent in the treasure still within the cave. But the just man was satisfied. He paid his respects to Santu Cuonu, still on his knees in prayer, replaced the hammer at his side, and left the cave.

While leading the caravan of mules back down the mountain to Polizzi, the victorious seeker became lost in fantasy, imagining his new life as a man of wealth. Touching his head he realized that he had lost his cap. Certainly it had fallen off his head while paying his final respects to Santu Cuonu.

Not willing to hang up his hat, he returned to the cave, tied up his beasts, and re-entered. He searched and searched, walking deep into the mountain, but the cap could not be found. He became lost. He couldn't find the door, for Santu Cuonu had closed it—the Passion was over.

As death approached, the poor fellow grew more and more frantic. He fell to his knees, fervently praying to the Almighty. In his prayers, he swore a solemn oath. If he were granted the freedom to leave, he would build a church in the name of the Savior.

All but dead, he felt something in his pocket. He reached in and, surprisingly, his fingers touched a blade. Holding it before his eyes, he knew that the ancient knife was not his. Perhaps, he thought, God has answered my prayer. He tapped the walls of the cave with the handle, looking for a thin place in which he might make a hole. He scratched the surface of the wall with the blade, chipping the stone away bit by bit. He did not lose hope, and kept faith in God's justice. After many hours of prayer and work, he had made a small hole, squeezed himself through, and escaped, praising the Lord.

Outside, in the light of day, he found his gold-laden mules undisturbed, just where he had left them. He quickly led them off the mountain and back home. The very next morning, he began building a church, as he had vowed, hewed into the face of the mountain. Above the altar he placed a golden statue of the Savior, made from gold coins of the treasure. The Little Church of the Savior still stands as a monument to one man's courage and faith. Some say that if it could be found, beneath the church's walls is the door to the treasure trove of the mountain of gold.

One evening, I was sitting in the overlook piazza with Nino. We were looking across to the Panhandle and discussing the legend. Just then, an old, lame man with a simpleminded expression began to cross the piazza. "They say," Nino began with the familiar disclaimer, "that his father actually saw the gold but failed to reach the cave before the door closed. Seven years later he returned, but he couldn't find the door. His preoccupation with refinding the gold became his only thought. He lived from one seventh-year Good Friday to the next. His neglected his farm, and the family grew poorer and poorer.

"He became a terrible drunkard, cursing and fighting with everyone. Finally his obsession turned into cruel madness. Those who are old enough to remember say it was very sad. The police, even the priest, couldn't stop him. He abused his wife and brutally beat all his children. This one, they say, he beat so badly that he became lame and senseless." As the old man drew nearer, he gave us a pathetic, glassy-eyed grin, then moved aimlessly away, dragging his leg behind him. "The sins of the father," Nino sighed.

More lighthearted, and sometimes satirical, are the legends and fables that illustrate relationships between men and women. The overbearing or pompous husband and the shrew wife amusingly show desirable qualities of wisdom, strength, and resourcefulness gone awry, as the next two fables illustrate.

### THE OLD MISER (*u Vecchiu Avaru*)

There was an old miser who married three times for the purpose of gaining his wives' goods. On his first wedding night, he said to his bride, "If we are to stay together, you must do as I say." The innocent girl, wishing to be a good wife, agreed.

The next morning, he put three lentils in a pot and boiled them. When they were cooked, he poured the meager broth into two bowls and divided the lentils. "This," he said, "is our meal." That evening he bought one salted sardine, ordering her to prepare only the tail section. The rest was to be saved for another day. The obedient wife did exactly as her husband wished and ate her half of the sardine tail. Little by little, the wife grew thinner and thinner, until she passed away.

The old miser married again and disposed of his second wife in the same way as the first. With his third wife, however, it turned out differently. She was a bit more worldly and a great deal smarter than the first two, and she quickly figured out his scheme.

Every morning, the old miser went to the country "to work," he said. But in reality he went to eat. Before leaving, he ordered either the three lentils or a part of a sardine for lunch. She would walk him to the front door and wave good-bye as he rode away. When he was well out of sight, she'd go to the backyard where the stingy man kept a large coop filled with chickens. She'd kill a nice, plump chicken and make soup, nourishing herself well.

When the husband returned from the country, he found only the three-lentil soup or a part of a sardine ready for lunch. The wife would bring out, perhaps, the head of a sardine, the husband would divide it, and they'd both pretend to dine together.

One morning, the wife realized that she had eaten all the chickens. The coop was empty, except for the rooster. She decided to cripple the old cock. When her husband returned she said to him, "The rooster is lame. You know what I say? Let's eat him."

"Yes, let's," said the husband, adding, "but this rooster will have to last for two months."

"But how?" she inquired, with feigned innocence.

"First," he said, "we'll cook the feet, then half the breast, and so on, so that this rooster will be on our dinner table for two months."

As soon as the husband left for "work" the next day, the wife cooked the whole rooster and saved it. Upon his return, he asked, "Did you cook the rooster?"

"Of course," she responded.

"But what did you cook? The feet? A piece of the breast?"

"I did just as you said," she obsequiously answered.

She went into the kitchen, took the rooster out of the broth, and put it on a plate. She then heated the broth with only the feet and carried it to the table. As the kitchen door closed behind her, the old miser glimpsed the whole, cooked rooster on the plate. Also, for the first time he noticed that his wife was not growing thin and realized that she had outsmarted him.

He became apoplectic and, barely finding the breath, screamed out, "Ai-eee! All of it, Catarina!! . . . Ai-eee! All of it, Catarina!!" When the wife saw that he was about to die saying these words, she ran into the street and brought back four witnesses. After they heard the husband's cries, she said to them, "My name is Catarina. This is my husband, whose dying words, as you can hear, are 'All of it, Catarina.' Clearly he is leaving me all his wealth." The notary was called, but by this time the dying man could no longer speak. He gestured feebly in his wife's direction. With every gesture, she said, "You see? He's leaving it all to me."

The old miser died. Catarina took his wealth and married again.

### THE ARGUMENT IS ALWAYS OVER THE COVERS
#### (TUTTA LA SCIARRA É PI LA CUTRA)

Once there was a married couple. Whenever the husband heard anyone in the town quarreling or fighting, he ran to break up the disagreement. He never took sides, and his only motive was to make peace. Indeed, the altercating parties themselves often called for his intervention. In time he became known as *Mastru Paci*, Maestro Peace.

Not everyone in town, however, appreciated his endeavors. A gallery of rogues, annoyed by his good works, decided to play a trick on him. One cold, wintry night, they stood on the street under Mastru Paci's balcony window, pretending to argue and beat each other.

The commotion roused Paci and his wife from a sound sleep. She groaned with annoyance, but the earnest man whispered to her, "Be still! I will go down and end this uproar." The tired wife responded, "What's it to you? Whoever kills, let them kill." She continued, her anger growing. "Oh! Injustice! Isn't the daytime enough for you? Now, even at night, Mastru Paci has to disturb me with his terrible habit!"

"No!" he insisted gravely. "Let me go! For if not, there's sure to be a murder tonight." The husband knew his wife was probably right, but refusing to give in to her entreaties, instead looked for matches to light the lamp. He stumbled about, not able to find them in the dark bedroom. Then he looked for his clothes, but couldn't find them either. Realizing he wouldn't find much in the darkness, he grabbed the only cloak he could surely find—the bedcovers. He flung them around his neck and wrapped himself well, leaving his wife completely naked on the bed. The wife screamed, "Why did you pull away the covers and leave me like this? As it is, I have no peace day or night!"

Ignoring her, Mastru Paci went down to the street to make peace among the strangers. "My dear gentlemen, what have we here?" he said in a conciliatory tone. "Must you argue so late into the night?" Using the Mastru's words as a cue, the scoundrels fought their pretend rumble even harder. They took advantage of the confusion to snatch the covers from around the Master of Peace and run away, laughing and mocking, carrying off the covers around their own necks.

Mastru Paci, seeing he was now naked, filled with despair and climbed back upstairs to his wife. "Ai-ai!" he lamented as he sat on the edge of the bed. "The good one tries to do is always turned to bad." The wife had had enough of this business. "It serves you right!" she wailed at her naked husband. "And worst of all, *you* took all the covers!"

Cold, tired, naked, and mad as hell, she commanded him to "Wait right here!" In all her glory, she marched into the kitchen and returned, brandishing a rolling pin. Still naked, she chased her naked husband through the house. She whacked him out the door and locked it. The husband, thrown out of his own house by his own wife's anger, found himself naked and battered in the cold night air.

Thus the husband's career as Mastru Paci came to an ignoble end. But from this very event was born the Polizzani household proverb: The argument is always over the covers.

The idea of pure romantic love came to Sicily with the Saracens in the ninth century. Polizzani are still in love with love, even when it is as fanciful as in the next fable.

### THE LITTLE MAGPIE ('A CIAULIDDA)

Once upon a time, there was a rich landlord who lived in a great house. He was alone in the world, without relatives or offspring. His only companion was his pet magpie. She was a good pet, attending her master well. In return for this faithfulness, he left the bird uncaged, and she could do as she pleased. Every time the kindly master went out, however, the magpie, mischievous by nature, would sneak into the neighbor's garden. In it stood a fig tree resplendent with ripe fruit, of which she ate heartily.

There was even more to this magpie than met the eye, for she was enchanted. Before leaving the house, she would drop her feathers and turn into a beautiful young woman. After consuming her fill of figs, she would climb down the tree, return home, and wait for her master with feathers in place, seemingly the trustworthy and attentive little magpie.

The master would sing out, "Little magpie, little magpie, come to your master." She would climb onto his knee, he would give her sweet little caresses, and together they made a happy little scene. Still, whenever the master left the house, she'd drop her feathers and go eat figs.

One day while the magpie was up the tree, the master returned unexpectedly and discovered all her feathers on a chair. He called and called for his sweet little magpie, but there was no response. Panicked, he searched the house but his only friend could not be found—only her feathers. In an act of grief, he threw the feathers into the fire. Now truly alone in his great house, tears of loneliness rolled down his face.

Suddenly he heard footsteps at the door. Fearful that it might be the same villainous murderer returning to kill him, he hid in the pantry. It was, of course, the magpie, in the form of a beautiful young woman. Realizing that her feathers were no longer where she had left them, the color drained from her fair cheeks. The master, witnessing all this from his hiding place, gasped, "Ah! *You* are my little magpie?" And with that, he stood in speechless wonder.

Regaining his senses, he said, "Since you are already my sweet little magpie, will you be my wife?" The young woman fairly chirped with joy, and the couple ran quickly to the church to exchange their marriage vows.

The next morning, the new husband planted a fig tree in his own garden. It grew lush and bore the sweetest fruit, reflecting the sweet love between the old landlord and the little magpie. And they lived happily ever after.

Food, the cornerstone of Polizzani culture, has a sure place in legends and stories. Sarafinu di Bella, a sportsman and hunter, told me of an ancient recipe.

## PASTA WITH SNAILS (PASTA CHI VAVALUCCI)

First you must forage the snails. After it rains, go to any wild fennel patch and collect the snails. Take them one at a time by hand. Do not use a trowel or shovel. Gently place them in a deep basket, and cover it securely so the snails don't escape on your way home.

Clean the snails very carefully and gently. Do not shake or rinse them in a colander, but rather hold them one at a time under a trickle of cold running water. Count the number of cleaned snails, and silently put them into a large pot. Cover them with cold water and bring the water slowly to a boil.

As the water comes to a boil, the snails will get hot and poke their horns out of their shells. At that exact moment, throw in an amount of *italieddi* [a small tube pasta]. Now, the snails are hot in their shells, the pasta is cold. So the snails, looking for relief, will leap out of their shells and insert themselves into the pasta. The snail-stuffed pasta is heavy and will sink to the bottom. The light, empty shells will float to the top, and you can remove them with a slotted spoon. When the pasta is cooked, drain, sauce, and serve.

I cannot stress enough how important it is to treat the snails with the utmost care and gentility. Rough handling might blind them, and then they wouldn't be able to find the holes in the pasta tubes.

Choose pasta tubes that are considerably smaller than the average snail shell opening. (Remember that the pasta will grow when cooked.) Don't worry if the snails seem too wide to fit. They can always stretch longer and become thinner.

An accurate counting of snails and pasta is a must, to ensure that every snail has a place to go. An empty pasta tube or a loose snail will ruin the dish. One time, a friend of mine made the dish, precisely following all of my directions. But in the end, one pasta tube remained empty. He couldn't figure it out, but the moment I saw the platter, I knew what had happened. In their haste to escape their hot shells, two snails had entered the same pasta tube, one from each end, like stuffing a cannoli.

Sarafinu takes great pleasure in seriously offering this absurd recipe to pretentious foodie folk, seeing how long he can keep them hooked.

I told him about a Japanese recipe that really does employ a similar process: Tiny live fish are placed in cold broth. As the broth heats, the fish swim around faster and faster, looking for escape. Just before the fish expire, a perfect rectangle of cold tofu is placed into the pot, whereupon, in desperation, the fish embed themselves inside.

Sarafinu shrugged. "It's only a question of culture."

## Pasta chi Civa

# *Baked Pasta with Almonds*

*Pasta chi Civa* is baked rigatoni in a pork ragù with chopped toasted almonds. It is traditionally prepared in Polizzi Generosa for *Carnilivari*, Mardi Gras. Every evening of this festival, the whole town assembles in the piazzas of Polizzi to dance. *Pasta chi Civa* is served to fortify the dancers for this great expenditure of energy.

Although the list of ingredients seems more likely to pin someone to an armchair than to inspire a whirling dervish, every time I serve the dish it has the most remarkable effect on my guests: Within 20 minutes of having eaten it, they are dancing, and they continue to feverishly prance away until the small hours of the morning!

*For 6 servings*

Sea salt
One 35-ounce can peeled whole Italian plum tomatoes, undrained
3   tablespoons extra-virgin olive oil
1   medium-sized yellow onion, finely chopped
12  ounces lean pork, ground
1   tablespoon tomato paste dissolved in ⅓ cup water
    Black pepper
2   teaspoons sugar
    Pinch of ground cinnamon
½   cup unflavored bread crumbs
6   ounces (1⅓ cup) shelled whole raw almonds
½   teaspoon almond extract
1   pound rigatoni
¾   cup grated imported pecorino cheese, preferably Locatelli brand
4   sprigs Italian parsley, chopped

Fit a food mill with the disk with the smallest holes (1 millimeter), and place it over a bowl. Pour the tomatoes and their liquid into the mill. Puree the tomatoes to remove the seeds, which can make the sauce bitter. Scrape the pulp from underneath the mill into the bowl. Reserve the milled tomatoes until needed.

Put 2 tablespoons of the oil and the onion in a heavy saucepan, and place over medium heat. Sauté just until the onion turns translucent, about 4 minutes. Raise the heat and add the ground pork. Sauté until it is lightly browned, about 3 minutes. Keep it moving with a wooden spoon, breaking up any clumps that may form.

Reduce the heat and add the thinned tomato paste. Scrape up any bits of pork or onion that may have stuck to the bottom of the pot. Cook the paste for a couple of minutes, until it thickens slightly.

Remove the pot from the heat (to avoid splattering), and add the milled tomatoes. Stir it all together very well. Return it to medium-low heat and season with salt to taste, a few grindings of black pepper, the sugar, and the cinnamon. Simmer, uncovered, for the remainder of the preparation time, stirring occasionally.

Toast the bread crumbs by placing them together with the remaining 1 tablespoon olive oil in a small heavy skillet. Turn on the heat to very low, and stir to distribute the oil. Nothing will happen at first, but then the crumbs will brown quite quickly. Toast them until they are a deep rich brown. To prevent the bread crumbs from burning, transfer them to a bowl the moment they are done.

Preheat the oven to 400°F, with a rack positioned in the center. Fill a large pot with 6 quarts water, add 2 tablespoons salt, and bring it to a boil over high heat.

Toast the almonds on a baking sheet in the oven for 10 minutes, making sure they don't burn. As soon as the nuts are removed from the oven, while still in the pan, sprinkle the almond extract over them. Reduce the oven heat to 375°F. When the nuts are cool enough to handle, chop them to the size of ice-cream topping.

Cook the rigatoni in the boiling water until it is 2 minutes underdone. Drain it thoroughly. Turn it into a bowl, and toss with about ½ cup of the liquid from the ragù.

Very lightly coat the bottom of a 12- by 8-inch baking pan with a small amount of the ragù. Place half of the rigatoni in the pan in a neat layer. Cover it with half of the almonds, half of the remaining ragù, half of the toasted bread crumbs, and finally half of the grated pecorino. Assemble a second layer in the same way, starting with the remaining rigatoni.

Bake for 15 to 20 minutes, until very hot and slightly browned at the edges. Sprinkle the top with chopped parsley before serving.

## Sosizza chi Linticchi

# *Sausage and Lentil Stew*

The hearty, warming goodness of this one-course meal is only increased by its utter simplicity of preparation. Accompany the stew with crusty bread.

*For 4 servings*

1½ cups lentils
1¼ pounds thick or thin sweet (mild) Italian sausages without fennel seeds
3   ribs celery plus their leaves
1   medium-sized yellow onion
5½ cups spring water
½   teaspoon sea salt
    Black pepper

Rinse the lentils and cull them for small stones and debris. Put them in a heavy 4-quart pot with a tight-fitting lid. Cut thick sausages into 1-inch lengths or thin ones into 2-inch lengths, and put them in the pot. Clean and thinly slice the celery, chop the leaves, peel and finely chop the onion, and add it all to the pot.

Pour in the water, and add the salt and a few grindings of black pepper. Stir all the ingredients together, cover, and bring to a boil over medium heat, stirring occasionally.

Reduce the heat and cook at a lively simmer for about 1 hour, stirring from time to time to prevent the lentils from burning. When the sausages and lentils are cooked and the liquid has thickened, serve piping hot in bowls.

## Torta 'i Nuciddi

### *Hazelnut Cake*

Hazelnut trees abound in Polizzi Generosa, and their produce quite naturally finds its way into delicious sweet baked goods. From autumn to spring, this hazelnut cake is the dessert that is served most often in homes in the area. In the United States, hazelnuts are sometimes called filberts.

It is essential that the nuts be chopped barely in half. If they are chopped too fine, the nut powder will absorb the liquid ingredients and cause the cake to become too dry.

*For one 9-inch round cake*

6   ounces (1½ cups) shelled whole raw hazelnuts (filberts)
2   cups cake flour, plus additional for dusting the pan
1½ teaspoons baking powder
1½ teaspoons baking soda
    Pinch of salt
½   cup (1 stick) unsalted butter, plus additional for greasing the pan
1   cup granulated sugar
3   eggs, lightly beaten
⅓   cup milk
1   teaspoon vanilla extract
    Zest of 1 lemon, chopped
    Confectioners' sugar in a shaker

Preheat the oven to 400°F, with a rack positioned in the center.

Spread the nuts out on a sheer pan and toast them in the oven for about 10 minutes. Take care that they do not burn. Remove the pan from the oven, wrap the nuts in a dishcloth, and let them steam for a couple of minutes. Then rub them together to remove as much of the brown skin as possible. Chop the nuts in half, and reserve until needed.

Reduce the oven heat to 375°F. Grease and flour a 9-inch round cake pan with 2- or 3-inch-high sides.

Sift the flour, baking powder, baking soda, and salt together in a bowl.

Put the ½ cup butter in a different bowl and, using an electric mixer or by hand, cream the butter until it becomes pale yellow. Add the sugar and continue to beat until the mixture is fluffy. While continuing to beat, add the eggs very slowly. Continue to beat until the mixture turns a whitish color.

Beat in a small amount of the flour mixture. When it is absorbed, add more. Continue in this manner until all of the flour has been beaten in and absorbed.

In a small bowl, mix together the milk and vanilla. Pouring it in a slow, steady stream, beat it into the other ingredients to form a thick batter. Stir in the nuts and lemon zest.

Turn the batter into the cake pan and gently smooth the top with a rubber spatula. Give the pan one quick, gentle tap on the counter to displace any large air pockets. Bake for 35 to 40 minutes, or until the cake is a rich golden brown and a toothpick inserted in the center comes out clean.

Let the cake cool in the pan for 5 minutes. Then run a small, sharp knife around the top edge to free it, and turn it out of the pan onto a cooling rack (it will be upside-down).

When the cake has cooled thoroughly to room temperature, transfer it to a serving plate, leaving it upside down. Just before serving, dust the cake with confectioners' sugar.

# Pira 'Ncilippati

## Sugared Pears

The Sicilian word *'ncilippati* literally means "cooked in sugar." It is derived from the Italian *giulebbe*, which has its root in the Persian word for rosewater, *gulab*. The English word *julep* derives from the same root.

The very thick cooking syrup brings out the pears' wonderfully sweet character, but at the same time the flavor is not cloying. Sugared pears can be eaten on their own or cut in half and topped with vanilla ice cream. They are also the perfect topping for *Torta 'i Meli*, Honey Sponge Cake (page 153).

A candy thermometer is helpful in preparing this dish.

*For 6 servings*

6  firm Anjou pears (about 2¼ pounds total)
   Juice of 2 lemons
4  cups sugar
1  cup spring water

Bring a large pot of water to a boil.

Clean the pears. Cook them in the boiling water, covered, for 10 minutes. Drain, and cool them quickly in four changes of cold water. Leave them in a bowl with enough cold water to cover. Make ready another bowl with enough cold water to cover the pears. Add the lemon juice to the water in the second bowl.

Peel the pears with a sharp paring knife or with long, gentle strokes of a vegetable peeler. Core each from the bottom, leaving the stem intact. As each pear is peeled and cored, put it immediately into the lemon-water to prevent oxidation. Leave the pears in the lemon-water until needed.

Put the sugar and the spring water in a heavy pot that is large enough to accommodate the pears in 1 layer. Turn on the heat to medium-low and stir until the sugar is dissolved, about 10 minutes. Stop stirring, raise the heat to medium, and let the sugar water boil for 5 to 8 minutes, until the syrup turns clear. Then remove the pot from the heat and let the syrup cool to room temperature.

Remove the pears, one at a time, from the lemon-water. Shake off the excess water, and put them in the syrup.

Spoon a good quantity of syrup over the pears. Cover, and let them macerate for 24 hours at room temperature, spooning the syrup over the pears several times.

Put the pot back on the stove. Uncover, and bring the syrup to a boil over medium heat, turning the pears in the syrup from time to time. When it begins to boil, raise the heat to medium-high. Boil for about 15 minutes, turning the pears, until the syrup reaches the thread stage, 230°F on a candy thermometer. If you don't have a candy thermometer, drop a small amount of the boiling syrup into a glass of cold water. The syrup should form a soft thick thread.

Immediately transfer the pears to a serving bowl and pour the syrup over them. Let them cool, uncovered, to room temperature. Chill slightly and serve.

# Five

# A Little Piece of Earth

*T*he first day of August is the first day of winter," or so they say in Polizzi Generosa. The adage dates back a thousand years, to a time when agriculture first became the principal occupation in this mountain community. Throughout the spring and summer, *cuntadini* (tenant farmers) would plant and nurture their crops. By August, attention would turn to the harvest and preserving summer's bounty for the cold winter ahead. As each crop was gathered, this process of "winterizing" turned the landscape from green and lush to brown and empty.

Post–World War II land reforms broke up the baronial feudal estates. The land, now available on the open market, was purchased by the former *cunta-dini*. During the second half of the twentieth century, however, people farmed less and less, and much of the land has gone fallow. Even though Polizzi no longer has an agrarian-based economy, many people still tend their own *pizzuddu 'i terrenu* (little piece of earth).

The cornucopia of these farms, orchards, and vegetable gardens is boundless. A portion of each crop is prepared fresh, but the major part is preserved for use during the rest of the year. The wisdom of history has taught the Polizzani to be frugal, and every gift of the earth is put to delicious use. Each crop is picked at the peak of ripeness, for the distance between cropland and the dinner table is a short walk.

During one of my summer visits to Polizzi, I'd hear the morning shouts of a fruit-grower on my street in the center of town. Selling his produce from a Lambretta, a three-wheeled motorcycle-truck, he'd sing out in Sicilian, "Pears! Peaches! They were fresh." I thought his choice of tense odd, and puzzled over its meaning. Nino Gianfisco explained this curious usage.

"Every morning at first light," Nino began, "the fruit-grower goes into his orchard, picks the ripest pears and peaches, and loads the Lambretta. Then he takes breakfast coffee with his wife." Adding a wry smile, Nino continued, "By the time he gets to town, it's already eight o'clock. The fruits *were* fresh at dawn, but by then there's no guarantee."

Polizzi has a mighty harvest of deep-red, velvety plum tomatoes, the type called *san marzano*. Smoke billows from country sheds and city garages as huge cauldrons of these tomatoes are cooked into sauce over wood fires. The sauce is then canned in recycled mineral-water bottles.

The work is accomplished by entire families. Small children, supervised by grandparents, wash the fruit, gleefully splashing their hands in the washtubs of cold water. Women tend the cauldrons, knowing exactly when and how much onion and salt to add. Young men carry the steaming pots across the shed to a milling machine that separates pulp from seeds and skins. Older men feed the small hopper and refill the pots with the tomato sauce.

Stationed at a different cooking fire in the cramped shed, the most fastidious woman of the household is put in charge of bottle sterilization and canning, maintaining strict quality control. Over the course of two days, a large family can process a thousand bottles of tomato sauce.

During the tomato harvest, the hills around Polizzi streak with crimson, as women in straw hats keep careful vigil over plywood sheets covered with tomatoes. In one day, the Mediterranean sun will dry the tomatoes into a thick paste. Seeds are carefully saved for next year's planting. Ripe cherry tomatoes still on the vine are hung in cool sheds, where they will remain fresh for months. All tomatoes that have not had enough time to ripen are eaten green in salad, pickled in vinegar, or cooked into marmalade.

By this time of year, *cucuzza*, a long Sicilian squash, is beginning to go to seed. Some of these are candied into a sweet confection called *cucuzzatu*; some are dried, primarily to be used as an important ingredient in *cunigghiu*, the traditional Christmas Eve dish of salt cod and vegetables.

In preparation for drying, the *cucuzza* is peeled and split. The seeds are removed and saved, and the squash is well covered with sea salt. After a few days, a ring of thread is sewn through the end of each half, and they are suspended from bamboo poles and put in the sun to dry.

Small groups of old women gather in their gardens to accomplish this task. Sometimes the matriarchs are joined by their daughters or granddaughters. If a young girl makes a stitch too close to the edge or ties a bad knot, the squash falls. The grandmothers smile and laugh, offering the same instructions given to them in the long-ago past. Their still-nimble, strong fingers easily demonstrate the technique they've used for decades. Seen from across the garden, the hanging squash look like primeval wind chimes in the late afternoon sun. One can imagine that they are ringing with the voices of this chorus of womanhood.

By late August, eggplant is in the produce spotlight. Spears of it are pickled in vinegar. Some is conserved as *capunatina*, a medley of eggplant, the previous season's green olives, celery, some almonds and raisins, tomato sauce, and a bit of red pepper and vinegar. Following an eighteenth-century tradition, unsweetened cocoa powder is added to counter the piquant sweetness with its bitter flavor.

Eggplant is technically a fruit, a member of the nightshade family, cousin to the tomato and the potato. It is indigenous to China and India. Arab traders introduced it to the Mediterranean area a millennium ago. Of the four varieties grown in Polizzi, the most common is called *nostrali*, that is, "ours." It is the same variety found in American markets, although slightly smaller.

Second in abundance is the *tunisina* (Tunisian) variety, long and thin, resembling an oversized Japanese eggplant. The Tunisian is a botanically older variety, close to the original type brought by the traders.

A close third is the *viuletta* or *missinisa* (Messina) type. Medium-sized and more round than oval in shape, this type is not the common aubergine color, but rather violet and white. It has a more delicate, less acidic flavor than the other two.

The *bianca* are the rarest of Polizzi's eggplants. Small, white, and nearly round, they are the inspiration for the American-English word, "egg-plant." The other varieties require salt-leaching to draw out their bitter liquid. Fresh white eggplant, however, is almost completely nonacidic and does not require this procedure.

During the ten or so days of the eggplant onslaught, home cooks prepare course after course of the fruit for lunch and dinner, employing a prodigious repertoire of recipes. The true mark of a good cook is how interested she can keep her family at mealtime with the daily repetition of the same ingredients. In this regard, the Polizzani cook achieves high marks indeed.

First among these is my friend Nino's mother, Stefana. An invitation to lunch at the Gianfisco family country house is highly prized, and I am always thrilled when one comes my way. The house, built by Nino and his father, Turiddu, lies in the center of a massive property that includes a large kitchen garden, several stands of fruit, nut, and olive trees, and a sizable vineyard.

On one part of the patio is a pergola roofed with bamboo matting and walled on the southwest side with flowering vines as protection against the hot afternoon sun. The table inside, large enough for twenty, is often filled with a gathering of family and friends. Lunch is the main meal of the day, and guests often volunteer to help Turiddu skin the peppers that have been roasted in the cinders of a hazelnut-wood fire.

On a different part of the patio, others stand near a large copper pot of water set on a wood fire, where pasta will be cooked. They try to cajole Stefana into giving up her cooking secrets. "Pasta always tastes sweeter when it's cooked outdoors on a wood fire" is all Stefana will say, with a shy country smile. She has held on to her secrets.

The grand lunch begins with an antipasto of more than ten dishes. Bowls of olives are placed at the edges of the table. Some are black, some oil-cured, and some green, cured in brine flavored with cloves, lemon peel, and wild fennel seeds. A platter of pungent, chewy salami and one of young, soft pecorino cheese pass in praise. The roasted peppers are delicious. We eat them with our fingers in one bite, using a piece of bread as a charger to catch fruity olive oil drizzle.

In this season, four of the antipasto dishes are made with eggplant. A fresh *capunatina* is scooped up with bread, Moroccan-style. Thinly sliced violet-skinned eggplants are eaten hot off the wood-fire grill. The tart flavor of raw white eggplant marinated in lemon juice is offset by curls of aged pecorino scattered on top. Little balls of eggplant fried in olive oil require a refreshing sip of Turiddu's dry white wine to neutralize the oily richness.

Stefana is somewhat embarrassed by the compliments she always receives, but at the same time she knows we're right; her food is great. And whichever dish is lauded, Turiddu responds, "That's from here." Adding special emphasis by tapping his strong, old farmer's finger on the table, he repeats, "From *here*." Only the cheese is not from his domain. He flatly comments, "*That's* not from here." Holding the moment just long enough to set up the punch line, he then gestures to a nearby hillside and says, "It's from *there*."

The first course is rigatoni in tomato sauce with pieces of fried eggplant cut to the size of the pasta. Stefana's eggplant is fried in her own extra-virgin olive oil, its sweet-pungent taste and frothy texture a counterpoint in this hearty dish. A large piece of pressed salted ewes'-milk ricotta, *ricotta salata*, is passed around the table. We coarsely grate it over our pasta. The flakes fall into the bowl like gentle snow, melting slightly in the heat.

The second course brings Turiddu back to the wood fire, where he covers the grill with thinly cut mutton chops. Stefana joins him and together they grill the chops, turning them often to prevent the surface from being charred and bitter. The mutton chops are carried to the table, mounded on a platter. For accompaniment, there is a just-picked mixed green salad. We delicately eat the chops off the bone with the aid of our fingers and folding knives. Almost as a footnote, Stefana sets down her final masterpiece of the day, a baked eggplant omelet cut in small squares, "just to try."

After a dessert of very fresh ripe fruit and a toast of wild-strawberry liqueur, the entire company takes a postprandial walk through the vineyard. Arm in arm, Stefana and Turiddu lead the strolling parade down a sunny

dirt road. Soon we are wandering through the rows of vines crowned by their lush canopies. Turiddu and Nino casually sample grapes from different vines, beginning to think about the grape harvest and the wine-making work ahead.

In the center of the vineyard is an ancient hazelnut tree, a collection of battered outdoor chairs nestled in its shade. We all settle in. Conversation slows and our breathing meanders like the gentle, balmy afternoon breeze. We fall into siesta, content and grateful for the gifts of this little piece of earth.

Choose an eggplant that has a bright green stem and calyx. If this part is brown, it is a sure indication that the fruit has been off the plant too long and may be bitter, or even rotten inside. The skin should be smooth and tight, and the eggplant itself should feel heavy for its size.

According to Sicilian folk wisdom, the way to find an eggplant with few seeds is to examine the shape of the mark at the blossom end. If this mark is a line or a narrow oval, there will be fewer seeds than if it is a circle.

## Mulanciani sutta Limuna

# Lemon-Pickled Eggplant

This amazingly simple dish is bursting with flavor. Baby white eggplant is macerated in lemon juice and olive oil, then served with thin slices of pecorino cheese. In Polizzi, it is served as a tangy component of a summer antipasto. Serve it with good crusty bread.

*For 6 servings*

- 4   **baby white eggplants (about 4 ounces each)**
-     **Sea salt**
-     **Juice of 2 small lemons (about ¼ cup)**
- ¼   **cup extra-virgin olive oil**
- 2   **ounces imported pecorino cheese**

Peel the eggplants and cut them from blossom to stem end in thin slices, about ⅛ inch thick. Lightly salt each slice on both sides.

Arrange the slices on a large platter in a single, slightly overlapping layer. Sprinkle with the lemon juice and then the olive oil. Cover with plastic wrap, and let pickle in a cool place (not the refrigerator) for 2 hours. Turn the eggplant once during this time and tilt the platter to ensure even distribution of the dressing.

Just before serving, cut the pecorino into very thin slices with a sharp knife or a cheese slicer, and scatter them over the surface of the eggplant.

Purpeteddi 'i Mulanciani

## Little Eggplant Balls

In Polizzi, eggplant patties are made in a variety of shapes and styles with a diversity of ingredients. This recipe uses almond meal instead of the more common bread crumbs as a binding agent, and is flavored with a small amount of chopped prosciutto. The mixture is shaped into small balls, and then breaded before frying to prevent the balls from absorbing too much oil.

As with most eggplant dishes, this one is best eaten at room temperature or slightly chilled. If you want to prepare a greater quantity than this recipe provides, do not double it; a larger batch is difficult to control. Instead, prepare one recipe-size batch at a time, frying all the eggplant balls in the same oil.

Do not lose any time between shaping the mixture into little balls and breading them. If the mixture stands, it becomes quite wet and unmanageable.

*For 30 little eggplant balls*

2½ **pounds eggplant (2 or 3 fruits)**
**Sea salt**
4 **ounces (¾ cup) shelled whole raw almonds**
2 **slices prosciutto cut ⅛ inch thick (about 3 ounces total)**
½ **cup finely chopped Italian parsley**
¾ **cup grated imported pecorino cheese, preferably Locatelli brand**
**Black pepper**
4 **eggs**
½ **cup all-purpose flour**
2 **tablespoons milk**
2 **cups unflavored bread crumbs**
3 **cloves garlic, peeled**
1½ **cups pure olive oil, for frying**

Peel the eggplants, and cut them lengthwise into ½-inch-thick slices. Salt the slices on both sides and arrange them in two stacks of equal height in a large shallow bowl. Place an upside-down plate on top. Press the eggplant under a light weight, such as a can of tomatoes or a container of salt, for 2 hours to express the bitter liquid.

Rinse the eggplant of excess salt under a trickle of cold running water. Pat dry with paper towels, and layer the slices on a platter with two sheets of paper towels between the layers. Leave the eggplant like this until needed.

Grind the almonds in a food processor or with a mortar and pestle into a very fine meal. Reserve until needed.

Line a sheet pan with waxed paper, and set it aside.

Remove and discard the fat from around the edge of the prosciutto. Cut the meat into ⅛-inch squares.

Chop the eggplant to the consistency of ground meat. If using a food processor, first cut the slices into 2-inch pieces and then pulse each batch of eggplant for only a few seconds.

Place the chopped eggplant on a large piece of doubled cheesecloth. Form a package, and twist and squeeze it until all of the liquid has been expelled.

Put the eggplant in a large bowl. Using your hands, thoroughly but gently mix in the almond meal, then the prosciutto, parsley, grated cheese, and several coarse grindings of black pepper. Lightly beat 2 of the eggs and mix them in to make a paste.

Without delay, form the mixture into 30 round balls, 1½ inches in diameter, and place them on the prepared sheet pan. Lightly dust each one with flour, returning them to the pan.

In a shallow bowl, beat the remaining 2 eggs with the milk. Put the bread crumbs in a different bowl. Coat each ball with the egg wash, then lift it out with a slotted spoon and roll it in the bread crumbs. Return each to its place on the waxed paper.

Slightly crush the garlic cloves with a wooden spoon or the flat of a large knife blade. Place the garlic and the oil in a heavy 9-inch skillet. Sauté the garlic over medium-high heat until it is golden brown on all sides. Then remove and discard it.

Fry the eggplant balls in the hot oil, in 2 batches, turning them frequently to prevent burning, until they are a rich golden brown on all sides, about 8 minutes. Remove them with a slotted spoon, leaving behind as much oil as possible. Immediately place them on brown paper or paper towels to drain the excess oil.

Serve at room temperature or slightly chilled.

Capunata 'i Meluni e Mulanciani

## *Cantaloupe and Eggplant Caponata*

The extraordinary combination of flavors in this ancient dish tricks the palate into tasting the eggplant as if it were in the same family as the cantaloupe. Santo Lipani told me about the dish, and he and I developed the recipe.

It is widely believed that cantaloupe originated in Cantalupo, the Italian town for which it is named. Literally translated, the name means "singing wolf." Cantaloupes in the United States are actually muskmelons, but the difference is not critical in this context. It is important, however, that the melon be 3 days underripe. A perfectly ripe melon will disintegrate when cooked, and a too green one will have an unpleasant squashlike flavor.

The remarkably refreshing flavor of this caponata makes it a perfect summer's antipasto, but it can be served at other times of the year as well. Be sure to always serve it with good crusty bread.

*For 6 servings*

| | |
|---|---|
| 1 | slightly unripe cantaloupe (about 2½ pounds) |
| 1 | or 2 eggplants (1½ pounds total) |
| | Sea salt |
| ¾ | cup plus 2 tablespoons extra-virgin olive oil |
| 2 | teaspoons sugar |
| ⅓ | cup red wine vinegar |
| | Black pepper |

Halve the cantaloupe, and scoop out and discard the seeds. Cut the halves into 1-inch-thick slices. Then remove the skin and cut the flesh into pieces about 1½ inches long. Place the pieces on a platter, uncovered, and set aside until needed.

Peel the eggplant and cut it into 1-inch cubes. Place the pieces in a bowl, liberally salting each layer. Place a plate over the eggplant and press it under a light weight, such as a can of tomatoes or a box of salt, for 2 hours to express the bitter liquid.

Quickly rinse the eggplant under cold running water to remove the excess salt. Pat the pieces dry with paper towels.

Pour the ¾ cup oil into a heavy, well-cured 9-inch skillet over medium heat. When the oil is hot, sauté the eggplant for about 10 minutes, until cooked yet firm, turning it with a spatula to prevent burning.

Remove the eggplant with a slotted spoon and place it on brown paper or paper towels to drain off the oil. Thoroughly clean the skillet.

Mix together the sugar and vinegar. Reserve until needed.

Return the skillet to the stove and add the remaining 2 tablespoons oil. Turn the heat to high, and when the oil is nearly smoking, add the melon. Sauté for about 3 minutes, until it gains a bit of color and begins to expel its orange liquid.

Reduce the heat to low, and add the eggplant. Gently turn the melon and eggplant pieces with a spatula. After about 1 minute, when the eggplant is hot, pour in the vinegar in an even stream. Turn again. Let the vinegar bubble for a minute, until its aroma rises. Then turn the caponata onto a serving platter and sprinkle it with a few grindings of black pepper. Serve at room temperature.

Frocia 'i Mulanciani

## Baked Eggplant Omelet

I managed to get Stefana, Nino's mother, to give me her recipe for this rustic, delicious omelet. Serve it at room temperature, so that all the flavors will be in full flower.

*For 6 servings*

1   eggplant (about 1½ pounds)
    Sea salt
1   cup pure olive oil
8   eggs
½   cup grated imported pecorino cheese
4   teaspoons tomato paste dissolved in ½ cup water
    Black pepper

Peel the eggplant. Cut it lengthwise into thin slices, ³⁄₁₆ inch thick. Salt the slices on both sides and arrange them in two stacks of equal height in a large shallow bowl. Place an upside-down plate on top. Press the eggplant under a light weight, such as a can of tomatoes or a container of salt, for 2 hours to express the bitter liquid.

Rinse the eggplant of excess salt under a trickle of cold running water. Pat it dry with paper towels, and layer the slices on a platter with two sheets of paper towels between the layers.

In a heavy, ovenproof 9-inch skillet, heat the oil over medium-high heat until very hot. Fry the eggplant, in batches, for about 2 minutes on each side, until they are a pale golden color. Drain the eggplant on brown paper or paper towels.

Preheat the oven to 350°F, with a rack positioned in the center.

Beat the eggs and cheese together.

Pour all of the oil out of the skillet, and carefully, to avoid burning your fingers, wipe it of excess oil, leaving a light coating. Place a layer of eggplant in the skillet, slightly overlapping the slices to cover the bottom surface right up to the edge. Position a second layer in the same way.

Place the skillet over medium heat, and when it is hot, pour in the beaten egg mixture. Using a spatula, gently lift the eggplant to make sure the eggs have reached the bottom. Reduce the heat to low and cook for about 7 minutes, until the eggs begin to set. Slowly pour the thinned tomato paste over the surface in a spiral pattern, and transfer the skillet to the oven. Bake for 20 minutes, until the omelet is cooked and pale golden on top.

Cool to room temperature, and add a few grindings of black pepper. Cut the omelet into 1¼-inch squares, and serve.

Cavatuna ca Sarsa e 'i Mulanciani

# *Rigatoni with Tomato Sauce and Eggplant*

There are many versions of pasta with tomato sauce and eggplant, but this one from Stefana's table is the most fundamental and the most delicious I have ever tasted. The eggplant, cut to the same size as the rigatoni, gives a great mingling of flavors to each bite.

*For 6 servings*

**For the eggplant**
2   eggplants (2½ pounds total)
    Sea salt
1½ cups pure olive oil, for frying

**For the tomato sauce**
    One 35-ounce can peeled whole Italian plum tomatoes, undrained
½   medium-sized yellow onion, finely chopped
2   tablespoons extra-virgin olive oil
1   tablespoon tomato paste dissolved in ⅓ cup water
    Black pepper
2   teaspoons sugar
⅛   teaspoon dried basil

**For the pasta**
2   tablespoons sea salt
1   pound rigatoni

**To finish**
1¼ cups coarsely grated *ricotta salata* or Greek *myzithra* cheese
    Black pepper

Prepare the eggplant: Peel the eggplants, and cut them lengthwise into ½-inch-thick slices. Salt the slices on both sides, and arrange them in two stacks of equal height in a large shallow bowl. Place an upside-down plate on top. Press the eggplant under a light weight, such as a can of tomatoes or a container of salt, for 2 hours to express the bitter liquid.

Rinse the eggplant of excess salt under a trickle of cold running water. Pat it dry with paper towels, and layer the slices on a platter with two sheets of paper towels between the layers.

In a heavy 9-inch skillet, heat the oil over medium heat until very hot. Fry the eggplant slices, in batches, until they are a rich golden color and cooked through, 2 to 3 minutes each side. Drain them on brown paper or paper towels.

When the eggplant has cooled to room temperature, cut it into strips about 1 inch wide and 2¼ inches long. Spread the strips on fresh brown paper or paper towels to further absorb any oil, and set aside until needed.

**Prepare the tomato sauce:** Fit a food mill with the disk with the smallest holes (1 millimeter), and place it over a bowl. Pour the tomatoes and their liquid into the mill. Puree the tomatoes to remove the seeds, which can make the sauce bitter. Scrape the pulp from underneath the mill into the bowl.

Put the onion and the olive oil in a heavy 4-quart pot over medium heat, and sauté the onion until it turns translucent, about 5 minutes. Stir in the thinned tomato paste. Cook for about 1 minute, and then add the milled tomatoes. Season with grindings of black pepper, and add the sugar and basil. (Do not salt the sauce, as there is enough salt in the eggplant and the *ricotta salata*.)

Reduce the heat to low and simmer the sauce, uncovered, stirring from time to time, for 40 minutes.

**Prepare the pasta and assemble:** Fill a large pot with 6 quarts water, add the 2 tablespoons salt, and bring it to a boil over high heat. Add the pasta and cook until al dente, about 10 minutes.

About 5 minutes after the pasta begins cooking, place the eggplant pieces in the sauce to heat them. When the pasta is cooked, drain it thoroughly and put it in a warmed serving bowl. Toss it with the sauce and eggplant, and with the *ricotta salata*. Serve very hot, with additional grindings of black pepper to taste.

## Maccaruna cu Tabbacchieri 'i Mulanciani

# *Macaroni with Eggplant "Tobacco Pouches"*

The resemblance between the shape of baby eggplants and that of tobacco pouches gives this classic Sicilian summertime dish its whimsical name.

The small eggplants are slit and stuffed with cheese, basil, garlic, and a piece of anchovy, and then the slit is closed with a strip of onion. The eggplants are lightly sautéed and then slowly simmered in tomato sauce. This sauce, infused with the flavors of the eggplant and its stuffing, is used to dress a first course of macaroni. Serve the eggplant as a second course out of the same bowl. The macaroni and the eggplant can also be served as the first two courses of a more elaborate meal.

*For 8 servings*

**For the eggplant pouches**

6   ounces imported aged *caciocavallo* cheese or imported pecorino, preferably Locatelli brand, in 1 piece

4   cloves garlic

10  flat anchovy fillets

10  small, plump eggplants (5 to 6 ounces each)

20  fresh basil leaves, torn in half

2   large red onions

1   cup pure olive oil, for frying

**For the tomato sauce**

Two 35-ounce cans peeled whole Italian plum tomatoes, undrained

2   tablespoons extra-virgin olive oil

2   tablespoons tomato paste dissolved in ⅔ cup water

3   teaspoons sugar

Sea salt

Black pepper

**For the pasta**

2   tablespoons sea salt

2   pounds *mezza rigatoni* (half-rigatoni) or any other short, fat tube pasta with ridges

4   ounces imported aged *caciocavallo* cheese or imported pecorino, preferably Locatelli brand, grated

**Prepare the eggplant pouches:** Using a cheese slicer or a sharp knife, thinly slice the cheese into 40 pieces. Peel and thinly slice the garlic. Cut the anchovies into quarters.

Rinse the eggplants and pat them dry. Tear off the calyx and cut off the remaining stem. Using a small sharp knife, make four deep equidistant incisions along the length of one side of each eggplant, leaving about ½ inch at the top and bottom intact. The incisions may meet inside the eggplant, but it is important that it is not cut open at the top or bottom.

Gently spread open each slit and stuff it with a slice of cheese, a piece of anchovy, a slice of garlic, and a piece of basil leaf. Be sure that none of the stuffing is sticking out.

Peel the onions and cut them into slices about ⅛ inch thick. Use a strip of onion to seal each incision. Finely chop enough of the remaining sliced onion to make 1 cup, and reserve it for the tomato sauce.

**Prepare the tomato sauce:** Fit a food mill with the disk with the smallest holes (1 millimeter), and place it over a bowl. Pour the tomatoes and their liquid into the mill. Puree the tomatoes to remove the seeds, which can make the sauce bitter. Scrape the pulp from underneath the mill into the bowl.

Put the reserved chopped onion and the extra-virgin olive oil in a heavy 6-quart pot over medium heat, and sauté the onion until it turns translucent, about 5 minutes. Stir in the thinned tomato paste. Let it cook for about 1 minute, and then add the milled tomatoes. Season with the sugar, salt, and pepper. Reduce the heat to low and simmer the sauce, uncovered, stirring from time to time, while you sauté the eggplant.

**Cook the eggplant pouches:** Pour the pure olive oil into a heavy 9-inch skillet and place it over medium-high heat. When it is very hot, sauté the eggplants in two batches, rolling each in the pan to sauté every side until the incisions are well sealed and the skin is slightly puckered, about 6 minutes.

Remove them with a slotted spoon, roll them on brown paper or paper towels to drain off the excess oil, and then slip them into the sauce. Reduce the heat to very low, cover, and cook at a very gentle simmer for 2 to 2½ hours. Stir from time to time to prevent the sauce or eggplants from sticking.

**Cook and serve the pasta:** When the eggplants have cooked for about 1¾ hours, fill a large pot with 6 quarts water, add the 2 tablespoons salt, and bring it to a boil over high heat.

When the eggplants have cooked for about 2 hours, remove the cover so that the sauce will reduce a bit while the pasta cooks.

Cook the pasta in the boiling water until al dente, about 10 minutes. Drain it thoroughly, put it into a large bowl, and toss it with a small amount of sauce to keep it from sticking together.

Divide the pasta among individual pasta bowls, and top with more sauce and grated cheese to taste. Serve the eggplant as a second course in the same bowl.

# 'Nsalata Mista

## Mixed Salad

A mixed salad is the most favored accompaniment in Polizzi, perhaps in all of Italy. As my grandfather, Papa Andrea, taught me, its preparation is more an art than a science. Polizzani cooks never measure the amount of oil or vinegar; rather, they use their eyes and noses.

This art of salad-making is not a difficult one to master. The ingredient amounts listed here are really an approximation. Use them as a guideline to develop your own signature mixed salad.

*For 6 servings*

| | |
|---|---|
| 1 | head romaine lettuce |
| 1 | red onion |
| ½ | English (hothouse) cucumber |
| 8 | green or red plum tomatoes |
| | Sea salt |
| 2 | tablespoons red or white wine vinegar |
| ¼ | cup extra-virgin olive oil |
| | Black pepper |

Cut the lettuce into 1½-inch-wide pieces, and thoroughly wash and dry them. Put the lettuce in a large salad bowl (one with plenty of room for tossing). Peel the onion, cut it in half, and thinly slice it into half-circles. Separate the pieces and add them to the bowl. Rinse and dry the cucumber, score the skin with a fork, and slice it into thin rounds. Put them in the bowl. Rinse and dry the tomatoes, and cut each into 6 slices. Add them to the bowl as well.

Salt the salad well (to bring out its flavor), and toss it. Add the vinegar (to open the pores of the lettuce), and toss again. Drizzle in the oil and toss one more time. Coarsely grind a small amount of black pepper over the top, toss it in, and serve.

# Alivi Salati

## *Savory Olives*

The uniquely flavored olives we ate at Stefana Gianfisco's table were handpicked and then cured for 40 days. Since most of us do not have access to an olive grove, I have developed a 3-day method for dressing already cured olives in an infusion of the same herbs and spices. The result gives a good indication of the colorful flavor of Stefana's olives.

*For 1 pound of olives*

¼ teaspoon fennel seeds
16 whole cloves
⅛ teaspoon coarsely ground black pepper
1 pound large green olives
2 tablespoons extra-virgin olive oil
   Zest of 1 lemon, chopped

Put the fennel seeds, cloves, and black pepper in a very small pot. Add ½ cup water. Boil gently for 10 minutes, and then cool to room temperature.

Soak the olives in a large bowl of cold water for 15 minutes to remove the strong salt taste, changing the water 3 times.

Drain the olives and crack each one with a meat pounder or a kitchen mallet. Do not remove the pits. Put the cracked olives in a bowl. Pour the cooled contents of the pot over them. Toss. Evenly coat the olives with the oil, and sprinkle in the lemon zest.

Cover the bowl with plastic wrap and marinate for 3 days in a cool place (not the refrigerator) before serving.

# Six

# *Sweeties and Sweets*

*S*ugar and the art of pastry-making have existed in Polizzi for twelve hundred years. Sweets were introduced to Polizzi during the North African occupation of the island. Today the largest single group of businesses in Polizzi is pastry shops, numbering almost one for each of the seven sections of the small city.

Although the Polizzani are extremely dedicated to their sweets, the usual dessert in most homes is fresh fruit. Pastries are eaten as a part of lunch or dinner only on special occasions. Breakfast, however, is most popularly a horn-shaped pastry filled with cream or marmalade. For a midmorning snack, one might eat a canoli, or a piece of the unique Polizzani cheesecake, *u sfuagghiu*. After siesta, a cup of espresso with some biscotti tastes very good. Whenever a Polizzani has the urge for a snack, he usually looks for something sweet.

Every Polizzani has his own favorite pastry shop, and supporters of the various establishments argue passionately the merits of their choice. These discourses hold a place only slightly less important than the topic of soccer, beating out political discussions by a landslide.

I have a favorite pastry chef in Polizzi: Pino Agliata. His party of supporters is quite large and his position as the best needs little defense. I met Pino for the first time in 1996, when I went to his small shop to thank him for the pastries he had sent over to Santo's restaurant for the mayor's dinner. Pasticceria al Castello is located on the far side of the Piazza Castello, off the Via Roma. The shop is tucked into one end of the enormous Palazzo Notarbartolo, an old baronial residence now owned by the pharmacist, Dr. Cannata. Next to the shop is the ruin of the Byzantine fortified castle, from which both the piazza and the pastry shop get their names.

As I entered the shop, I was treated with the pervasive aromas of toasted nuts, citrus, chocolate, and baking pastry, all mixed together. The place was filled with the diamonds of Pino's art. Sparkling glass cases held the pleasures of many varieties of delicate pastries, ranging from canoli to *cigaretti*, a small tube of rich dough filled with whipped cream. An entire section was filled with almond paste sculptures that looked exactly like dishes of pasta with tomato sauce, or tins of sardines, or bowls of ripe fruit.

Antique chocolate keys, rubbed with cocoa powder to create "rust," filled several trays. The real keys from which the molds were made hung on a nearby hook. This "metal" section also included chocolate monkey wrenches and large nuts and bolts that actually work. Around the room were some of the almond-paste and chocolate sculptures that have won Pino first prizes at contests throughout Sicily, Italy, and other European countries. In the place of honor was his almond-paste model Ferrari F1, encased in a Plexiglas cover like a sculpture in a museum.

Pino emerged from the back, a man of average height and rather chubby, as a good pastry chef should be. He has gone prematurely bald and the fair skin on his face and head is permanently flushed, perhaps from being near the heat of his ovens. He extended his hand and I introduced myself, thanking him for the pastry. "It was my pleasure," he said, adding, "Would you like a piece of *sfuagghiu?*" I accepted without hesitation.

• • •

*U sfuagghiu,* or *lo sfoglio Polizzano* as it is called in Italian, is a type of cheesecake unique to Polizzi Generosa. More than three hundred years ago, the nuns of the Benedictine convent, known as the Old Abbey, invented a grand pastry for the feast of their patron, Saint Benedict. They decided that this sweet should be rich with all of the flavors representative of their epoch and of the region.

The good sisters decided to spotlight ewes'-milk cheese, a Polizzani artisanal product. Usually ewes'-milk ricotta is used for pastry filling; the soft, fluffy, unformed loose curds of this whey-cheese give pastries a creamy, delicate flavor and texture. The nuns, however, chose to use *tuma,* an extremely fresh, unsalted ewes'-milk curd-cheese, so rubbery in texture that it needs to be finely chopped for use as a pastry filling. Their reason is forgotten in time, but to this day, *tuma* is not used in any other pastry recipe in all of Sicily.

To complete the filling, chopped *tuma* was mixed with sugar, cinnamon, and cocoa powder—at that time precious, expensive ingredients, and the gustatory fashion of the age. (Later on, bittersweet chocolate replaced the cocoa.) For the crust, the nuns used the traditional pie crust of Sicily and Italy, *pasta frolla,* a soft, rich, short pastry dough. The filling ingredients were bound with beaten egg whites and turned out into a cake pan lined with the *pasta frolla.* The cake was closed with a top layer of crust and baked, cooled, and then dusted with powdered sugar.

At the back of the counter, Pino took a small knife and cut a generous piece of *sfuagghiu,* handing it over on a paper napkin. I bit off the point, filling my mouth with an explosion of flavor and texture. The richness of the *tuma* cushioned the stronger impact of cinnamon and the direct pleasure of chocolate. In the smooth yet slightly sandy center was a flavor like hazelnuts. The butterfat in the *tuma* had been baked to that flavor, similar to *buerre noisette.* After each swallow, I could only be satisfied by another bite. Those Benedictine nuns knew their stuff.

Inspired by my appreciation of his art, Pino offered me samples of every small pastry and sweet in the shop. Among them were *ramuzzi,* "sweet little branches": A channel is made in a rope of *pasta frolla* and filled with a paste of hazelnut, semolina, and honey. The dough is then cut into the shape of tree branches. I sampled delicate almond paste cookies that Pino called *muzzicuni d'amuri,* "love bites."

Leading me to the other side of the shop, Pino gave me a taste of the best almond nougat, *turruni*, I had ever eaten. Green and black olives, made of almond paste, were glazed with a special edible varnish that gives the appearance of glistening oil. It was disconcerting to the palate to justify their sweet almond flavor with their perfect olive appearance. Then I tasted a key—a bittersweet chocolate trick to the eye and palate. I was in a child's dream of fantastic sweetness.

When it became clear to Pino that I could not sample one thing more, he said with a grin, "*Allura* (so) let me show you something." He snatched one of the real antique keys off the hook and led me to a house across the piazza. Inside a storage room, opened with the rusty key, I could see the unmistakable outline of a model Chiesa Madre, the main church of Polizzi. After Pino turned on the light, I saw that this scale model was made of chocolate.

A moment later the church glowed with small lights, positioned inside. The model stood 3½ feet high, 4 feet long, and 3 feet wide. Pino told me it was made of 150 pounds of chocolate molded over a structure of cardboard wafer boxes, and weighed at least 200 pounds. Pino and his brother, Antonio, had created it two years earlier for a Christmas celebration, and the chocolate was now stale. With a slight tone of regret, he added, "So we can't eat it."

Pino Agliata began to learn about pastry-making when he was fourteen. He took an after-school job at the shop of *Mastru* (Maestro) Nunziu Lima, at that time the finest pastry chef in Polizzi. Pastry-making had been in the old master's family for five generations, but his children weren't interested in that life, and soon Pino became his apprentice.

Under the *mastru*, Pino became a fine journeyman pastry chef. Among other things, the old master shared with his young apprentice the secrets of his authentic *sfuagghiu* recipe. After fifteen years together, Mastru Nunziu wanted to retire, and offered to sell Pino the business on very easy terms. But Pino felt that he did not yet possess a broad enough mastery of his craft to open his own shop.

By this time, Pino had married and started a family. Encouraged by his wife, Elena, he made a hard financial decision and moved his family to Cefalù, a bustling seaside city forty miles away. Recommended by his longtime employer, he was offered a position at the famous pastry shop and café Bar

Duomo. There, as he had hoped, he was exposed to a much broader repertoire, including the techniques of almond-paste sculpture.

After ten years of hard work, Pino felt he was ready to open a shop of his own. Six years before my visit, he rented the space from Dr. Cannata and established the Pasticceria al Castello. A spacious second-floor apartment in the palazzo, owned by Pino's mother-in-law, is where he, Elena, and their two children, Mariangela and Domenico, reside.

In some years business has been good, in others not so profitable, but Pino has never stopped creating his almond-paste and chocolate sculptures. Several years ago, ancient Greek amphorae were found at Polizzi's archeological dig. The actual pottery was taken to Palermo until a special museum could be built in Polizzi's city hall to house them permanently. Before it opened last year, replicas made of white chocolate, colored with edible glazes to reproduce the original glazes, could be seen at Pino's shop.

Devotion to Padre Pio, the modern priest believed to have stigmata, is growing throughout southern Italy and Sicily. A photograph of this candidate for sainthood is prominently displayed in homes and businesses of the devoted. In Pino's shop there is such a portrait above the cash register, but his is sculpted in bas-relief of white chocolate on a chocolate "wood" background.

One day, as I walked into the shop, Pino poked his head out of the back and with a gleeful chuckle gestured me to join him. "Look at my new creation," he called out. My eyes opened wide when I saw the cake on the work table. On top of a whipped-cream-covered, liqueur-soaked sponge cake were

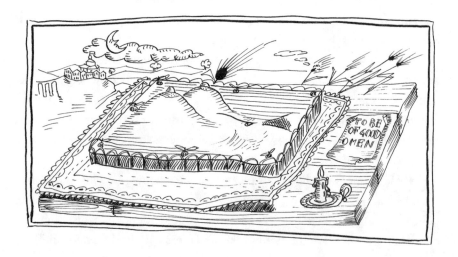

a pair of enormous breasts, made of lemon pudding covered with flesh-colored gelatin. One of his workers nudged the table, and the breasts jiggled. We all laughed like teenagers.

Elena, who was also working in the shop that day, said, "Pino made the silly thing for a bachelor party, because all men are boys." To further prove her point, she asked if we all would like to meet the model. She went to the sink and returned brandishing a large funnel. We laughed harder. Pino grabbed the funnel out of her hands, saying, "My dear, don't give away all my secrets."

One summer, when business was slower than usual, Pino decided to sponsor a beauty contest, guided by the good business sense that at such an event he would sell a lot of pastry. His plan was to invite the participation of the young women of Polizzi, as well as those of four neighboring towns: Scillato, Fasanò, Campofelice, and Castellana. The winner would receive a silvered loving cup, a cash prize, and the title "Miss Madonie."

For the event, the piazza in front of his shop was filled with tables and chairs for the friends and relatives of the contestants to sit at and, surely, buy pastry and coffee. At its center, jutting out from the ruins of the Byzantine fortress, a low construction scaffold was erected, decorated with flowers and covered with oriental carpets, provided by a local rug dealer for promotional consideration. This ramp would serve as a runway for the beautiful young ladies to parade in their formal and casual attire. The clothing was lent to the pageant by a local dress shop, also for promotional consideration.

After several weeks of intensive planning, the evening of the contest arrived. Just as dusk fell on the warm summer evening, the crowd poured into the piazza. There was a mad scramble for places, as there weren't enough tables and chairs. Many people settled for eating their pastries standing up. Pino was overjoyed by the turnout.

The sight of one of the contestants, a stunningly beautiful young woman from Scillato, named Daniela, sent the buzz around the piazza: She was sure to win. I thought it odd that the idea of her winning seemed exciting to Pino and the other Polizzani organizers. After all, she wasn't from Polizzi.

Golden spotlights were fired up and aimed at the runway. The crowd settled down as the jury members took their places close to the runway. They included the mayor, a priest, a medical doctor, a lawyer, a partner in the dress shop that had lent the clothing, a butcher from Campofelice, and me. We were each given a ballot with all the contestants' names and a space to grade them from one to ten. I was seated next to the mayor, and we were served, of course, Pino's pastry.

The mistress of ceremonies was Lucia, the other partner in the local dress shop. She conducted the event with great poise. After the appropriate welcome and jury introduction, she brought two teenaged brothers up to the runway. They were half Polizzani, half French, and lived in Paris; their family was in Polizzi for summer vacation. These young men were to escort the beauties on their walks to glory. Their style, sun-tanned good looks, and bleached-out shoulder-length hair raised a cheer from the crowd not equaled the rest of the evening.

The contestants began to parade one by one down the runway on the arm of one of the young Frenchmen. Lucia gave name, age, and town as each young woman stood atop the ruined parapet of the Byzantine fortress, bathed in golden light, nervous and uneasy. The truth of the matter is that the contestants, mostly forced into competition by proud parents, did not want to be there. Many clomped down the runway like donkeys. They would pause in front of the jury with arms folded in defiance and with the facial expressions of children who had just been administered a bitter medicinal tonic.

As the contestants paraded, the mayor would nudge me and whisper discreet instructions. That summer he and I had often played *briscola*, a Sicilian card game of trumps. Cheating between partners is expected even in serious matches, and verbal communication of strategy is permitted in friendly games like ours. If one wished his partner to play one of the two higher-point cards, he would say *caricu*; for cards with lower points, *punti*; for cards with no points at all, *carti lisci*.

"Vicenzu, *punti*," the mayor might whisper of one beauty, or "Vicenzu, *carti lisci*," he might say of another less classically defined. When Daniela, the beauty from Scillato, hit the parapet, the crowd hushed. The mayor whispered, "Vicenzu, *caricu, caricu!*"

In the second part of the pageant, the contestants paraded in formal attire. Walking in unfamiliar high heels, they leaned heavily on the arms of their attentive escorts. Each paused in front of the jury to say a few words about themselves, have a brief interview conducted by Lucia, and respond to her inane beauty pageant questions. Beaming and teary-eyed mothers and fathers cheered their daughters, proudly screaming out, "That's my baby!"

Regrettably, the interviews revealed that all most of the young women wanted to do was dance, listen to recordings, and talk to their friends on cell phones. In contrast, Daniela, the ringer, wanted to study hard, go to college, and become a translator. She was asked the hackneyed pageant question: "You're walking down the street with two friends and it starts to rain. You have the only umbrella. What do you do?" Her poised, smiling answer met with thunderous applause: "I'd walk in the middle."

At the end of the parade, the ballots were collected. We waited a long time for the tally. Maybe this interval was designed by Pino to give people an opportunity to buy more sweets. Finally Lucia took the spotlight. Everybody held their breaths. Third place was awarded to a very pretty, well-spoken contestant from Castellana. A real charmer from Polizzi took second place. Daniela, of course, was crowned Miss Madonie.

Pandemonium broke out as tears of joy from contestants, relatives, and friends filled the winners' circle. Parents comforted daughters who had lost. Even though they hadn't been much interested at first, by the end of the pageant they had regretted their indifference, promising more interest next year.

Pino and four assistants emerged from the shop carrying an enormous cake and bottles of Spumante. On the cake in colored fondant was drawn the old fortress, the runway decorated with flowers, and the intricately patterned rugs. Across the top was written *Miss Madonie*. Daniela, loving cup and check in one hand, made the first cut with the other. The tumultuous crowd toasted her crown.

Something—and not just the mayor's instructions to me—told me that the outcome of the pageant had been fixed, but I couldn't figure out why. I was hesitant to ask, but putting myself in a truly Polizzani frame of mind, I came up with the answer.

A Polizzani contestant could not win. People from other towns would say, "You have a beauty contest and your girl wins. Why did you invite us to participate?" A contestant from Polizzi had to take second place. Otherwise, they would say, "What? You have a beauty contest and you don't have any beautiful girls? Why did you bother?" Third place really didn't matter, and that prize could go to the most deserving contestant. In the end, however, the crowd certainly approved the outcome, securing the date for next year.

Months after this visit to Polizzi, I received a letter at my home in Los Angeles. I did not know the writer. A short note asked me to contact him as soon as possible; he had something from Pino Agliata for me. I phoned immediately and reached a man who told me the following story.

He, originally from Sicily, and his American wife went back to the island for a visit. While touring, they discovered Polizzi Generosa. Charmed by its beauty and the hospitality of its people, they stayed for several days. During this time, they wandered into Pino's pastry shop. Pino, as is his custom, gave them the grand tour of tastes and showed them the chocolate church, as he had done for me, as he does for every interested visitor.

When Pino learned that the couple lived in Los Angeles, he asked them if they would bring a little something to his friend Vincent Schiavelli, who also lived there. Pino then carefully packed two *sfuagghiu*, one for them and one for me, and gave them my address. (He had misplaced my phone number.) The couple dutifully and carefully carted around my *sfuagghiu* for the last ten days of their trip. (Their cake was eaten long before those ten days had elapsed.) The moment they arrived home, the man sent the note. Fortunately, I lived nearby.

I picked up the package, thanking the couple profusely, although I was doubtful that after such a long journey the cake would still be edible. But as I undid the final paper covering, my dining room filled with all the luscious aromas of Pino's pastry shop. I took a small knife and cut myself a large piece. My senses filled as they had that first time at Pino's. The sweetness of life in Polizzi floated all around me, like clouds of spun sugar.

## Crostata 'i Miennuli

# *Almond Pie*

As Pino began to make this wonderfully rich almond pie in his shop, he used an amount of already prepared *pasta frolla*, soft short pastry dough, for the crust. He asked, "You have my recipe for *pasta frolla*, don't you?" I answered affirmatively.

When I began to test the cake recipe months later at home in Los Angeles, I reviewed Pino's *pasta frolla* recipe as printed in an Italian pastry chefs' trade magazine. The ratio of flour to shortening and egg yolks was quite different from any other *pasta frolla* recipe I had ever used.

I telephoned Pino, curious about the differences. After I told him I'd gotten it from the trade magazine, there was a pause on the line. Then Pino said, "Vicenzu, we never give them the right recipes."

For the filling of this pie, fine almond meal is mixed with sugar, butter, and eggs to create a delicious sweet paste. In former times, the almonds were crushed with a mortar and pestle. By using a food processor instead, the time required for this preparation is reduced to minutes.

Due to the time needed for the crust and the filling to set, it is best to prepare this pie the day before it is to be served.

*For one 9-inch pie, 12 to 16 servings*

**For the pasta frolla *crust***
2½ cups cake flour, plus additional for dusting
¼ teaspoon baking soda
Pinch of baking powder
¾ cup granulated sugar
¾ cup (1½ sticks) unsalted butter
4 egg yolks
1 to 2 tablespoons milk

*For the filling*
1   pound (about 3 cups) shelled whole raw almonds
1¼ cups granulated sugar
1   tablespoon cake flour
¾   cup (1½ sticks) unsalted butter
3   eggs, lightly beaten
1   teaspoon almond extract
⅔   cup bitter orange marmalade
4   ounces (about ¾ cup) whole blanched almonds
    Confectioners' sugar, in a shaker


Prepare the crust: In a large bowl, sift together the flour, baking soda, baking powder, and sugar. Using an electric mixer fitted with the paddle on low speed, or by hand, cut or rub in the butter until the flour has the consistency of cornmeal, about 2 minutes. Lightly beat the egg yolks and quickly work them into the mixture with the mixer or a spatula. Add enough of the milk to form a soft dough.

Turn out the dough onto a lightly floured surface and knead it just enough to form a very soft dough with a slightly sticky surface. Depending on climatic conditions, it might be necessary to add some extra sprinklings of flour for the dough to come together. Remember that overkneading pastry dough will make it tough. Form the dough into a ball, cover it with plastic wrap, and let it rest, refrigerated, for 2 hours.

Prepare the filling: Coarsely chop the 1 pound almonds in a food processor by pulsing for a few seconds. Add the granulated sugar and process for about 1½ minutes, until the almonds turn into a very fine meal. Add the flour and pulse once or twice to mix it in. Add the butter and pulse a few times until it is thoroughly mixed in. Combine the eggs with the almond extract in a small bowl, and add this to the almond paste; pulse to amalgamate.

Transfer the paste to a bowl, smooth the top, and refrigerate, uncovered, for about 1½ hours, until well set.

Assemble the pie and bake: Preheat the oven to 375°F, with a rack positioned in the upper third.

On a lightly floured surface, roll the dough out to form a 13-inch circle, and use it to line a 9-inch springform pan or a pan with a removable bottom and 2-inch sides. Coat the bottom of the crust with a thin, even layer of the marmalade. Spread the filling over the marmalade in an even layer. Smooth the top, and then score it with the tines of a fork or a pastry tool.

Place a blanched almond at the center of the pie. Starting at the outside edge, cover the top with blanched almonds arranged end to end in concentric circles. There will be space between the last circle and the center almond, revealing the filling.

Bake for 25 to 35 minutes, until the crust around the top edge is quite browned. Cool the pie in the pan for 10 minutes, and then remove it. Cool to room temperature. Do not refrigerate. Just before serving, lightly dust the top with confectioners' sugar.

# Torta 'i Frutta

## Fruit Torte

For this dessert, sponge cake, *pan 'i spugna* in Sicilian (literally "sponge bread"), is split in half and sprinkled with Strega, an Italian liqueur flavored with herbs and flowers. The center is then spread with a layer of *crema pasticciera*, the yellow custard cream so popular in Sicilian and Italian pastry.

The top of the torte is covered with a beautiful arrangement of fresh fruit. I have chosen to use sliced strawberries and kiwis. Although native to New Zealand, kiwis are now grown all over the world and are used in the sweets of much of Europe, including Pino's, at his pastry shop in Polizzi.

In other seasons, different fruits can be used, such as peeled sliced peaches or nectarines, or very ripe pears, or sections of small oranges or tangerines. To deliciously finish the sides of the torte in any season, they are coated with chopped pistachios.

To preserve the fresh flavor and color of the fruit, gelatin is spread over the top. The recipe given is for more gelatin than is required, but it is easier to work with the larger quantity.

Prepare this torte the day before it is to be served so that the custard cream and the gelatin have time to set before assembly and so that all the flavors have time to mingle.

*For one 10-inch cake, 16 to 20 servings*

**For the sponge cake**
Unsalted butter for greasing the pan
1   cup cake flour, plus additional for dusting the pan
6   large eggs, separated
1   cup sugar
1   teaspoon vanilla extract

**For the custard cream**
4½ cups milk
¾   cup cake flour
6   egg yolks
1   teaspoon vanilla extract
Zest of 1 orange, finely chopped (about 2 teaspoons)
¾   cup sugar
Rounded ½ teaspoon unsalted butter

*For the gelatin*

2    **cups water**

¼    **cup sugar**

2    **envelopes (½ ounce total) unflavored gelatin**

*For the fruit topping and assembly*

3    **kiwis**

8    **ounces ripe strawberries**

¼    **cup Strega liqueur**

⅔    **cup (about 2 ounces) chopped unsalted pistachios**

**Prepare the sponge cake:** Preheat the oven to 350°F, with a rack positioned in the center. Butter and flour a 10-inch round cake or springform pan. Sift the 1 cup flour.

Using an electric mixer or a wire whisk, beat the egg yolks, ½ cup of the sugar, and 2 tablespoons warm water together until the mixture turns pale yellow and forms ribbons, about 7 minutes. Mix in the vanilla extract. Beat in the sifted flour a little at a time, adding more only when the previous addition has been thoroughly absorbed.

In a clean grease-free bowl, copper if possible, begin to beat the egg whites with a clean mixer or whisk. (If any oils from the egg yolks touch the egg whites, they will not stiffen.) Beat until the whites form peaks that are stiff but not dry. Continue to beat, sprinkling in the remaining ½ cup sugar a little at a time.

Beat a few tablespoons of the whites into the yolk mixture to loosen it. Quickly but gently fold the rest of the whites into the yolk mixture with a rubber spatula. Turn the batter into the pan and bake for 30 to 40 minutes, or until the cake is light golden and a toothpick inserted near the center comes out clean. Refrain from opening the oven door as much as possible, since a sudden gush of cold air or even a heavy thud of the door can cause the cake to collapse. If you must, peek in and close the door gently.

When the cake is baked, turn off the oven and let the cake cool in the oven with the door ajar for 10 minutes. Then remove the cake from the pan, and put it upside-down on a wire rack to cool to room temperature. (Using the flat bottom as the top of the torte ensures an even surface for the custard and fruit topping.) Store the sponge cake, unrefrigerated, loosely covered in waxed paper, until needed.

**Prepare the custard cream:** Pour the milk into a small saucepan and heat it over medium-low heat to scalding, the temperature (185°F) at which small bubbles form around the edge of the pot. Do not boil the milk. Remove the pot from the heat, cover, and let it rest for 10 minutes.

Sift the flour and set it aside until needed.

Using an electric mixer or a wire whisk, beat the egg yolks, vanilla extract, orange zest, and sugar together in a bowl until the mixture turns pale yellow and forms ribbons, about 7 minutes. Beat in the sifted flour a little at a time, adding more only when the previous addition has been thoroughly absorbed.

Mix in the scalded milk a little at a time, so that the flour does not form lumps. Pour this mixture into a heavy 4-quart pot, and set it over medium-low heat. Stir constantly with a wooden spoon while bringing the mixture slowly to a boil. Continue to boil until the flour taste is cooked away and the mixture has thickened to the consistency of thin yogurt, about 7 minutes.

Remove the pot from the heat, let the custard settle for a minute, and then stir in the butter. Transfer the custard to a bowl and allow it to cool to room temperature, stirring from time to time to prevent a skin from forming on the top. Then refrigerate it for 3 hours to set into a smooth custard that will just hold its shape.

**Prepare the gelatin:** After the custard has set, put 1½ cups of the water and the sugar in a small saucepan over medium heat. Stir just until the sugar is dissolved, and then bring the sugar-water to a boil.

Meanwhile, put the remaining ½ cup water in a small stainless-steel bowl. Sprinkle the gelatin over the water and let it dissolve, about 1 minute. Add the boiling sugar-water to the bowl. Stir together. Let the mixture cool for 5 minutes and then refrigerate, uncovered, for about 1 hour, until it has partially set but is still spreadable.

**Assemble the torte:** As soon as the gelatin is refrigerated, peel and slice the kiwis into rounds. Clean, hull, and slice the strawberries. Reserve until needed.

Cut the sponge cake in half horizontally, making sure the layers are equal. (This is easily accomplished with a large serrated knife: Cut around the edge first to maintain the center line, and then cut the cake through. An alternative is to use an adjustable cake cutter. These methods will make a straight cut and keep the cake from crumbing excessively.)

Smear the center of a 12-inch cake platter with a dab of the custard. Set the bottom half of the sponge cake on the platter. It will be held in place by the custard. Using a pastry brush, sprinkle the cake evenly with half the Strega. Do not, however, moisten it to the point that the liqueur leaks through. Spread the top of this half with three fourths of the custard cream in an even layer.

Fit the other cake half in place, and sprinkle with the remaining Strega. Coat the sides of the cake with a very thin layer of custard, and smear custard on the top to later hold the fruit in place.

Lift one edge of the platter and prop it up on an upside-down plate. (The cake will not slide off because it has been stuck to the platter with custard.) Sprinkle that side of the cake with chopped pistachios. Gently push the pieces into the custard to hold them in place. Rotate the cake platter on the upside-down plate and apply pistachios until the entire circumference of the cake is coated.

Arrange all of the kiwi slices in a slightly overlapping layer at the center of the top of the torte. Cover the remainder of the top with a slightly overlapping layer of sliced strawberries. Refrigerate the torte, uncovered, until the gelatin is ready.

Using a pastry brush, seal the fruit in a thin, even coat of gelatin. Refrigerate, uncovered, until set 1 or 2 hours. Then cover with plastic wrap and re-refrigerate until 15 minutes before serving.

## Muzzicuni d'Amuri

# *Almond Love Bites*

First planted in Sicily by the Arabs in the tenth century, almonds are used frequently in Polizzani desserts, as well as in savory dishes. This love affair has been going on for a thousand years.

For these "love bites," almond paste is mixed with egg whites, formed into cookies, and refrigerated overnight to dry and set. The cookies are then baked at a low heat, more to dry completely than to cook. To prevent browning, the cookies are removed from the oven, cooled off, and then rebaked to achieve their chewy surface and soft center.

Almond paste is traditionally colored green because originally it was a cheap substitute for pistachio paste.

*For 36 cookies*

12 ounces (2¼ cups) whole blanched almonds
1½ cups granulated sugar
1 teaspoon honey
½ teaspoon almond extract
6 to 7 drops green food coloring
2 egg whites, lightly beaten
  Confectioners' sugar, for dusting

Coarsely chop the nuts in a food processor by pulsing for a few seconds. Add the granulated sugar and continue to process for about 2 minutes, until the almonds turn into a meal as fine as the sugar. Transfer the almond mixture to a bowl, breaking up any clumps.

In a small bowl, thin the honey with the almond extract and food coloring. Using an electric mixer fitted with a paddle on a low speed, or by hand, thoroughly mix the honey mixture and the egg whites into the almonds to form a sticky, heavy paste.

Lightly dust a work surface with confectioners' sugar, and with dusted hands form the paste into a ball. Knead it, adding pinches of confectioners' sugar as required, until the paste is cohesive and the surface is less sticky.

Line a sheet pan with kitchen parchment. Place the paste in a pastry bag fitted with a ½-inch fluted tip. Pipe the paste onto the pan in 3-inch squiggles, close together. Place the pan in the refrigerator, uncovered, and chill overnight.

Remove the cookies from the refrigerator, and preheat the oven to 300°F, with a rack positioned in the center.

Bake the cookies for 20 minutes. Remove them from the oven and allow to cool for 10 minutes. Then rebake them for an additional 10 minutes. Let the cookies cool to room temperature before removing them from the pan.

Ramuzzi Duci

## *Sweet Little Branches*

The filling in these "branches" is made of finely chopped hazelnuts mixed with semolina and honey, certainly deriving from some ancient North African source. The dough is *pasta frolla*, a less rich version than the one used for a crust, as in the recipe for Almond Torte. This dough must rest in the refrigerator for 3 hours before the cookies are formed, to ensure workability.

These cookies taste great dunked in morning coffee, or on their own.

*For 12 large cookies*

**For the dough**
3⅓ cups cake flour, plus additional as needed
¼ teaspoon baking soda
Pinch of baking powder
1 cup sugar
¾ cup (1½ sticks) unsalted cold butter, cut into pieces
2 whole eggs
1 egg yolk
1 tablespoon sweet Marsala

**For the filling**
4 ounces shelled whole raw hazelnuts (filberts)
½ cup semolina (pasta flour)
½ cup honey

Prepare the dough: In a large bowl, sift together the 3⅓ cups flour, baking soda, baking powder, and sugar. Using an electric mixer fitted with the paddle on low speed, or by hand, cut or rub in the butter until the flour has the consistency of cornmeal, about 2 minutes. Lightly beat the eggs and yolk in a small bowl, and quickly work them into the mixture with the mixer or a spatula. Add the Marsala to form a soft dough.

Turn out the dough onto a lightly floured surface and knead it just enough to form a very soft dough with a slightly sticky surface. Depending on climatic conditions, it might be necessary to add sprinklings of flour for the dough to come together. Remember that overkneading pastry dough will make it tough. Form the dough into a ball, cover with plastic wrap, and let it rest, refrigerated, for 3 hours.

**Prepare the filling:** Preheat the oven to 400°F, with a rack positioned in the center.

Toast the hazelnuts on a baking sheet in the oven for about 10 minutes. Take care that they do not burn. Remove the nuts from the oven, wrap them in a dishcloth, and let them steam for a couple of minutes. Then rub them together to remove as much of the brown skin as possible. Using a food processor, finely grind the nuts to the same consistency as the semolina. Mix the nuts and semolina together in a bowl.

Pour the honey into a small saucepan. Heat it over low heat until it just begins to come to a boil, about 3 minutes. Mix the thinned honey well into the semolina mixture to form a smooth paste with the consistency of brown sugar. Cover the bowl loosely with waxed paper, and let the paste rest at room temperature until needed.

**Form the cookies and bake:** Preheat the oven to 375°F, with a rack positioned in the upper third.

Flour a work surface. Be sure that it remains lightly but well floured throughout this step by adding pinches of flour as needed.

Remove the dough from the refrigerator, and divide it in half. Re-cover one half and return it to the refrigerator.

Roll the dough with your hand against the work surface to form a rope 24 inches long and about 1¼ inches in diameter. Flatten it with your fingertips into a 2-inch-wide strip.

Divide the filling in half. Compress it with your hand, and place a ½-inch-diameter mound down the center of the length of the dough strip. Cut the strip in half for easier handling. Now, while gently pushing on the filling, stretch the dough around to cover it. Roll it against the well-floured surface to create a cylinder about 1½ inches in diameter. Slightly flatten the cylinder, and cut it into 6 slices. Place all 6 cookies, evenly spaced, on a sheet pan.

Using a wet dough scraper or sharp knife, make two equidistant cuts on one side of each cookie from the center to the outer edge at a 45° angle. Make one such cut on the other side, so that the cookie resembles the sprig of a branch.

Bake for about 20 minutes, until the top is barely colored. Cool the cookies for 5 minutes in the pan, and then transfer them with a spatula to a wire rack to cool to room temperature.

Prepare the second batch while the first one bakes.

Turruni 'i Miennuli

# Almond Nougat

Turruni, or *torrone* in Italian, is nougat that ranges in texture from very soft to a hardness that seems designed to break one's teeth. It can be made with a variety of nuts. This nougat from Pino is tender and is made with almonds.

Preparing this *turruni* is not complicated. One part of the process, however, involves beating the hot honey and sugar syrup into the egg whites. A stand mixer with a stainless-steel bowl is essential for this task.

The *turruni* is then cooked in this bowl over a pot of water, creating a double boiler. Before you begin, determine the amount of water needed in the pot by filling it with enough water to touch the bottom of the bowl.

Stored in an airtight container lined with waxed paper, *turruni* will keep fresh for 2 months on average.

*For about 36 pieces*

1    pound (about 3 cups) shelled whole raw almonds
    Solid vegetable shortening, for greasing the pan
1    cup honey
1    tablespoon light corn syrup
1¼ cups sugar
2    egg whites
1    teaspoon vanilla extract
¼   teaspoon almond extract
¼   teaspoon ground cinnamon

Preheat the oven to 400°F.

Toast the almonds on a sheet pan in the oven for 10 minutes. Be sure the nuts don't burn. Set aside until needed.

Very lightly grease a marble slab or a sheet pan with vegetable shortening.

Put the honey, corn syrup, and 1 cup of the sugar in a heavy 1½-quart pot over low heat. Stir with a wooden spoon until the sugar is melted. Stop stirring, raise the heat to medium, and boil until the honey stops frothing and goes flat, about 7 minutes.

Meanwhile, start beating the egg whites in a large stainless-steel bowl with an electric stand mixer on high speed until they form peaks that are stiff but not dry. Continue to beat, sprinkling in the remaining ¼ cup sugar a little at a time.

As soon as the syrup is ready, reduce the mixer speed to medium and pour in the syrup. Add the vanilla and almond extracts, and the cinnamon. Beat for 5 minutes, until the mixture is smooth, elastic, and well aerated.

Meanwhile, bring a pot of water (see headnote) to a boil; then adjust the heat to keep it at a lively simmer.

When the *turruni* is ready, set the mixing bowl on the pot of simmering water. While it is cooking, constantly turn the *turruni* away from the sides and bottom of the bowl with a hard, heat-resistant spatula. Cook for 20 minutes. The *turruni* is ready when a small amount dropped on the slab or pan and cooled to room temperature can be formed into a firm yet tender ball.

Remove the bowl from the pot and mix in the almonds. Turn out the *turruni* onto the prepared slab or pan. Using a wet dough scraper or metal spatula, form it into a 9-inch square, 1 inch thick. Smooth the top. Let it set for at least 4 hours.

Serve the *turruni* from the slab, or cut it into 1½-inch squares and store it in an airtight container.

Amarena Cotta

# Sour Cherries in Syrup

This recipe calls for a type of sour cherry called Morello. These are available from specialty produce markets during cherry season. An excellent alternative is to use wild "backyard" cherries. The recipe has also been tested with Bing cherries with good results.

Use these cherries as a topping for cake or ice cream. The syrup can be mixed with cold sparkling mineral water to make a refreshing drink.

Stored in a closed glass jar in the refrigerator, the cherries will last for several months.

*For 3 cups*

1   pound cherries (see headnote)
⅓   cup spring water
1½ cups sugar

Stem and wash the cherries. Pit them with a cherry pitter, leaving them whole.

Put the water and sugar in a heavy 1½-quart saucepan. Stir gently over very low heat until the sugar is melted. Stop stirring, raise the heat to low, and boil for 3 minutes. Then stir in the cherries and continue to stir gently for about 15 minutes, until the liquid turns a deep, dark cherry color.

Remove the pot from the stove and cool the cherries and syrup to room temperature. Pour it in a clean glass jar, cover, and store in the refrigerator.

*tarting* with Cain and Abel, man has gained earthly power by violence and treachery. If the genealogy of every aristocratic, noble, or royal family in the world were traced back to the years before courtly gentility, the founder would surely have been a chicken thief, or worse.

In Polizzi, from the Middle Ages until after World War II, the aristocracy controlled agriculture through huge hereditary holdings called *latifondi*. Even after the turn of the twentieth century, virtually feudal *baruneddi* (barons) lorded over poor tenant farmers with absolute, sometimes cruel, authority. The Polizzani still tell stories of one such baron who lived less than a hundred years ago.

Whenever the mood struck him, this baron would ride into the fields, point his bony, blue-blooded finger at one of his working farmers, and order the man to follow him. The baron (on horseback) would lead the farmer (on foot) to the highest hill in the terrain and say, "Look! Everything you see with your eyes is mine. Now, go back down and work."

During one wheat harvest, this same baron rode into the fields and gestured one of his tenants join him. With a broad, seemingly genuine smile on his face, and speaking as to a child, he said, "I have been watching you. You are a very good worker, and I have something for you." The baron produced a paper bundle from one of his saddlebags. The farmer accepted it, eyes lowered subserviently. But when the baron had ridden off, the farmer quickly opened it to find an egg. This egg, beaten into the farmer's meager evening meal of soup or pasta, would provide a delicious bit of protein for his whole family, and he was happy to have it.

The next day, the farmer worked harder. When one of his co-workers told him to slow down, the farmer said, "The *baruneddu* noticed my hard work and gave me an egg."

"An egg?!" the other responded. He thought, "I'll work harder, the baron will notice, and he'll give me an egg too."

Two days later, the baron returned to the field, gestured over the same farmer, and with the same ceremony gave him another egg. Word quickly spread throughout the fields: The baron is giving away eggs for good work. Sickles sparked as that wheat harvest became the fastest, most meticulous, and richest in memory. But the promise of eggs remained only that, and the close-fisted baron gave away not one egg more.

At one time, Polizzi boasted the residences of fifteen barons, two counts, and a prince. In the late fifteenth century, the daughter of one of the *grandes familles* of Polizzi, La Matina, entered the old cloistered Benedictine convent, which had been completed in 1330 today known as *'a Badia Vecchia*, the Old Abbey. The reason for her confinement is still a topic of eyebrow-raising speculation among the people. Nevertheless, it is no surprise that she quickly rose to the position of abbess.

Noble indiscretion must have been pandemic in fifteenth-century Polizzani society, for soon after, the daughter of another great house, Signurino, entered the same convent. Count Signurino demanded that the bishop replace La Matina's daughter, the abbess, with his own daughter. The bishop refused.

This rift escalated to such proportion that the Count finally built a new convent, installing his daughter as abbess. Completed in 1499, the New Abbey, *'a Badia Nuova*, was far more splendid than the Old Abbey.

With malicious purpose, the count had his daughter's bedroom positioned so that it faced that of the abbess of the other convent. The two good sisters, however, did not share their fathers' animosity, and took every opportunity to silently smile and wave at each other.

The idea that one man possessed enough power and wealth to build an entire monastery just to prove a point was incomprehensible to the common people. It made them laugh over the foolishness of the aristocracy, but it also showed them the powerlessness of their own position.

These days, what aristocrats are left return for the summer season, when they take up residency in their hereditary palazzi. Some return to their country estates in the autumn just to play at harvesting olives. Many of these *barunali* (baronial estates) are in crumbling disrepair, and the titled owners camp out, living in tents and using sleeping bags, to the amusement of the people. One Polizzani friend ironically commented to me, "*Poveri blasunati* (the poor titled ones); if they need a roof over their heads, they can stay with me."

There is a certain reality that some of these "poor titled ones" are indeed useless. Paradoxically, the people take pity on *them*. An older friend, Guidu, recalls that when he was a boy, his mother would say, "Take these oranges to the baron. It's Christmas Eve, and the poor man is all alone in that big house."

Santo and I were hiking one morning in the countryside when we came upon a *barunali* with a party of olive pickers. Santo said hello to the baronet, whom he had known since childhood. The man was standing in front of a small campfire, and in his hand was a large plastic sack of sausages. He was beside himself, for he had forgotten to bring along a grill or a pan, and did not know how he was going to cook lunch.

Santo calmed him down and asked me to reach my long arm on top of what was left of the roof and grab a loose terra-cotta tile. Santo washed the half-round tile in a nearby stream and set it on the fire, curved side up. When it was hot, he put the sausages in it. The baronet thanked Santo for his help, but the hospitable concept of inviting us to lunch never occurred to him. As we walked away, Santo, knowing what I was thinking, commented, "Forget about it. That's the way they are."

Since 1948, Italy has been a democracy and titles are, in fact, outlawed on mailing addresses or official documents. Aristocratic Polizzani attitudes have changed in modern times. For several generations now, many aristocrats have felt a civic and personal responsibility to use their wealth and position for the common good. As a group, they have gone from being dabblers and dilettantes to doers and true artists. Their academic pursuits have produced a fine crop of professionals in every discipline from medicine to agronomy. Some of the finer modern Sicilian writers, painters, and musicians have emerged from their ranks, through serious exploration of the artistic process.

But for a few who still view themselves as upper-class, subtle reminders of the past remain. They speak to shopkeepers and tradesmen in loud, slow voices, the way one speaks to a small child. They always try to go to the front of the line in the bank or the post office, and even crowd people in the first pew at church, behaving as if these places have been permanently reserved for them.

My roots are from the people, but as a Sicilian-American movie actor, I have access that crosses class lines. Even so, that old unconscious attitude is as plain as the large "aristocratic" nose on my face. While pointing to an old man busy baking bread, a Sicilian countess once said to me, "Your grandfather, did he look like that peasant, that one there?" She was completely unaware of the significance of what she said.

I am acquainted with a Polizzani baron from one of the "lesser" families. He and I have met for coffee from time to time, and judging from his conversation, this baron seems to be a modern, egalitarian person. I saw a different picture, however, after I described to him the fun of a family dinner at my cousin Moffu's country house. His response came from a deep-seated attitude that I am sure he is not conscious of. After listening to my account with an amused smile, he said, in earnest, "Ah, the humble folk."

Beginning in the 1880s, and for nearly fifty years after, thousands of Polizzani emigrated to America. For poor tenant farmers, the golden opportunities of the great freedom across the sea presented the only way out of a life under the boot heel of the local barony.

It was from this life of locked-in poverty that Gannuarfu Picchiu (an *'ngiuria* meaning "woodpecker"), a boy of twelve, was saved by a ticket to America, sent by his "rich" uncle. Settling in Brooklyn with his uncle (who turned out not to be rich at all), Gannuarfu spent his boyhood growing up on the streets, working in textile factories, and living from hand to mouth. His only thought was to save enough money to return to Polizzi, buy a grand house, and live like a baron.

By the 1930s, he was working as a manual laborer. The uncle had passed away and Gannuarfu lived alone, without wife or family. His co-workers and neighbors, many of them Polizzani immigrants as well, taking pity on him, would often invite him to have dinner with their families. He always refused, saying, "Tonight I was planning to eat pasta with chicken." To manual laborers during the Great Depression, chicken was fortunate Sunday fare, not a weeknight thing. As time passed, it seemed that this fellow was eating pasta with chicken every night of the week.

Gannuarfu, or "the man who eats pasta with chicken," as he became known, was a topic of intense neighborhood gossip. One man said, "He works digging in the hole right next to me. So from where is he getting the money to buy all this chicken?"

The neighbors began to suspect that some secret criminal life accounted for this endless supply of chicken. It occurred to them that no one had ever been invited to his home, concluding that clues to the nature of his double life could be found there. If only they could gain entrance for a thorough snooping.

One summer evening, a group of neighbors gathered quietly in front of his building. They had devised a plan to settle their curiosity. Pretending Gannuarfu wasn't home, they would burst in (nobody locked their doors in those days) under the feeble pretext of closing his windows against an impending thunderstorm. Of course the timing was set to surprise him at table.

The neighbors did burst in, screaming warnings of deluge, but were frozen silent in the doorway by what they saw. The man was sitting with a humble bowl of spaghetti in front of him. He was slicing a clove of garlic over it, and then carefully adding a few drops of olive oil. Gannuarfu answered the question on his neighbors' faces with a simple explanation: "You know how the rich give fancy names to different dishes? Well, I call this one pasta with chicken."

Although it took him thirty years of hard work and frugality to fulfill his dream, Gannuarfu did return to Polizzi to live out the rest of his years in baronial luxury. And pasta with *real* chicken filled his plate whenever he desired.

A traditional outdoor cooking method in Polizzi, especially at grape-harvest time, this technique can be easily adapted for barbecuing in this country. Sausages or lamb chops work best; pork chops or steaks are usually too large to fit down in the curve. Chicken requires too long a cooking time and will char before it is ready.

In the southwestern United States, where tiled roofs are common, curved, unglazed terra-cotta roofing tiles can be found easily at building supply stores. In other parts of the country, finding them might involve a bit of research. Be sure the tiles are made of terra-cotta and not concrete or glazed ceramic.

Terra-cotta tiles are generally 2½ inches high and 18 inches long, tapering an inch along the length. There is a hole at the center of the wide end for nailing it in place on the roof. When cooking meat on the tile, this hole allows the grease to run off. Before using a roofing tile for the first time, rinse it clean and soak it in cold water for 2 hours.

Build a fire in the center of a barbecue grill, following the manufacturer's instructions. It is best to use real wood charcoal rather than briquettes. When the charcoal turns white, set the grill rack in place and put the tile on the rack, curved side up. Close the cover and heat the tile for about 30 minutes, until it is very hot.

Cut thin sausages into 7-inch lengths, or separate thick ones into single links. Place them in the curve of the tile and cook, uncovered. Turn the sausages with long-handled tongs until browned all over, a total of 15 to 25 minutes. Cook lamb chops for about 3 minutes on each side. Be aware that grease will drain out of the hole onto the hot coals, and might flare up.

A dramatic serving idea is to bring the tile directly to the table. Be very careful to protect your hands with oven mitts while transporting the hot tile. Also be sure to protect the tabletop from burning. Note that anything that comes in contact with the bottom of the tile will blacken from the charcoal.

To clean the tile after use, wait until it has completely cooled and then scour it under running water with steel wool or a plastic scrubber.

## Pasta ca Gaddina

### *Pasta with Chicken*

While Gannuarfu was eating his meager bowl of pasta with garlic and olive oil, this might have been the pasta with chicken that filled his imagination.

This recipe will serve four as a one-course meal, or six as a first course.

*For 4 or 6 servings*

4    chicken thighs (about 1½ pounds total)
2    tablespoons extra-virgin olive oil
2    medium-sized yellow onions, finely chopped
1    cup dry white wine
    Sea salt
    Black pepper
3    scrapes of nutmeg
1    pound rigatoni
2    eggs
¾    cup grated imported pecorino cheese, preferably Locatelli brand
⅓    cup chopped Italian parsley

Rinse the chicken thighs and pat them dry.

In a heavy 6-quart pot, heat the olive oil over medium-high heat. Brown the chicken well on all sides, about 8 minutes. Transfer it to a plate. Remove the pot from the heat and pour off half the fat.

Put the onions in the pot, adjust the heat, and sauté for about 4 minutes, until golden. Return the chicken to the pot and mix it with the onions. When the chicken is hot, pour the white wine over it. While the alcohol evaporates for a minute or two, deglaze the pot by scraping up all the bits that have stuck to the bottom with a wooden spatula. Season with salt, a few grindings of black pepper, and the nutmeg.

Reduce the heat to low, cover, and cook at a simmer for 45 minutes, until the chicken is cooked. Turn the chicken and onions twice to prevent sticking.

During this time, fill a large pot with 6 quarts water, add 2 tablespoons salt, and bring it to a boil over high heat.

When the chicken is cooked, remove it from the pot. Let it cool a bit for easier handling. Then discard the skin, and use a fork to remove the meat from the bones in strips. Put the meat back into the pot, and continue to cook over very low heat, partially covered, for the remainder of the preparation time.

Cook the rigatoni in the boiling water for about 10 minutes, until al dente. Beat the eggs and cheese together in a small bowl. Reserve until needed.

When the rigatoni is ready, add ½ cup of the starchy pasta water to the chicken in the pot. Drain the pasta very well, and toss it in the pot with the chicken. Let the flavors mingle for a minute. Then turn off the heat, and thoroughly mix in the eggs and cheese, and then the parsley.

Serve directly from the cooking pot in pasta bowls, topped with grindings of black pepper to taste.

## Pasta ca Sarsa d'Ova

# *Pasta with Tomato-Egg Sauce*

In former times, the clever Polizzani cook found a way to extend the treasure of 2 eggs for her entire family. By adding them to a simple, ordinary tomato sauce, she changed it into something bursting with richness and new flavor. For poor farmers, this might have been the only source of protein for the day.

*For 4 servings*

| | |
|---|---|
| | Sea salt |
| | One 35-ounce can peeled whole Italian plum tomatoes, drained |
| 1 | small yellow onion, finely chopped |
| 2 | tablespoons extra-virgin olive oil |
| 1 | tablespoon tomato paste dissolved in ⅓ cup water |
| | Black pepper |
| 2 | teaspoons sugar |
| 1 | pound linguine |
| 2 | eggs, beaten |
| ¾ | cup grated imported pecorino cheese, preferably Locatelli brand |

Fill a large pot with 6 quarts water, add 2 tablespoons salt, and bring it to a boil over high heat.

Meanwhile, prepare the sauce: Fit a food mill with the disk with the smallest holes (1 millimeter), and place it over a bowl. Puree the drained tomatoes to remove the seeds, which can make the sauce bitter. Scrape the pulp from underneath the mill into the bowl.

Put the onion and olive oil in a heavy medium-sized pot over medium heat, and sauté the onion until it turns translucent, about 5 minutes. Stir in the thinned tomato paste. Cook for about 1 minute and then add the milled tomatoes. Season with salt and pepper, and add the sugar. Reduce the heat to low and simmer the sauce, uncovered, stirring from time to time, for 20 minutes. Do not let it boil.

When the water boils, cook the linguine until al dente, about 10 minutes. Drain it thoroughly, and put it in a warmed serving bowl.

Remove the sauce from the heat and let it settle for a minute. Then stir in the beaten eggs, doing so quickly to be sure they don't seize or separate.

Toss the linguine with the sauce. Serve immediately, with a grinding of black pepper and grated cheese to taste.

# Farsu Magru

## Stuffed Meat Roll

The idea of stuffing a thin piece of meat is an old and thrifty Sicilian culinary tradition. In centuries past, poor country folk who were lucky enough to get a piece of muscle meat could extend its serving capacity by rolling it around more common ingredients. As the meat roll moved from the kitchens of the poor to the kitchens of the rich, these fillings became quite lavish.

Based on these rich, aristocratic versions of the dish, the Sicilian term *farsu magru* may have been derived from the Italian *falso magro* (false lean). A more likely explanation, however, is that it is a Sicilianization of the French term *farce maigre* (meatless stuffing). This theory is supported by the lighter, more meager versions, like this very old Polizziani recipe.

This stuffed meat roll is cooked in tomato sauce, sliced, and served at room temperature without the sauce. It can be served as part of a buffet or as a second course. The sauce makes an excellent stock for a first-course risotto (see *Risuttu 'i Pumadamuri*, page 148).

A note on the meat: In the original Polizziani recipe, the meat is veal flank from *vitellone*, an older calf, similar to what we call a yearling. Since this type of veal is virtually impossible to find in this country, flank steak has been substituted. Purchase a young, tender flank steak weighing about 1½ pounds. Have the butcher butterfly it, remove the surface fat from both sides, and pound it to ¼-inch thickness, without tears or holes. (If there are holes, the meat must be patched before stuffing it.) After pounding, the piece should measure about 10 by 12 inches.

*For 6 to 8 servings*

5   eggs
    One 35-ounce can peeled whole Italian plum tomatoes, undrained
4   ounces *caciocavallo* cheese, coarsely grated (about 1½ cups)
1   cup grated imported pecorino cheese, preferably Locatelli brand
4   *cipollini* (small flat Italian onions) (4 ounces total) or 4 ounces
    new yellow onions

Sea salt

Black pepper

1½ pounds beef flank steak (see note on the meat)

3 tablespoons extra-virgin olive oil

1 cup dry white wine

2 teaspoons sugar

Hard-boil 4 of the eggs: Pierce the large end of each egg with a pin (to prevent cracking). Put the eggs in a small pot, cover with cold water, and cook for 10 minutes after the water comes to a boil. Drain the eggs and run them under cold water to stop the cooking and loosen the shells. Peel the eggs and set them aside until needed.

Fit a food mill with the disk with the smallest holes (1 millimeter), and place it over a bowl. Pour the tomatoes and their liquid into the mill. Puree the tomatoes to remove the seeds, which can make the sauce bitter. Scrape the pulp from underneath the mill into the bowl. Reserve the milled tomatoes until needed.

Put the *caciocavallo* and pecorino in a bowl. Peel and chop the onions, and mix them with the cheeses. Beat the remaining egg, add it to the bowl, and mix the ingredients into a chunky paste. Season with salt and several grindings of black pepper.

Cover a work surface with a length of waxed paper. Place the meat on it with the narrow edge facing you. Salt and pepper it on both sides. Cut 3 lengths of sturdy kitchen twine about 16 inches long. Slip them, evenly spaced, lengthwise under the meat. Spread the paste over the meat, leaving a 1-inch border around the edges.

Cut off the ends of the hard-boiled eggs just until the yolks are exposed. Place them, end to end, along the nearest edge of the meat. Use a thin 10-inch-long bamboo skewer to hold the eggs together. Now firmly roll up the meat, starting at the near edge. Tie it securely with the strings. Remove the skewer and fold the ends closed. Wind string around and from end to end of the roll to be sure it is tightly closed.

Pour the olive oil into a heavy pot that is large enough to accommodate the rolled meat. Heat it over medium heat until hot. Stand the roll in the pot, leaning it against the side, to lightly brown and seal the end. Do the same at the other end, and then lightly brown it all over, about 3½ minutes a side.

Turn off the heat, remove the roll, and deglaze the pot with the wine, scraping the bottom and sides. Turn the heat back to medium-high and return the meat to the pot. Roll it in the wine for a couple of minutes while the alcohol evaporates.

Add the milled tomatoes, salt and pepper to taste, and the sugar. Stir well. When the sauce comes to a boil, turn down the heat, cover, and simmer for about 1½ hours, until the meat is very tender when pierced with a fork. Turn the meat in the sauce several times while it simmers.

When the roll is cooked, transfer it to a platter and allow it to cool, uncovered, for at least 45 minutes.

Meanwhile, degrease the sauce by cooling it to room temperature and then skimming off all the fat that pools on top. Do not degrease it any further. Save the sauce for another use, such as the Tomato Risotto (page 148). After it has been degreased, well covered, and refrigerated, the sauce will keep for several days, or it can be frozen for 2 months.

Remove the strings from the meat roll. Turn it so it is seam side down, and cut it with a very sharp or serrated knife into thin slices, about ¼ inch thick. Arrange the slices in slightly overlapping layers on a platter, and serve.

# Risuttu 'i Pumadamuri

## *Tomato Risotto*

The liquid used to make this risotto is the tomato sauce from *Farsu Magru*, Stuffed Meat Roll (page 145). It contains all the flavors of the meat roll, which are then infused into the rice.

The process for making risotto is simple but requires attention. The basic concept is to slowly add just enough liquid to the raw rice to cook it. Adding the liquid in too large quantities will cause the risotto to be gummy and porridge-like; adding too little at a time may cause it to burn. The proper consistency is creamy, but with each grain individuated and cooked all the way through.

Only two types of rice will produce this result, both imported from Italy: *canaroli* and *arborio*. The latter is easier to find in this country. Both of these rices have enough starch content to produce the necessary creaminess, and they take a longer cooking time to become al dente.

Finishing a risotto with raw eggs gives it a rich, mouth-filling creaminess. This is a secret I learned from my grandfather, Papa Andrea.

The cooking time from the first addition of the liquid is approximately 18 minutes. Risotto cannot be held at the ready and must be eaten within minutes of completion.

This risotto can be served as a first course for a meal in which the meat roll is served, or it can be served at a different meal.

*For 6 to 8 servings*

 

Sauce (about 6 cups) from 1 recipe *Farsu Magru*, Stuffed Meat Roll
(page 145)
1    pound (about 2½ cups) *arborio* rice
1    medium-sized yellow onion
2    tablespoons unsalted butter
1    tablespoon extra-virgin olive oil
1    cup dry white wine
2    eggs, beaten
⅓    cup chopped Italian parsley
¾    cup grated imported pecorino cheese, preferably Locatelli brand
      Black pepper

Pour the sauce into a saucepan. If it has not been degreased already, cool it to room temperature and skim off all the fat that pools on top. Do not degrease it any further. Thin the sauce with 1 cup water. Cover the pot and bring the sauce to a boil. Adjust the heat, and keep it covered at a lively simmer for the remainder of the preparation.

Rinse and drain the rice, checking it for debris. Put it aside.

Peel the onion, cut it in half, and thinly slice it into half-circles. Put the butter and olive oil in a heavy 4-quart pot. Turn on the heat to medium-low, and when the butter stops foaming, add the onion. Sauté just until the onion turns translucent, about 5 minutes.

Add the rice, and turn it in the pot until it is well coated with the fat. Continue stirring until it is hot. Do not let it brown, which would inhibit its ability to absorb liquid.

Raise the heat to medium-high, and pour in half of the white wine. Stir gently but constantly until it is completely absorbed by the rice. Add the remaining wine, proceeding in the same way.

If at any time during the cooking process, the rice begins to stick to the bottom of the pot, adjust the heat immediately to keep it from burning.

Pour in about ½ cup of the sauce, and continue to stir until it has been absorbed. Repeat, always stirring constantly. When the rice is half-cooked, after about 9 minutes, begin to add the sauce ¼ cup at a time. When the rice is nearly cooked, add the sauce in spoonfuls at a time. The rice may cook before all the sauce is used. If it is not cooked when all the sauce has been used, add boiling water until it reaches the proper consistency (see headnote).

If the rice remains ever so slightly dry in the center, stir in 2 tablespoons of sauce (or water) just before proceeding to the next step.

When the rice is cooked, remove it from the heat. Stir for a moment longer, until it stops boiling. Quickly and thoroughly mix in the beaten eggs, then the parsley and grated cheese. Cover the pot and let the risotto rest for 3 minutes before serving.

At the table, add grindings of black pepper to taste.

## Stufatu 'i Cacuocciuli

# *Braised Artichoke Hearts*

These artichoke hearts are slowly cooked with onion perfumed with melted anchovy, garlic, and mint. They are then dressed with lemon juice and mixed with toasted bread crumbs. The dish is served slightly chilled as an antipasto or as part of a buffet, or as an accompaniment to meat or fish.

Use artichokes that are fresh and tender. Choose ones that are closed and that squeak when rubbed between your hands. This will ensure that the inner leaves are moist and soft.

*For 6 servings*

| | |
|---|---|
| 3 | lemons |
| 9 | artichokes, about 4 inches long and 2½ inches in diameter at the widest part |
| ¼ | cup plus 1 tablespoon extra-virgin olive oil |
| 1 | medium-sized yellow onion, finely chopped |
| 2 | anchovy fillets |
| 2 | cloves garlic, finely chopped |
| | Sea salt |
| | Black pepper |
| 2 | tablespoons chopped fresh mint leaves |
| ¾ | cup unflavored bread crumbs |

Fill a medium-sized bowl two-thirds full of cold water. Juice 2 of the lemons, and add the juice and rinds to the water.

Working with 1 artichoke at a time, cut off ½ inch from the top of the artichoke. Pass a knife through the remaining lemon prior to each cut; this will help prevent the artichokes from turning black. Remove the outer leaves to the place where the leaves are thin and pale green. Cut the artichoke and stem into quarters. If the stem is curved, pay special attention while cutting. With a sharp paring knife, trim away the dark green base of the leaves around the heart. Peel the stem and cut away the end. Carefully remove and discard the spiny choke and the purple leaves with a paring knife or a spoon, and place the quarters in the lemon-water. Let the artichokes macerate in the lemon-water for 20 minutes.

Pour the ¼ cup olive oil into a heavy 9-inch skillet over medium heat.

When it is hot, add the onion and sauté until it is a bright golden color, about 7 minutes. Push the onion to one side of the pan and add the anchovies to the oil. Cook for about 2 minutes, mashing with a fork to form a paste. Stir the anchovies into the onion.

Drain the artichokes and add them and the garlic to the skillet. Fold all the ingredients together and sauté for 3 minutes to sear the artichokes. Season with salt and black pepper. Cover, reduce the heat to very low, and simmer gently, stirring occasionally, for 20 minutes. Add the mint and simmer for another 15 to 20 minutes, until the artichoke hearts are tender and some of the fragile leaves have fallen away.

If at any time the liquid in the pan evaporates and the artichokes start to crackle, add water in spoonfuls down the side of the pan.

While the artichokes are cooking, toast the bread crumbs: Place the bread crumbs with the remaining 1 tablespoon olive oil in a small heavy skillet. Turn on the heat to very low, and stir to distribute the oil. Nothing will happen at first, but then the crumbs will brown quite quickly. Toast them until they are a deep rich brown. To prevent the bread crumbs from burning, transfer them to a bowl the moment they are done.

When the artichokes are cooked, remove them from the heat and fold in the juice of the remaining lemon (the one you used to coat the knife) and then the bread crumbs. Transfer to a serving bowl and cool, uncovered, to room temperature. Cover and chill slightly before serving.

## Pùarri Fritti

### Fried Leeks

The utter simplicity of this preparation is all that is necessary to bring out the vitality of this native Mediterranean vegetable. Choose leeks that have crisp, bright leaves and an unblemished white portion.

*For 6 servings*

**12  leeks, 1¼ inches in diameter at the root end**
   **Sea salt**
**1½ cups pure olive oil, for frying**
   **Flour, for dusting**

Cut off the leeks' green leaves and the root ends. Peel away one or two of the outer layers, which are tough and fibrous. Split the leeks lengthwise and rinse them under cold running water to remove all the dirt from between the layers.

In a medium-sized pot, bring 3 quarts lightly salted water to a boil over high heat. Blanch the leeks in the boiling water, uncovered, for 4 minutes. Drain, and cool the leeks to room temperature under cold running water. Pat them dry and arrange them on a platter with paper towels between the layers.

Put a baking pan in the oven and preheat it to 300°F.

Pour the oil into a heavy 9-inch skillet over medium-high heat. When the oil is very hot, lightly dust with flour as many leeks as will fit comfortably in the pan. Fry them for about 3 minutes on each side, until the edges are well browned and crispy. Use tongs to remove them from the skillet, and place them on brown paper or paper towels to drain the excess oil. Then put the fried leeks in the baking pan and leave in the oven, uncovered, to stay hot while you cook the rest.

Place all the fried leeks on a serving platter, season with salt, and serve.

## Torta 'i Meli

# *Honey Sponge Cake*

Sponge cake was introduced to Sicily in the ninth century by the North Africans. Along with eggs and flour, sugar is a basic ingredient of this baked delight. Until the mid-nineteenth century, however, refined sugar was expensive, available only to the rich; substituting honey produced by local beekeepers made this sponge cake affordable to all.

Fruit salad in syrup, a modern topping for this cake, turns it into a special dessert. The fruit salad may be substituted with canned sliced fruit in heavy syrup or with halved *Pira 'Ncilippati*, Sugared Pears (page 90). Another seasonal alternative is to use fresh strawberries soaked in sweet vermouth: Halve the strawberries, dust them with confectioners' sugar, and macerate in vermouth for several hours.

For centuries, powdered eggshell has been the secret of pastry chefs for keeping beaten egg whites from collapsing. To prepare an eggshell for this purpose, peel away and discard the inner lining of the shell, wash it with warm water, and let it dry thoroughly. Keep it in a small jar, and pulverize a small piece as needed in a mortar and pestle or between two spoons. The shell will keep for many years, and will be enough for many batches of egg whites.

*For one 9-inch round cake*

Unsalted butter for greasing the pan
2 cups cake flour, plus additional for dusting the pan
1 teaspoon baking soda
Pinch of sea salt
6 eggs, separated
1 cup mild-flavored honey
Juice (about 3 tablespoons) and chopped zest of 1 small lemon
⅛ teaspoon powdered eggshell (see headnote), or a pinch of cream of tartar
2 pounds fruit salad in heavy syrup, chilled

Preheat the oven to 375°F, with a rack positioned in the center. Butter and flour a 9-inch round cake pan with 2- or 3-inch sides.

Sift the flour, baking soda, and salt together in a bowl.

153

Using an electric mixer or by hand in a large bowl, beat the egg yolks with the honey until the mixture is pale yellow. Add the lemon juice.

While continuing to beat, add a small amount of the flour mixture. When it is absorbed, add more. Continue in this manner until all of the flour has been beaten in and absorbed. Stir in the lemon zest.

In a clean grease-free bowl, copper if possible, begin to beat the egg whites with a clean mixer or whisk. (If any oils from the egg yolks touch the egg whites, they will not stiffen.) When the whites begin to change and color, add the powdered eggshell or cream of tartar, and continue beating until the whites form peaks that are stiff but not dry.

Vigorously beat about 3 generous tablespoons of the stiffened egg whites into the egg yolk mixture to loosen it. Quickly but gently fold the remaining egg whites into the yolk mixture with a rubber spatula. Turn the batter into the pan and smooth the top with a spatula.

Bake for 30 to 40 minutes, until the top is a deep golden brown and a toothpick inserted near the center comes out clean. Refrain from opening the oven door as much as possible, since a sudden gush of cold air or even a heavy thud of the door can cause the cake to collapse. If you must, peek in and then close the door gently.

When the cake is baked, turn off the oven and let the cake cool in the oven with the door ajar. When it is completely cooled, run a small, sharp knife around the top edge to free it, and turn it upside-down onto a serving plate. Arrange the fruits and syrup on top just before serving.

# Eight

# The Polizzani Circle of the Night

*S*ummer! Glorious, brilliant summer! In the rest of Italy, the word for summer is *l'estate*. In Polizzi it is *'a stasciuni*, the season. The population doubles as native Polizzani return from northern Italian and European cities, even from America, for summer vacations. Friends and relatives renew acquaintanceships, compare and evaluate the growth of children, and exchange stories (not all true) from foreign places. The city blazes with the joy and frivolity of summertime.

The weather is usually more balmy than hot. The Madonie Mountains provide breezes and clean, fresh air. But when the hot winds from the Sahara, *u scirroccu*, blow across Sicily, it becomes like the inside of a bread oven. While Polizzi is spared the worst of it, on occasion the air can become extremely hot and heavy.

Adding to the discomfort is the universal belief that *'a currenta purta mali*, "the draft brings evil." This notion dates to the Middle Ages, when people mistakenly believed that the Black Plague was carried on the wind. To this day, windows are kept closed against the blowing wind, making indoors unbearably stuffy. Most everyone relocates to summer homes in the nearby countryside, where the temperature is a bit more bearable.

In the city, men can be seen in public wearing undershirts, and women might undo a top button or appear in shorts, relaxing traditional modesty. In the morning and evening, the glistening population moves about town in slow motion, but during the afternoon heat, not one soul is on the streets of Polizzi Generosa.

During one of these periods of extreme summer heat, I was staying at my cousin Moffu's unused house on the Via Roma. In the morning, as the heat waves began to reach high tide, I would walk the several blocks to Pino's pastry shop. At this hour, housewives would be on their hands and knees in front of their houses, washing their front sidewalks with scrub brushes, backsides swaying from the pressure they exerted on their hands and arms. All wiggling stopped, however, as their heads peeked over their shoulders to bid me good morning, discretely wiping sweat from their brows.

At Pino's I'd sit outside and enjoy a *café latte*, the laughter of children engaged in a gleeful game of street soccer the accompaniment. Pino would join me for a coffee and weather talk, trading his ovens for the one heating outside. "Don't you know how hot it is?" was his rhetorical question to the children, who were far too exhilarated to listen.

From Pino's shop I'd backtrack on sidewalks that seemed, somehow, cooler now, in their freshly washed state. As soon as I turned into the stepped alley leading to Santo's restaurant, my nose told me whether or not he had begun to prepare the luncheon *antipasti*. The main midday meal is the one aspect of daily Polizzani life that even fire from hell can never alter.

As I entered the cool of the shaded courtyard, Santo bellowed his familiar " 'Ell-oo." While exchanging pleasantries, I'd wash my hands and join him on the line. I had learned that he would turn down any offer of help but was pleased to have my aid. We boiled or sautéed a garden of vegetables into salads and caponatas. We beat eggs with pecorino and bread crumbs, frying dollops into small patties. Just-picked radicchio and arugula were cleaned and tossed together with red onion, ready to later receive a dressing of vinegar and olive oil. Once we found our rhythm, we worked in silence, moving from one task to the next, as the Franciscan monks might have done in this very building centuries ago.

Purveyors stopped by, reporting the progress of the weather, their wilting vegetables confirming current conditions. One egg-seller insisted that we all share a beer to protect our health against the heat. Good manners and a Polizzani sense of hospitality gave Santo no choice but to offer the drink.

Around one, the guests, locals and tourists, would arrive, settle themselves in the garden, sigh at its coolness, and eat. At about two-thirty, when the last dishes came out of the kitchen, Santo and I would lunch together. Our friend Nino, and perhaps Santo's sister Mimma, would join us. The afternoon heat gathered, making us a bit woozy at the last bites. As we dropped peeled slices of perfect peaches into our wineglasses, the need for siesta became our paramount thought. I would walk the few hundred feet to the house on the Via Roma, climb the stairs to the bedroom, and fall into a warm, mellow summer nap.

One afternoon, the hot, thick silence was pierced by church bells. An old woman on the balcony opposite mine called out in a craggy voice, to no one in particular, "*Cu murivu?*" "Who died?" The answer came from a nearby balcony, and the two old women had a lengthy conversation, balcony to balcony, about the long illness of their neighbor and his demise. They agreed that God had graciously put an end to his suffering. As the balcony doors squeaked shut, I could hear the funeral band with its mournful trumpet crescendos escorting the man to his final resting place. It soon faded to the sound of birds in the afternoon stillness.

Evening is always a grand spectacle. From seven until midnight, with an hour and a half break for dinner, the main street is crowded with strollers enjoying and creating its atmosphere. Groups of families, children on bicycles, gaggles of giggly teenage girls, mobs of randy teenage boys, indeed everyone in town strolls the circuit from the main piazza to the overlook. Appointments are made by simply saying, "I'll see you in piazza."

Each evening, the overlook piazza, *u chianu*, fills with spectators waiting to view the sunset, as the sky glows with shades of crimson and mauve and violet. Sometimes public dances are held in this large open space after dinner. The theme could be folk, or ballroom, or rock-and-roll. On occasion, a portable bandshell is set up, and free concerts are given by popular singers, their music ranging from opera to teenage heart-throb goo.

The Bar Cristallo, at the center of the main street, is packed on summer nights. Most come for a coffee or a cold soft drink. For a special treat, my friends and I might sample one of the house cocktails. Invented by the owner, Gasparinu Iovino, these concoctions have the most brilliant phosphorescent colors. We all know that these drinks are designed to startle by their appearance and not their taste, but we are charmed by them nonetheless.

Gasparinu is a man in his forties with matinee-idol good looks. He sports a thin, perfectly trimmed mustache. His wavy, jet-black hair is also perfectly groomed; biweekly visits to my cousin the barber keep him well shaved and with every hair in good control. Majestically he stands behind his bar, with the bearing of a flamenco dancer, shaking his cocktails with strong, sharp beats.

When saluting a passerby through the open glass doors, he counters this rhythm with a slow, imperious nod. But as are all things in Sicily, his studied stance is not only what it seems. One evening, while in the middle of a cocktail shaking, Gasparinu stopped suddenly, leaned over, and confided in me, "When I shake the cocktails, my balls dance." He burst into slightly embarrassed laughter, then composed himself and returned to his task, more serious than ever.

Sometimes Mimma would say to me at lunch, "Vicenzu, tonight we will go out. Meet me here at ten." I'd appear at the appointed hour, dressed in nice summer sports clothes. Mimma would appear in similar attire. We would walk to the center of town, where we'd be joined by other friends, who would comment, "Oh, you're going out tonight." We'd all stroll together, and people would turn their heads, looking at us with smiles and nods. As we all stepped into Gasparinu's bar, he would look at Mimma and me, inquiring, "Going out tonight?" On other nights, we could go through exactly the same ritual but dressed more casually, and attract little attention, except an occasional "What? Not going out tonight?"

As the bars and restaurants began to close and the throng of strollers thinned, *Circulu Notturnu Polizzanu*, the Polizzani Circle of the Night, would come to session. That summer Nino, Santo, and I would often meet at DA . . . DA . . . CI . . . CCIO for a nightcap. In short order, this spot became the late meeting place for everyone in the food trade, as well as for other Polizzani creatures of the night. I had christened the group with its grand-sounding name, and on nights when it was to meet, word spread—"*Circulu* tonight!"

The founding members were we three, plus Gasparinu, Francesco Ficile, at whose café we met, and a dozen other men. Mimma, Nino's sisters, and some other women friends attended sometimes, but usually it was just we men. We'd sit in the piazza in front of the café. A fountain gently flowed near a side wall of the city hall, formerly a Jesuit monastery. Behind us, the grand Palazzo Rampolla was quiet and shuttered. The white plastic tables and chairs at which we assembled glared in contrast to the very old surroundings.

Francesco offered little glass bowls of his perfect granita, cold and slushy, with frozen bits like crushed granite, the source of the dessert's name. The flavors included wild strawberry, bilberry, and mulberry, with whole frozen berries throughout the juicy slush. We drank Spumante out of plastic champagne flutes. At first our conversation was whispered—we wouldn't want to disturb the neighbors—but soon the sugar in the granita and the alcohol in the Spumante made our voices louder. Still, no one ever complained.

Within our company was a shepherd named Sebastianu. He was a tall, wiry man with an alpha ram look in his eyes. He portrayed himself as a real ladies' man, but his boasting mostly produced rolling of eyes from the more genteel members. No one liked the coarse way in which he talked about women, and we did our best to steer him clear of the topic. When ladies were present, he did behave like a gentleman, even seeming a bit bashful.

One night, I recounted the story of a very funny but dark comedy script I had once read. It was about a rich aristocrat who falls profoundly in love with a sheep. Everyone laughed as I told of the scenes in which their eyes met through the window, and how it was love at first sight; how the man leaves his wife for the sheep; how he is even driven to murderous jealousy over the presumed attentions of another man.

When the laughter subsided, Sebastianu said very seriously, "Sometimes it happens like that." All froze in open-mouthed surprise until Gasparinu said, "Now I understand, boys, why this 'lady killer' spends his nights with us in piazza." Everyone roared. Even Sebastianu laughed at himself.

There were performances, too. Pippinu, a tattooed truck driver from a nearby town, was a great joke-teller. In Sicily there is a fine art to joke-telling. All the characters are burlesqued with broad pantomime, and the comedy is more in the telling than in the punch line. We each had our favorites from his repertoire, and we asked for them regularly. Pippinu was a bit of a ham, and one never needed to ask twice. Laughter bounced off the ancient stone buildings, bursting high into the night sky, giving the stars more twinkle.

The church clock struck four, and sometimes five, but we were still in session. A momentary pause in conversation was caused by the aroma of hot bread snaking under our noses. Nino and I walked the few yards to the open bakery door and asked to buy a loaf or two. The busy baker would not take our money, explaining that the laughter of *u Circulu* made his work go faster.

While passing the bread around the circle and tearing off bites, our words turned to exhausted half-babble, but no one ever wanted the night to end. Francesco snubbed out his final cigarette and took the initiative by locking up his café.

As a closing gesture of camaraderie, someone always suggested a walk down to the *canula*, the "big pipe," for a drink of water. At this fountain near the entrance to the city, the water comes directly from the mountains, clear and cold, flowing into a rectangular fountain from a three-inch pipe. Each in turn, we held on to the pipe with one hand and swung our mouths under it to get a good long drink. My eyes, looking skyward in this position, could see the yet dark mountains, the mysterious source. I thanked the gods of heaven and earth for this refreshment.

We all stood in silence for a while, in preparation perhaps for the new day, perhaps for the rest of our lives. The members of the Polizzani Circle of the Night said goodnight, as first light outlined our way home.

# Pipi Chini

## *Stuffed Peppers*

The peppers used in this recipe are long, thin green or red frying peppers. The stem is removed like a cork, the seeds removed, and the pepper is stuffed; then the stem is put back in place. After the peppers have been cooked, they simply look like whole fried peppers. The surprise of a wonderfully rustic stuffing is revealed at the first bite.

*Pecorino purmintiu* is a key ingredient in this recipe. It is a table pecorino, younger and softer than the kind used for grating. It comes in small wheels, about 8 inches in diameter and 3 inches thick. Versions from Tuscany, Sicily, or Lazio can be found in certain cheese or Italian specialty shops. A good substitute is domestic sharp provolone.

In Polizzi, these stuffed peppers are served as part of an antipasto or as a summertime second course.

*For 4 to 6 servings*

| | |
|---|---|
| 8 | long green or red Italian (frying) or Hungarian peppers, 5 to 6 inches long and about 1½ inches in diameter at the stem end, with no deep dents and with a bit of stem attached |
| 4 | ounces *pecorino purmintiu* (see headnote) or domestic sharp provolone, in 1 piece |
| ¾ | cup unflavored bread crumbs |
| ½ | cup grated imported pecorino, preferably Locatelli brand |
| 1 | medium-sized yellow onion, finely chopped |
| 2 | small, ripe but firm plum tomatoes, chopped |
| | Black pepper |
| ⅓ | cup extra-virgin olive oil |
| 1 | egg white, lightly beaten |
| ¾ | cup pure olive oil, for frying |
| | Sea salt |

Clean the peppers and pat them dry. Using a small, sharp knife, cut a circular opening around the stem of each pepper. Remove the stem with the core, like a cork. Shake out the seeds but do not cut off the core; reserve these "corks."

Cut the *purmintiu* or provolone into small dice and put it in a mixing bowl. Add the bread crumbs, grated cheese, onion, tomatoes, a few grindings of black pepper, and the extra-virgin olive oil. Mix together well with a wooden spoon.

Stuff the peppers right up to the top but not too tightly. Gently shake them to make sure the stuffing has reached the bottom. Dip the stem-plug in the egg white, to serve as glue, and push it through the stuffing into place.

When all the peppers have been stuffed, pour the ¾ cup oil into a well-cured 9-inch skillet over medium heat. When the oil is hot, slip in half the peppers. Adjust the heat so the skin doesn't scorch before the peppers are done. The frying peppers should make a lively tinkling sound rather than a roar. Cook for 16 to 20 minutes, turning them often with tongs, until they are a deep brown. Then remove the peppers from the pan, supporting their length on a metal spatula. Place them on brown paper or paper towels to drain the excess oil. Fry the second batch the same way.

Arrange the peppers on an oval serving platter, season with salt, and serve at room temperature or slightly chilled.

## Ministruni

# *Summer Minestrone*

*Ministruni* is Sicilian for "big soup." There are many variations, with specific ingredients determined by the seasons. Summer *ministruni* uses all the freshness and fragrance of the kitchen garden's bouquet. Oftentimes, a pot of water will be set on the fire to boil, and then the cook will go into the garden to pick that day's *ministruni* ingredients. One possible result is the recipe that follows.

*For 6 to 8 servings*

5   quarts spring water
22  whole black peppercorns
2   pounds broad flat Italian green beans (romano beans)
1   bunch collard greens (about 1 pound)
2   small zucchini (about ½ pound)
2   carrots (about ½ pound)
1   small yellow onion
1   white rose (long white) potato (about ½ pound)
1   rib celery
4   teaspoons coarse sea salt plus additional
1   pound *ditali* or *ditalini* (small tube macaroni about ¼ inch in diameter
    and ½ inch long)
    Extra-virgin olive oil, for drizzling
    Crushed red pepper
    Black pepper

Fill a stockpot with the spring water, add the peppercorns, cover, and bring to a boil over medium-high heat. While waiting for the water to boil, prepare the vegetables:

Clean the beans, snap off the ends, and cut them into 1½-inch lengths.

Cut off and discard the fibrous end of the collard greens. Thoroughly clean them in a sink full of cold water. Drain, and cut the stalks into 1½-inch lengths. Halve the larger part of the leaves crosswise.

Clean and peel the zucchini. Cut them in half lengthwise and then slice across into ½-inch-thick pieces.

Peel the carrots, halve them lengthwise, and then slice across into ¼-inch-thick pieces.

Peel the onion. Cut it in half and then into thin slices.

Peel the potato and cut it into 1-inch cubes.

Clean and thinly slice the celery.

When the water comes to a boil, stir in the salt. When the water returns to a boil, add all of the vegetables, stir, and cover. When it again returns to a boil, reduce the heat and cook, covered, at a lively simmer for 40 minutes, until the beans and potatoes are cooked through. Stir occasionally.

Raise the heat, bringing the soup to a boil once more. Add the pasta. Stir to prevent sticking. Place the cover ajar, and cook at a gentle boil for 10 to 15 minutes, until the pasta is cooked al dente. Check for salt.

Serve the *ministruni* from the cooking pot. Drizzle each serving with a little extra-virgin olive oil, and sprinkle with crushed red and freshly cracked black pepper to taste.

# Linguini Picchii-Pacchiu

## *Linguini with Fresh Tomatoes, Basil, and Mozzarella*

Originally from Catania, this simple dish has been adopted by the Polizzani as part of their summer kitchen. The term *picchii-pacchiu* (pronounced *pick-ye-pack-you*) is an onomatopoetic expression of the sound of the knife as it chops the tomatoes and basil.

The tomatoes used are vine-ripened cherry tomatoes. In this country, small mesh bags of cherry tomatoes on the vine are now widely available. However, ordinary ripe cherry tomatoes may be substituted.

Diced fresh mozzarella, added as the pasta is tossed, melts from the heat, enhancing the luxury of this delicious first course for a summer day.

*For 4 servings*

Sea salt
12  ounces vine-ripened cherry tomatoes (about 20)
¾  cup chopped fresh basil leaves (1 large bunch)
3  cloves garlic, finely chopped
Black pepper
8  ounces fresh mozzarella packed in water
½  cup extra-virgin olive oil
1  pound linguini
Crushed red pepper

Fill a large pot with 6 quarts water, add 2 tablespoons salt, and bring it to a boil over high heat.

Meanwhile, clean the tomatoes, cut them in half, and coarsely chop them. Put them in a bowl. Prepare the basil and garlic, and mix them into the tomatoes. Season the mixture with salt, and add a few gridings of black pepper. Put the bowl near the stove.

Drain the mozzarella, pat it dry, and cut it into ¼-inch dice. Place it on a plate near the pasta pot. Pour the olive oil into a small saucepan, ready to be warmed.

When the water comes to a boil, cook the linguini until al dente, about 10 minutes, stirring occasionally. During this time, warm a large serving bowl with hot tap water, and dry it.

Just before draining the pasta, turn the heat on under the oil to warm it.

Drain the pasta and put it in the warmed bowl. Quickly toss it with the warmed oil, then the tomato mixture, and finally the mozzarella.

Serve with crushed red pepper to taste.

## Pasta chi Pipi Russi

# *Pasta with Sweet Red Pepper Sauce*

This summery first course has a deliciously refreshing quality. The peppers are first slightly charred to remove the skin, and then stewed with a bit of garlic, olive oil, and pancetta to enrich the dish.

The best pasta shape to use here is *casereccia*, a slightly twisted form about 2 inches long. It can be found amongst the artisanal pasta in Italian grocery stores and in some supermarkets. Good substitutes would be *gemelli* (twins) or *pennette lisce*, a small penne pasta without ridges.

*For 6 servings*

Sea salt
2¼ pounds red bell or Italian frying peppers, with as few dents as possible
Two 1-ounce slices pancetta
2  cloves garlic, peeled
¼  cup extra-virgin olive oil
Black pepper
Pinch of dried oregano
1  pound *casereccia, gemelli,* or *pennette lisce* pasta
⅓  cup grated imported pecorino cheese, preferably Locatelli brand

Fill a large pot with 6 quarts water, add 2 tablespoons salt, and bring it to a boil over high heat.

Preheat the broiler.

Put the peppers under the broiler, as close to the heat source as possible. Turn them frequently with tongs until the skin is slightly charred or puckered on all sides. Then put the peppers in a paper bag, close it, and let them steam for about 10 minutes to loosen the skin. When the peppers are cool enough to handle, skin, core, seed, and coarsely chop them.

Coarsely chop the pancetta. Put it in a heavy 6-quart pot along with the garlic and olive oil. Sauté over high heat until the pancetta turns translucent, about 3 minutes.

Add the peppers, stir, and sauté for a minute or so until they are well coated with oil. Season with salt, a few grindings of black pepper, and the oregano. Add ¼ cup water, reduce the heat to low, cover, and simmer for

15 minutes, until the peppers are quite soft and the mixture is sauce-like. Stir from time to time. Continue to simmer while the pasta cooks.

Cook the pasta in the boiling water until it is al dente, about 10 minutes. Before draining it, stir ¼ cup of the starchy pasta water into the pepper sauce.

Remove and discard the garlic cloves. Drain the pasta and toss it gently in the pot with the peppers for a minute or two, letting the flavors mingle.

Serve from the cooking pot. Lightly sprinkle each bowl with grated cheese.

Pasta ca Smuzzatura

## *Pasta with Broccoli*

*Smuzzatura* is the Polizzani word for broccoli. It means "cut off" and has more to do with the harvesting technique than with the vegetable itself.

Pasta with broccoli has become a standard in many of America's Italian restaurants. In that version, lightly sautéed broccoli florets are tossed with penne. This is not that dish.

Here the broccoli is partially cooked in the pasta water, chopped, and then sautéed into a chunky paste with garlic and salted sardines. Called *sarde salate*, this form of preserved sardines might be difficult to find in this country; in that case, sardines packed in olive oil or spring water may be substituted.

Cooked shell-shaped pasta is tossed with this chunky paste and becomes delightfully "stuffed." The dish is sprinkled with black pepper and grated pecorino cheese. Although the mixing of fish with grated cheese is not often found in traditional recipes, the result here is exquisite.

*For 6 servings*

Sea salt
4 salted sardines *(sarde salate)*, or 3¾ ounces (1 small tin) sardines packed in olive oil or spring water
2½ pounds broccoli
½ cup extra-virgin olive oil
3 cloves garlic, finely chopped
1 pound shell-shaped pasta *(conchiglie rigate)*
Black pepper
⅔ cup grated imported pecorino cheese, preferably Locatelli brand

Fill a large pot with 6 quarts water, add 2 tablespoons salt, and bring it to a boil over high heat.

While you are waiting for the water to boil, rinse the salted sardines, remove and discard the heads, and skin and bone them as well. It is not necessary to keep the fillets whole. If you are using tinned sardines, drain, skin, and bone them.

Cut off the dried ends of the broccoli stalks. Partially cook the broccoli, whole, in the boiling water, covered, for 5 minutes. Transfer the broccoli to a colander and rinse it under cold running water to stop the cooking. Keep the pot of water at a boil (covered if you wish), ready to cook the pasta. Coarsely chop the florets and finely chop the stalks. Reserve until needed.

Heat the oil in a heavy 6-quart pot over medium-high heat. Add the sardines and sauté for about 4 minutes, until reduced to a paste. Be aware that the water in the sardines may splatter, so stand well back.

Reduce the heat to medium and add the broccoli and the garlic. Season with salt to taste. Sauté for 5 to 7 minutes, until the broccoli can be chopped into a chunky paste with a wooden spatula. Cover, reduce the heat to low, and continue to simmer for the remainder of the cooking time.

Cook the pasta in the boiling water until it is al dente, about 10 minutes. Drain it, allowing the excess water to cling, and toss it in the pot with the broccoli. Sprinkle with a good amount of black pepper. Reduce the heat to very low, add the grated cheese, and cook, folding in the cheese, for about 2 minutes for the flavors to amalgamate. Serve in individual bowls, directly from the cooking pot.

Cucurummà

# Melody of Summer Vegetables

In the brilliant midday summer sun, the air in Polizzi Generosa is filled with the sounds of larks, and cuckoos, and roosters, and doves. It is as if the birds are giving a call to dinner, naming this dish.

This summer caponata is often served with bread, as a meal on its own. It is also served as an accompaniment to grilled meat or fish.

*For 6 servings*

1¾ pounds eggplant
    Sea salt
1    pound very red ripe plum tomatoes
1    hot green Italian pepper in vinegar *(pepperoncino)*
2    medium-sized yellow onions
1    rib celery
1    to 1¼ cups extra-virgin olive oil
1    teaspoon sugar
1    pound bell peppers, any or assorted colors
1    pound Yukon Gold, Yellow Finn, or russet potatoes
16    Kalamata olives
    Black pepper

Peel the eggplant and cut it into 1-inch chunks. Place the pieces in a bowl, liberally salting each layer. Place a plate over the eggplant and press it under a light weight, such as a can of tomatoes or a box of salt, for 2 hours to express the bitter liquid.

Meanwhile, prepare the tomato sauce: Blanch the tomatoes in boiling water for 1 minute. Peel them by spearing a tomato with a fork, holding it vertically in the air, slitting the skin with a paring knife, and peeling it away.

Put the peeled tomatoes in a shallow bowl and coarsely chop them. Chop the hot green pepper and add it to the tomatoes.

Peel and finely chop half an onion. Finely chop the celery. Put the celery and 3 tablespoons of the oil in a small heavy skillet and place over medium heat. Sauté for 3 minutes, until the celery turns a brighter green color. Add the chopped onion and sauté until the onion is translucent, about 4 minutes.

Add the tomatoes. Season with salt and stir in the sugar. Cook over very low heat, stirring occasionally, for about 20 minutes, until the tomatoes are reduced to a thick, pulpy sauce. Then remove from the heat and reserve until needed.

Wash, stem, and seed the bell peppers. Cut them into 1-inch-wide strips, about 2 inches long. Peel the potatoes, and cut them into ¾-inch chunks. Peel the remaining 1½ onions and slice into rings. Pit the olives with a cherry pitter. Keep the vegetables separate from each other.

Rinse the eggplant under cold running water to remove the excess salt. Pat the pieces dry with paper towels.

Have ready a 4-quart pot.

Pour ¼ cup of the olive oil into a heavy, well-cured 9-inch skillet over low heat. When it is hot, add the peppers and salt to taste. Sauté until cooked, about 10 minutes. Lift them out of the oil with a slotted spoon and put them in the pot.

Add ¼ cup of the oil to the skillet. When it is hot, add the potatoes and salt to taste, and cook to a rich golden brown, about 15 minutes. Transfer them to the pot with a slotted spoon.

Next, sauté the onion rings until they are a pale gold color, and transfer them to the pot.

Add about ¼ cup of the oil to the skillet. Raise the heat to medium and add the eggplant. Sauté until cooked but firm, about 5 minutes. Turn it with a spatula to prevent it from burning. Transfer it with a slotted spoon onto sheets of brown paper or paper towels to drain. Then put the eggplant in the pot with the other vegetables.

Add about 2 tablespoons of the oil to the skillet. Raise the heat to medium-high. When it is hot, sauté the olives for 2 minutes, until they are a bit crusty on the surface. Add them to the pot.

Stir the tomato sauce into the vegetables. Reduce the heat to low and cook, letting the flavors mingle, for 10 minutes. Gently turn the vegetables with a spatula to prevent scorching on the bottom. Check for salt.

Transfer the *cucurummà* to a serving platter and add a few grindings of black pepper. Serve warm or at room temperature.

Pisci sutta Sali

# Fish Baked in Salt

Since Polizzi is not near the sea, fresh fish is not a common part of its traditional cuisine. Today, with the sea a short car ride away, fish has found its way into everyday fare.

The flavor of an extremely fresh fish sealed in a casing of salt and steamed in its own juices is sublime. Its texture resembles lobster. Since the salt is coarse, it will not dissolve, so the fish is never salty.

The technique of baking a whole fish encased in salt is an ancient, traditional one, but I do recommend one modern convenience: baking the fish in a large, deep, disposable roasting pan set on a sheet pan so it doesn't bend when lifted. This will greatly simplify cleanup. The weight of salt should equal the weight of the whole fish before it is gutted.

The best varieties of fish to use are grouper, sea bass, or rock cod—in that order. Avoid cooking a fish that weighs less than 4 pounds, as they are too small for this process. Two or three fish of equal thickness can be cooked at the same time in one casing, but one large one makes a better presentation and is more economical.

*For 8 servings*

One 8-pound whole fish (see headnote), gutted and scaled
Black pepper
½ pound fennel (sweet anise) leaves and tender stems, wild if possible (see headnote, page 188)
8 pounds coarse kosher salt
1½ cups all-purpose flour
Lemon wedges
Extra-virgin olive oil, for drizzling

Preheat the oven to 425°F, with a rack positioned in the center.

Remove the fish's side and dorsal fins, and trim the tail. Rinse the fish under cold running water. Dry the cavity by filling it with wadded paper towels. Wrap the fish with paper towels to thoroughly dry the surfaces. The fish may be kept in the refrigerator in this wrapping for up to 3 hours.

Remove the paper towels, lay the fish flat, and make a note of its measurement at its thickest part. Season the cavity with a few grindings of black pepper, and stuff it with the wild fennel.

Fill a roasting pan (preferably disposable) with half the salt, about 1½ inches deep. Place the disposable roasting pan on a sturdy sheet pan. Gently put the fish on the salt, and cover it completely with the remaining salt. Smooth the top.

Whisk enough water into the flour to turn it into a thin paste. Pour it over the surface of the salt.

Using the thickness measurement of the fish, bake it for 12 minutes to the inch plus an additional 12 minutes.

Remove the pan from the oven by lifting the sheet pan, and let it rest for 10 minutes so the internal juices will adjust.

Crack the salt with a stiff metal spatula and lift it off in large pieces. (Use an oven mitt to handle it, as it will be hot.) Brush away all the salt from the surface of the fish, and remove the skin. Cut the fish down the center and transfer the fillet in 2 pieces to a warmed serving platter. Remove the spine and all the bones, and then transfer the bottom fillet, without the skin, to the platter. Carefully remove the cheeks from the head, placing them on the platter as well.

Serve the fish with lemon wedges and extra-virgin olive oil to drizzle on top.

## Vruacculu Accupatéddu

# *Cauliflower Under Siege*

As pleasing to the eye as it is to the palate, a whole cauliflower is put "under siege" by strips of dried Italian sausage, *pecorino purmintiu* (see headnote, page 161), and slices of garlic that are concealed in its interior. It is then drizzled with olive oil and steamed over water flavored with fennel seeds. Just before serving, the top is sprinkled with grated cheese and parsley. Cauliflower Under Siege may be served as an accompaniment to a meat or fish dish, or on its own as a lighter second course.

In Polizzi Generosa, the local cauliflower has a remarkably strong flavor. It must be blanched or partially cooked in salted boiling water before any other preparation can be undertaken. American cauliflower, however, is relatively mild-tasting; the traditional cooking method, therefore, has been adjusted to compensate.

Serve good, crusty bread with this, to sop up the flavorful pot liquor.

*For 4 to 6 servings*

1   large cauliflower (about 2½ pounds)
    Sea salt
1   link dried Italian sausage, about 4 ounces
4   ounces *pecorino purmintiu* (see headnote, page 161) or domestic sharp provolone, in 1 piece
¼   teaspoon fennel seeds
4   cloves garlic, peeled and sliced
¼   cup extra-virgin olive oil
⅓   cup grated imported pecorino cheese, preferably Locatelli brand
4   sprigs Italian parsley, chopped (leaves and stems)
    Black pepper

Clean the cauliflower under cold running water. Remove and discard the leaves. Trim the stem so that it does not extend beyond the bottom edge of the cauliflower. To ensure that the thick central stem will cook through, give it 10 or more jabs with a small sharp knife. Put the cauliflower upside-down in a large bowl and add enough cold water to cover it; lightly salt the water. Let it soak for 10 minutes.

Split the sausage and pull off the skin. Slice it into long strips slightly less

**175**

than ⅛ inch thick. Cut the rind off the cheese, and slice the cheese into wedges the same thickness as the sausage. Halve the wedges so that each one is about 2 inches long and ¾ inch at the wide end. Reserve both until needed.

Put 2 cups water and the fennel seeds in a heavy-bottomed 4-quart pot. Drain the cauliflower and put it in the pot, right side up. Cover, and cook over high heat for 15 minutes, until it is three-quarters done.

Keeping the liquid in the pot, remove the cauliflower with a large slotted spoon and transfer it to a colander. Rinse it under cold running water to stop the cooking. Transfer the cauliflower to a plate.

Push the sausage strips between the florets so that it mostly disappears into the cauliflower. Evenly distribute the strips over the entire head. Do the same with the cheese and the garlic.

Add 1 cup water to the pot and replace the cauliflower. Drizzle it with the olive oil, cover, and cook over high heat for 10 minutes, until it is quite soft but still maintains its shape.

Carefully remove the cauliflower with a large slotted spoon and put it on a shallow serving bowl, "flower" side up. Pour the pot liquor around it. Sprinkle the cauliflower with the grated cheese and parsley.

Portion it with a large spoon into bowls. Serve immediately, with a grinding of black pepper.

# Nine

# The Gatherers

*P*olizzi Generosa is situated on the southern boundary of a national park, the Parco della Madonie, which encompasses 39,475 hectares, roughly 100,000 acres. No mining, logging, or transportation of nuclear materials is permitted within its boundaries, as it is a designated watershed. The park is also home to an animal preserve and to the second largest tree farm in Italy.

Within its borders are numerous examples of rare indigenous flora and fauna, some to be found nowhere else in the world. Rarest amongst the flora is the Nebrodi Fir *(Abies nebrodensis)*. Locally it is known as *pinu a cruci-cruci*, because of the unique crisscross arrangement of its pine needles.

Before the ancient Romans clear-cut the forests of Sicily for lumber to build their warships, these stately trees covered much of the mountainous landscape. Today fewer than thirty trees remain, all within the Parco della Madonie.

Carnivorous animals still make their homes in this forest—among them foxes and martens, even wildcats and wolves. Herbivores include deer and wild boar, hares and wild rabbits. Green frogs and toads croak in proximity to wetlands. Vipers and other varieties of snakes slither about, hidden in the cool shade. The sky is filled with birds, large and small: royal eagles, peregrine falcons, and the nearly extinct imperial raven *(Corvus corax)* among the more than fifty species represented. More than ninety species of butterflies flutter here. One of the rarer species is the Sicilian Apollo *(Parnassius apollo* subsp. *siciliae)*, native to the Madonie.

This dense forest produces an abundance of edible wild delicacies. In spring and early summer wild fennel, asparagus, strawberries, and several varieties of mulberries give the forest floor a young green coloring dotted with red, yellow, and deep purple. Small-leafed piquant arugula rises from the ground straight up like a ready rocket, giving this desirable green its Sicilian name, *rucula*. In summer, tangles of thorny bushes bear sweetest berries. All of these fruits are picked, finding their way into summer granitas and gelatos. A portion of this wild harvest is used to flavor liqueurs.

At the end of summer, the forest yields great bunches of lavishly perfumed wild oregano, which soon hangs in sheds all over Polizzi, drying for winter use. Wild green hazelnuts fill shallow straw baskets and dry in the sun. After the autumn rains, the forest turns deep green with wild rapini, spinach, and cardoons. Camouflaged by the loam are several varieties of rich, pungent wild mushrooms, among them *chiuppu*, a kind of wild oyster mushroom *(Pleurotus ostreatus)* that grows at the base of poplar trees, and *ferla (P. fermlae)*, with a taste similar to porcini.

After it rains in any season, the damp earth is covered with a gliding of snails. *Vavaluci*, as they are called, are small, with brown and white shells. The

Polizzani prepare them boiled and then dropped in a tomato sauce, sweet with onion and hot with crushed red pepper.

Many Polizzani regularly venture into the countryside to find wild ingredients for the table. Some go on excursions in search of wild mushrooms. Generally, these hunters are extremely familiar with only one type of mushroom, knowing well how to distinguish their particular one from similar-looking poisonous ones. It is extraordinary that in modern Polizzi a portion of the daily food supply is still reliant upon wild rather than cultivated produce.

In Polizzi there are several indigent older men whose only occupation is to forage and then sell what they've found. Each morning at daybreak, these weather-worn, leathery-skinned fellows go out into the countryside to harvest the wild bounty of nature. The "crops" they seek are governed by the seasons. Each gatherer has his own secret places deep in the forest where he is likely to find what he seeks. There are no paths or maps to these places, and they find them only by their long experience and sure knowledge of the terrain.

Often the whole day passes before they're back in town, selling their goods to local restaurants, or to pastry shops and coffee-bars for sweets and granitas or gelatos. Sometimes they hawk these treasures in the piazza, where they are quickly snatched up by grateful housewives.

One day, I was rushing to Nino's house for lunch, not wanting to be late. One of the gatherers jumped in front of me and said in a low voice, *"Talé!"* (Look!). He opened a plastic grocery bag, revealing two bunches of wild asparagus, each bunch about eight inches around. This "harvest" surely took a whole day. Wild asparagus is sparse and difficult to spot on the verdant floor. An accomplished gatherer would do well to find ten in an acre.

These were at least sixteen inches long and no thicker than a pencil; the shoots were a deep, brilliant green turning to rich, dark purple at the tips. The perfume released as he opened the bag was intoxicating. We briefly negotiated a price and settled on 3,000 lire, about $1.50.

I brought this treasure to Nino's house. Upon seeing the asparagus, Nino's mother, Stefana, practically grabbed them out of my hand. First she carefully cleaned them, and then she blanched them to bring out their sweetness. She cut them into short lengths and quickly sautéed them with a hint of chopped garlic in good extra-virgin olive oil. Stefana added beaten eggs, gently turning all of this together just until the eggs were soft-scrambled. We ate this dish as a course of its own, accompanied by fresh semolina bread. We did not neglect to toast the forager who had made this unexpected treat possible.

• • •

One of the gatherers is called Moffu Mimidda. The surname is not actually his family name, but a nickname from childhood designating him as 'Moffu the son of Mimidda,' his mother's given name. Moffu Mimidda is now in his late seventies, thin as an asparagus and strong as a mule. He smokes a pipe, as do I, and whenever I see him I offer him a fill of my tobacco, which he has come to expect. I have seen him stuff all sorts of tobacco products into his pipe, including cigar and cigarette butts—paper, filter, and all. It is widely believed that he suffers from mild dementia, although he is clearly content in his own world.

On one balmy summer evening, a large crowd had assembled in the piazza to hear a debate among the candidates for Polizzi's city council. Nino and I were among them, listening to the various political arguments. Moffu Mimidda elbowed his way to a spot next to me, prominently displaying the empty pipe between his teeth. I offered him my tobacco pouch and he filled his pipe. Then he said something I didn't understand. As I was asking him to repeat it, Nino, at my other side, whispered to me, "You know, sometimes he doesn't make sense." At which Moffu Mimidda declared in a loud, sure voice, "I do it on purpose." At the risk of being rude to the politicians, we all three laughed deeply. As Moffu Mimidda walked away, he put his finger to his lips as if to say, "Don't tell anybody."

Another of the gatherers is named Turiddu Lavanco, who calls himself "King of the Mountains." Although he is a man of about sixty, decades of exposure to the elements and hard drinking have given him a much older appearance. He stands about five feet six inches tall and is squarely built. His year-round wintry clothing is so filthy that it is impossible to determine its original color. His uncut hair is matted with forest debris. He always wears a large knitted *baret* at an exaggerated angle, revealing a dent in his skull near his left temple. His face is covered in a long, tangled grayish beard, and what can be seen of his skin is smudged with dirt. When he speaks in his gravely growl, his piercing pale blue eyes lock you in their sadness.

The story of how Turiddu Lavanco came to this sorry level of existence is, indeed, a sad tale. As a young man, Turiddu and a good, beautiful young woman, Rosanna, fell deeply in love. After an appropriate courtship, they wed. Those who remember the wedding recall that the sweet love in the couple's eyes made all the guests feel happy, for themselves as well as for the young pair.

Their first home was a small house near the center of town. Although poor, Rosanna kept house in that immaculate, charming way for which Polizzani women are famous. Each day Turiddu took his motorcycle into the countryside, where he tended his small piece of land. They got by, but the joy of their love and their life together far outshined their station in life. In sum, they were very happy.

One morning, Turiddu went out at dawn as usual to work his land. It was during the time of spring planting, and the weather was still chill and fogbound. As he climbed onto his motorcycle, Rosanna ran out of the house to bring him an extra sweater. "Be careful driving this morning, *caru miu*. It's so foggy," she said as he rode away, blowing kisses.

An hour later, the police came to the door of the little house. They told Rosanna that while Turiddu was driving down the winding road from Polizzi, a truck was heading up in the opposite direction. Its driver, going too fast, did not see Turiddu on his motorcycle in the fog. The collision was head-on, the impact tossing Turiddu high in the air. His left arm and both his legs had been broken, and he had suffered multiple skull fractures. An ambulance was taking him to a hospital in Palermo, for his condition was very grave.

The good wife was immobilized by the news. Family poured into the little house as word of the accident spread throughout Polizzi. An uncle drove Rosanna to the hospital. She found Turiddu in a coma, his head in bandages and his limbs in plaster casts. The doctors prepared her for the worst, which seemed inevitable.

Rosanna visited her husband every day. She sat next to the bed as life slipped out of his grasp. Then, on a foggy night, as Rosanna and her uncle were returning to Polizzi, there was a terrible collision. The uncle walked away with minor bruises, but Rosanna died instantly. In a strange twist of fate, Turiddu regained consciousness the next day.

"I was supposed to die, not Rosanna," Turiddu lamented. "Why has God in heaven done this cruel thing to me?" This thought, and the permanent brain damage resulting from his injuries, sent Turiddu into dark insanity.

No one, not even his cousin, a brilliant priest, could help him. He began drinking heavily and wandering in the forests near Polizzi, searching in nature for some peace, and perhaps for the answer to his question. He'd spend weeks there, sleeping in the open air and foraging food. Whenever he'd return to town and the little house, he was sure to be well self-medicated with cheap wine.

All Polizzi knows Turiddu's tragic story. People shake their heads and sigh sadly when speaking of him. The townspeople look out for him as best they can, always welcoming him to city festivals and, uncharacteristically, never quibbling over his asking price for the wild produce he sells. But aside from that, there is not much more they can do.

In the winter of 2000, Turiddu Lavanco, husband, farmer, and King of the Mountains, passed away. Moffu Mimidda found him in the forest. All who learned of his death sighed in relief at the merciful end to his tortured life.

I imagine that he is now a gatherer in heaven, wandering Elysium. I am sure his beloved Rosanna awaited him in a field of golden mushrooms. Certainly he has gathered an understanding of the answer to his question and finally has found eternal peace.

Sparaci cu l'Ova

# *Asparagus with Scrambled Eggs*

It is difficult to match the intense flavor of the wild asparagus used in Polizzi for this dish. However, at the height of our cultivated asparagus season in the spring, it is possible to taste a different but still delicious dish. Be sure to use the freshest eggs from grain-fed, free-range chickens.

It is best to cook asparagus in a tall pot, with the stalks standing in an inch of water. In this way, the denser stalk ends cook at the same rate as the delicate tops. Asparagus pots are available at cooking supply stores. One can be improvised out of a tall percolator-type coffee pot with the spout covered with aluminum foil.

*For 4 servings*

1   pound fresh asparagus, the thinnest available
2   cloves garlic, finely chopped
¼   cup extra-virgin olive oil
    Sea salt
4   eggs
3   tablespoons grated imported pecorino cheese, preferably Locatelli brand
    Black pepper

Rinse the asparagus, and trim away the fibrous ends. Tie the stalks in a bundle, and cook them standing up in 1 inch of water, covered, over medium-high heat until bright green and almost tender, about 6 minutes. Quickly rinse them under cold running water to stop the cooking. Cut the asparagus into ¾-inch lengths.

Put the chopped garlic and olive oil in a heavy, well-cured 8- or 9-inch skillet over medium heat. When the garlic just begins to crackle, add the asparagus. Turn the pieces with a spatula to coat them with the oil. Season with salt to taste. Cover the pan, reduce the heat to low, and cook for 8 minutes, until very tender. Check from time to time, turning the asparagus to avoid burning.

Meanwhile, scramble the eggs and cheese together in a medium-sized bowl, using a fork. Use big looping strokes to beat in air, making the eggs fluffy.

When the asparagus are ready, uncover the pan, raise the heat to high, and slightly reduce the liquid in the pan by boiling it away for 1 minute.

Pour in the eggs. Remove the skillet from the heat, and quickly fold the eggs and asparagus together for about 30 seconds, until the eggs are barely soft-scrambled. (The eggs will continue to set even after taken off the heat.) Immediately lift the asparagus and eggs out of the pan, and put them on a warmed platter. Sprinkle with a grinding of black pepper, and serve.

# Pasta chi Sparaci e u Capuliatu

## *Pasta with Asparagus and Ground Veal*

The success of this recipe depends upon using asparagus with an intense flavor. Select the thickest asparagus spears available, at the height of the season. Be sure that the stems are crisp and not dried out at the bottom.

The use of what Santo calls *demi-glassa* gives a completeness to the flavors of this creation, which would otherwise just be a simmering of ground veal and asparagus. Although a lengthy preparation, Santo's *demi-glassa* is well worth the time and can be used in other dishes.

A close substitute is a product called Demi-Glace Gold, made by More Than Gourmet. A concentrated classic French *demi-glace*, it is available at fine specialty shops across the United States. Reconstitute the required amount following the instructions on the package.

*For 6 servings*

Sea salt
1½ pounds fresh asparagus, the thickest available
⅓ cup extra-virgin olive oil
1 pound ground veal
3 cloves garlic, peeled and finely chopped
1 cup dry white wine
Black pepper
1¼ cups Santo's Demi-Glassa (recipe follows) or purchased demi-glace (see headnote)
1 pound *gnocchetti* or shell pasta
1 cup (about 2 ounces) coarsely grated imported pecorino cheese, preferably Locatelli brand

Fill a large pot with 6 quarts water, add 2 tablespoons salt, and bring it to a boil over high heat.

Meanwhile, rinse the asparagus and pat dry. Cut off and discard the fibrous ends. Cut the asparagus into 1-inch lengths.

In a heavy 6-quart pot, heat the olive oil over medium-high heat until very hot. Add the asparagus and sauté for 2 to 3 minutes, until they are bright green. Remove them with a slotted spoon and put them on a plate until needed.

Put the ground veal in the same pot and sauté it for about 6 minutes, until it is well browned, using a wooden spoon to break up any large clumps. Return the asparagus to the pot and add the garlic; stir well. Deglaze the pot by adding the white wine and scraping loose the bits of browned veal that have stuck to the bottom. Let the alcohol evaporate for about 1 minute. Then add salt to taste and a few grindings of black pepper. Add the *demi-glassa*, stir, reduce the heat to very low, and gently simmer, uncovered, for 30 minutes, until the asparagus are quite soft.

After the veal and asparagus has cooked for 20 minutes, add the pasta to the boiling water and cook until al dente, about 10 minutes. Drain it very well and toss it in the pot with the asparagus-meat sauce and the grated cheese. Gently fold the mixture together over low heat for 2 or 3 minutes to let the flavors mingle. Serve in pasta bowls directly from the cooking pot.

## Santo's Demi-Glassa

Storage tip: Fill about 16 small paper cups with ⅔ cup each of the *demi-glassa*. Place the cups, uncovered, in the freezer. When the liquid is well frozen, bundle the cups in several layers of plastic bags. Stored in this manner, the *demi-glassa* will keep for up to 6 months.

*Makes 2½ quarts*

4   pounds beef soup bones, some meat attached
1   cup all-purpose flour
1½ cups dry white wine
5   quarts spring water
2   carrots, scraped and cut in half
3   ribs celery, cut in half
2   medium-sized yellow onions, peeled
1   leek, trimmed
4   plum tomatoes
12  sprigs Italian parsley
6   thick portabella mushroom stems (optional)

Preheat the oven to 500°F.

Place the bones in a roasting pan and bake for 3 to 4 hours, turning from time to time, until they are well browned but not burned.

Lift the bones out of the fat and transfer them to a 12-quart stockpot. Place the pot over low heat, and scatter the flour over the bones; toss to coat them. Add the white wine, stirring it into the flour to make a smooth paste. Cook until the flour is golden brown, about 10 minutes.

Pour in 2 quarts of the spring water, stirring to prevent lumps. Then add the remaining water and all the vegetables. Cover and bring slowly to a boil.

Uncover, reduce the heat, and cook at a tremble (barely boiling) for 4 hours. Pour the contents of the pot into a colander over a large bowl. Discard the solids. Remove the excess fat from the liquid with a skimmer or a fat separator. If necessary, reduce the liquid further until it measures 2½ quarts.

Cool the *demi-glassa* to room temperature, stirring from time to time so the steam will escape. Refrigerate, or freeze as suggested in the headnote.

## Ziti alla Ulrich

# Ziti with Sausage and Wild Fennel

One day in Polizzi Generosa, Santo Lipani prepared this amazing pasta dish for lunch. In honor of his nickname, I christened the dish *Ziti alla Ulrich*.

If you live in an area where fennel can be found growing wild, forage it for this recipe. The sweet leaves atop the anise bulbs sold in markets can be substituted, but the wild variety has a much more intense flavor.

*For 4 to 6 servings*

Sea salt
12 ounces plain sweet (mild) Italian sausage
2 cloves garlic, finely chopped
⅓ cup Pernod
Crushed red pepper
1 cup chopped fennel (sweet anise) leaves and tender stems, wild if possible
⅔ cup Santo's Demi-Glassa (see recipe, p. 186) or purchased demi-glace (see headnote, page 185)
1 pound *ziti tagliati* (cut ziti) or other small tube macaroni without ridges
3 tablespoons heavy cream
Black pepper

Fill a large pot with 6 quarts water, add 2 tablespoons of salt, and bring it to a boil over high heat.

Soak the sausages in ice water for 3 minutes. Slit the skin and press out the meat into a bowl.

When the pasta water is nearly at a boil, heat a heavy 6-quart pot over medium heat. Sauté the sausage meat until it is well browned, about 5 to 7 minutes. Add the garlic and deglaze the pan by adding the Pernod and scraping loose any bits that may have stuck to the bottom. Season with salt and add a small amount of crushed red pepper.

Stir in the fennel. Cook for 1 to 2 minutes, until it turns bright green. Add the *demi-glassa* and stir. Reduce the heat to low, and gently simmer for about 10 minutes, until the sauce thickens a bit.

During this time, cook the pasta in the boiling water until al dente, about

10 minutes. Drain it very well and toss it in the pot with the sausage and fennel sauce. Reduce the heat to very low and mix in the cream. Gently toss the pasta, letting the flavors mingle for a minute or two. Serve in pasta bowls, with a grinding of black pepper.

# Ten

# Andrea Goes to Polizzi

**G**rowing up as I did in a Sicilian-American Brooklyn neighborhood, the culture of Sicily surrounded our world. My grandparents and other immigrants had transported the day-to-day life of their mountaintop city of Polizzi Generosa, replanting it like ancient pine trees in the tenements of Brooklyn—*Bruculinu*, as they called it.

Andrea, my twelve-year-old son, is growing up in a vastly different world. The difference in our ages certainly contributes to this, but more important, Los Angeles, our home, couldn't be farther away from the *Bruculinu* of my childhood if it were in Siberia.

When I was a boy, if you wanted to go out and play, that's exactly what you did. The streets were filled with children and a game of stickball, or hide-and-seek, or cowboys and Indians could be organized ad hoc. For Andrea, going to play with a friend means a barrage of phone calls to set up the appointment and a car ride to bring the two youngsters together. Because of the complexities of modern city life, the boys are never far from someone's watchful eye. Their social life is, of necessity, far less spontaneous.

I maintain as many traditional Sicilian celebrations as I can, but the foods I prepare meet no fellow travelers in the "neighborhood," and the guests at our table are mostly Americans with roots in other places. Yet, since he was a small boy, Andrea's imagination has been sparked by my tales of *Bruculinu* and of Polizzi Generosa. When he was eight, I told him that when he was eleven I would take him to Polizzi Generosa. He would never forget this promise.

In 1999, Andrea's eleventh summer, it looked as if the trip would have to be postponed because of my work schedule. I was too mortified to speak of it, and he too noble. Then, toward the end of August, the start date for my new film was postponed; suddenly there were three free weeks before Andrea had to return to school. Four days later, we boarded a plane, beginning our journey to Polizzi Generosa.

To say we were excited doesn't quite express the pitch with which we soared through the embarkation process. Finally seated and belted, we settled in for the long flight from Los Angeles to Milano. Sort of eating, sort of sleeping, and truly dreaming, we passed the time uneventfully, the best way a flight could be.

As we collected our baggage in Palermo, Andrea tugged at my sleeve, asking, "Dad, are we really here?" So excited was I, all I could manage was "Yes, son, I think we are!"

We began the seventy-mile drive from Palermo to Polizzi Generosa, a route I know well, this being my eighth visit in eleven years. Even though the relatives I found on my first visit in 1988 have become close, and the friendships started then have become deep, each visit feels like the first time, filled with excitement and wonder. Andrea, going to Polizzi for the first time, seemed charged with the same magical expectations.

It was dark when we turned off the highway onto the winding road to Polizzi. We arrived just at dinnertime. The city was quiet, the streets empty. A gentle, warm, low fog was rolling in. The antique street lights barely dispelled the darkness as Andrea and I walked up the Via Roma. The only sound was our feet on the cobbles; the only evidence of habitation was the delicious cooking smells emanating from every house. We passed the great Palazzo Gagliardo, still inhabited by its hereditary owners, and the impressive Chiesa Madre, the main church, built in the thirteenth century. A bit farther along, the street surprisingly opens to a piazza in front of the ruins of the Byzantine fortress.

These places were familiar to me, but for a kid from Los Angeles, they were sights from movies or dreams. Again Andrea asked, "Dad, are we *really* here?"

We turned down the steps of the alley-like Via dei Cappuccini and into the courtyard of Santo Lipani's restaurant, Orto dei Cappuccini. "Oooh! 'Ell-oo!" Santo bellowed to us from the kitchen. "You are here!" As I translated the Sicilian for Andrea, Santo was racing toward us with outstretched arms. He and I hugged, with a kiss on each cheek. Andrea followed suit. Santo stood there smiling at Andrea, and while firmly pinching the boy's cheek, he said, "Oooh! What a handsome young fellow you are. You must be hungry."

Trying to be a good sport about the cheek-pinching, Andrea looked to me for translation. We were both, in fact, starving, but for sleep as much as for food. I called after Santo in Sicilian as he headed toward the kitchen, suggesting it would be best if we just ate a little something. "Of course," Santo called back, "I'll just make a simple pizza."

Most of the other diners were people I knew. They all gathered to welcome us to Polizzi, each re-enacting the cheek-pinching ritual. By the end, Andrea's healthy, rosy cheeks had acquired an even brighter hue.

Before the pizza, Santo brought in some *bruschetta* "to munch on while you wait"—semolina bread toasted in the wood-burning pizza oven and topped with the ripest chopped tomatoes mixed with fragrant fresh basil, and drizzled with local extra-virgin olive oil. Andrea's appreciation of this simple culinary delight was not unnoticed by Santo, who smiled, nodding approval.

With great nonchalance, Santo sauntered over to the fig tree next to our table. He picked a half-dozen of the ripest figs and returned to the kitchen. Moments later he was back with a small oval platter of paper-thin slices of prosciutto wrapped around the cleaned, halved figs. Andrea had never before eaten this combination, and I had never eaten it so close to the tree. After one bite, my son's eyes registered delight.

A plate of pungent salami arrived next, accompanied by slices of young pecorino cheese, *pecorino purmintiu,* and a bowl of green-black olives. A basket of semolina bread took its place next to the carafes of sweet Polizzani water and young wine from the nearby Regaliali winery.

An eggplant *palmigiana* came next, topped only with grated pecorino cheese and a dollop of tomato sauce. Santo made his little egg patties, made with bread crumbs and pecorino, covered in tomato sauce. Blanched oyster mushrooms appeared, drizzled with olive oil and a drop of vinegar. Zucchini was served in pieces, boiled in a small amount of water and enriched with beaten eggs and a dusting of grated pressed ewes'-milk ricotta.

Somewhere (I was starting to lose track during this feast) there was a plate of fried sweet rice patties, an ancient dish, North African in origin. Its preparation in Santo's kitchen began with a rice pilaf made with milk, a bit of sugar, and a pinch of cinnamon. When it had cooled, he added black pepper and formed the rice into flat oval patties, then fried them in olive oil. The counterpoint it made with the other flavors was sublime.

About this time, my good friend Nino Gianfisco bounded into the courtyard, his smile sparkling. At seeing Andrea, whom he had met several years before in Los Angeles, it nearly burst into flame. Andrea was excited to see him too. After a big hug, Nino stood glowing, with his hands on the boy's shoulders, evaluating his growth and maturity. No sooner had he joined us at the table than the courtyard was filled with the diminutive yet outsized presence of my eighty-four-year-old cousin, Zà ("Aunt," out of respect) Pasqualina. I had planned to bring Andrea to her house first thing in the morning, when we were refreshed and cleaned up, but she must have intuited our arrival and would not be deterred. She walked right up to Andrea, who leaped to his feet. While welcoming him in Sicilian, she drilled his cheeks with many kisses. One of her sons, Giuseppe, who had accompanied her, followed suit.

Our party grew to about twelve as the news of our arrival spread throughout Polizzi in the usual mysterious Sicilian fashion. Santo, his work mostly done in the kitchen, joined us with an enormous bowl of linguini with garlic, oil, and melted anchovy. He smiled at Andrea's enjoyment of this strongly flavored dish, one not likely to be appreciated by an American boy. A toast seemed in order. We lifted our glasses (Andrea's filled with water and a stain of wine) to my son's first night in Polizzi.

Then Santo asked if we still wanted pizza.

It was now 11:00 p.m., two in the afternoon in Los Angeles, twenty hours since our journey had begun the previous evening. I looked at Andrea just as he was rolling a grape around in his mouth, unable to bite it. We had hit the wall. Santo insisted on driving our car down the hill to the country inn where we were staying; Nino would follow in his. The parade to the car was led by Andrea and Zà Pasqualina. She held Andrea's arm in a grip of death, although her step on the downhill cobbles was as sure as a mountain goat's.

After fifteen minutes of hugs and kisses and *bona notti* at the car door, we descended into the countryside and soon turned onto the gravel road of our inn. Franca and Franco D'Anna, the owners, were there to greet us. Franca had grown up in Brooklyn and spoke an out-of-practice English. She welcomed Andrea to Donna Giovanna, the name of her inn. She then added in a soft, motherly voice, "My boy, you must be very tired from such a long, long trip. Go to bed now. I'll see you in the morning."

Our room was simple but lovely. From its balcony we looked up to Polizzi and its lights curled in the gentle fog. There were two beds, a double and a single. Andrea said, "Dad, since you're bigger and older, you should have the larger bed; I'll take the smaller one." I graciously accepted. Preparation for Franca's advice took no time at all. Just as my eyes closed, the stillness was broken by Andrea's excited voice. "Dad," he said, "we're really here!"

The next morning was bright with the glorious Sicilian sun. It filled our room, carrying with it the sounds of country life—sheep bleating, cocks crowing, bells tinkling around the necks of goats. A mare in the paddock below our balcony whinnied and stomped. She was bumping her head against a fig tree, causing the ripe figs beyond her reach to fall to the ground.

Franca was sweeping the already immaculate patio of what centuries ago had been a Jesuit monastery, and more recently the home of a nobleman's daughter, Donna Giovanna. She called up a good morning to me, adding that it was a fine day. Andrea and I were soon in the dining room, ready for food and for the day.

Breakfast was semolina toast with butter and homemade preserves. The one both Andrea and I liked best was green tomato. The beverage was rich black coffee served with a pitcher of hot milk, our ages determining the proportion of each in our cups.

Franco is a thin, wiry, handsome man with dark hair and sharp features.

His serious expression makes him look like a tough guy, but when he smiles, his face shows the gentle soul that he is. He carried two orange plastic baskets into the room and, handing one to Andrea, beckoned him to follow. Franco led the boy to a nearby zucchini patch, where they picked the largest zucchini flowers I have ever seen. Andrea is familiar with small backyard gardens, but he had never seen a zucchini patch so lush and large. Franco gave instructions, uselessly in Sicilian, more effectively by demonstration. They laughed as their steps turned into a game of hopscotch in order to avoid stepping on delicate shoots in their quest. Andrea returned very proud of his harvest, and zucchini-flower-picking with Franco became an activity Andrea enjoyed every morning of our stay.

Polizzi Generosa was bustling that morning. We met scores of friends and acquaintances as we walked from the car park through the center of town. All of them bid us welcome; all of them were happy to meet Andrea; all of them pinched his cheek.

Our first stop was City Hall, where I had hoped to introduce Andrea to the mayor. His Honor was locked in conference so we waited for a time in the busy grand hall of this imposing Renaissance structure. Finally Andrea needed to use the men's room. After a few minutes, he did not reappear. Spotting Captain Epifanio of the three-person Polizzi police force, I said excitedly, "I lost my son." With a calm, wistful smile, he responded, "Vicenzu, here in Polizzi, you cannot lose anyone."

The captain was right. Andrea had assumed I had left and had gone out onto the street to find me. He thought *I* was lost.

We brought flowers to Zà Pasqualina, and after a brief visit, we were back on the streets again, Andrea's eyes wide with wonder. At one point, Andrea stopped and asked with simple candor, "Did Bruculinu look like this?" Somehow my stories of the Brooklyn neighborhood of my childhood and Polizzi had become confused. I gently explained the difference, keenly aware of his disappointment at my answer.

By late morning the day was turning hot. We stopped in Gasparinu's coffee bar, Bar Cristallo, for a cold drink. Andrea sampled a uniquely Sicilian sandwich: his first gelato on brioche. Gasparinu, with the hands of an artist, piled hazelnut and chocolate gelato and whipped cream between the sliced

four-inch-round brioche in just the right proportion to be generous yet man-
ageable. Andrea's mouth watered with each enticing application. With his
brioche finally in his hands, Andrea and I moved to the grand stairway on the
street next to the shop and sat down. We licked around the creamy edges and
bit into the cold sweet-savory piece of heaven.

We wandered the city, I pointing out centuries-old churches and other
monuments. On our way, we stopped often to chat with *paisani*, proud to welcome a fourth-generation American returning son. By one-thirty we were
back at Donna Giovanna's crowded dining room for lunch.

Andrea went into the busy kitchen to find Franca. I could hear snippets
of their conversation above the clatter. "And then we saw the Commenda. It
was built by the Knights of Malta in the Middle Ages. . . . And do you know
the story of the Old Abbey and the New Abbey?"

"Tell me all about it," Franca said with smiling attention, ignoring her
work assisting Franco in the kitchen.

"Well, once there were these two noblemen, La Matina and Signurino . . ." Andrea continued, in specific detail, telling the tale in nearly the
same words I had used. Franco understood not a word of their conversation
but seemed respectful of the growing confidence between his wife and the
boy. I was gratified to hear how much my son had absorbed, and how he had
appreciated it all.

We sat down to lunch. There were no menus, every table enjoying the
same wonderful bill of fare. During the antipasto, when Franco presented
Zucchini Flowers Stuffed with Béchamel and Wild Mushrooms, he announced to the room that the flowers had been picked that morning by Andrea. As the crowd popped the warm, delicately rich delights into their
mouths, like bonbons, they all cheered, "*Bravu*, Andrea!"

After our magnificent and plentiful lunch, I introduced Andrea to the
most civilized custom of the Mediterranean world: the postprandial siesta. I
explained that the entire city stopped now. All the shops, even the banks and
the post office, were closed. We drew the curtains in our room to mellow the
light. The breeze gently billowed, the mare cavorted, and we fell into sweet repose.

When we returned to Polizzi, as we were parking in the piazza in front of
the Byzantine fortress, a group of children appeared. Mariangela, the beauti-

ful teenage daughter of Pino Agliata, came forward to greet us. I introduced her to Andrea. She spoke to him in her first-year high-school English. Mari was a good student. The other children crowded around, eyeing Andrea and he them. Domenico, Pino's ten-year-old son, came through the group holding a soccer ball. His question in Sicilian was obvious in any language, and Andrea's answer was easy: "*Sì*."

Teams were easily formed, girls against boys. I'm sure Andrea fully expected to be transported with all the others to a nearby soccer field, but Domenico tossed out the ball and the game began right there in the hilly cobbled piazza. Could it be that Polizzi is more like Bruculinu than I thought?

The children played and screamed until it was too dark to see the ball. Then they played a game of *mucciaredda*, hide-and-seek. And what places there are to hide in in a 2,500-year-old city! I left at one point to go see Santo, and my return found the children laughing, sweaty, and rosy-cheeked, enjoying a cold drink at the tables in front of Pino's. Mari asked, "Tomorrow you will bring Andrea?"

The next morning I dropped off Andrea as promised. When I returned at lunchtime, Mariangela said her mother wanted to know if Andrea could have lunch with them. Domenico added, "Andrea is with us now." And he was. He played with the children every day. I began to hear him speak phrases in Sicilian as he played soccer. When we walked down the main street, always with at least four of his new friends, he greeted people in Sicilian, saying, "*Bona sera, chi si dici?* (Good evening, what do you say?)." I'd never seen Andrea so safe or so free in his life.

Early one morning, we went out onto our balcony to greet the dawn. Bundled in our bathrobes against the chill, we sat looking at Polizzi perched above. We watched it turn from silhouette to positive image as the daylight gathered behind it and the streetlights went out. It was quiet. Then Andrea, in a clear, soft voice, said, "You know, Dad, in Los Angeles people have a lot of stuff. Here, in Polizzi, people don't have a lot of stuff. But they have their families, and their friends, and they work, and eat, and play, and sleep. And maybe you don't need to have all that stuff to have a nice life."

The days passed, and Andrea's birthday was just a day away. Pino asked Andrea if he would be interested in helping him in his pastry shop for a little while. Mariangela dressed Andrea in a white apron and pastry chef's hat. Andrea, standing at the massive marble pastry table, watched attentively as Pino split a large rectangular sponge cake in half. Then, with Pino's guidance, Andrea sprinkled the bottom half with Strega, an Italian liqueur. As Andrea held the bowl, Pino spread the surface with a layer of hazelnut cream. He fitted the other cake layer on top and plastered the surface with whipped cream.

Using a fine-pointed pastry bag, Pino drew a map of Sicily on top. The island had only one city, Polizzi Generosa. All of us, children and adults, watching the demonstration, laughed at this chauvinism. Pino and his new assistant covered Sicily with chopped-hazelnut mountain ranges. Azure-colored whipped cream created the sea around the island. Pino began to write on the surface in Italian, "Welcome to Sicily. Happy Birthday . . ." The room grew especially silent as he began to spell out the last word, "A . . . N . . . D . . . R . . . E . . ." Andrea gasped, "It's my cake!"

The next night, a surprise birthday party at Santo's was a real surprise and a huge success. More than thirty of our family and friends assembled at a serpentine table in the restaurant courtyard. This time Santo really did prepare pizza—delicious individual ones, Neapolitan-style, with rustic Sicilian toppings. The pizzas were cooked in about three minutes, baked in a hot wood-burning oven.

At one point, Gasparinu and five other friends, some in traditional costume, marched into the courtyard playing musical instruments. The leader played a short wooden flute to the accompaniment of a drum, two tambourines, a Jew's harp, and a most extraordinary drone instrument, *u cafuddu*. Its base is a half-gallon-size sardine tin. The bottom and sides are covered in decorative cloth. The open side of the tin is covered like a goatskin drum. Embedded in its center is a long cane shaft. The tin is held under the left arm, while the right hand is kept wet and slides up and down the shaft, emitting a droning sound. I still don't know if Andrea understood what was making the adults giggle.

Everyone—children, Zà Pasqualina, all of us—danced together into the morning hours. The figures were expertly called by Gasparinu, making the traditional steps easy for novice and expert alike. Watching Andrea prance around the courtyard, I thought of his question about Brooklyn from our first day. Holding him close, with my mouth next to his ear, I whispered, "You know, my boy, this *is* what Bruculinu felt like."

Andrea went to Polizzi, and he came back with more than I ever could have imagined. I know that he will return again and again. But I also know that he will carry that first experience with him for the rest of his life. One day, perhaps, he'll bring his own child to that wondrous place.

## Purpetti 'i Risu Ducu

### *Sweet Rice Patties*

Rice pilaf cooked with sugar, cinnamon, and black pepper—this recipe surely has North African roots. When cooled, the rice is formed into patties and pan-fried.

These rice patties are usually served as part of an antipasto. The recipe may be multiplied, using the same amount of oil for frying.

*For 18 patties*

1½ cups *arborio* rice
3   cups whole milk
4   teaspoons sugar
1   tablespoon plus ½ cup extra-virgin olive oil
¼   teaspoon sea salt
½   teaspoon ground cinnamon
    Black pepper

Preheat the oven to 350°F, with a rack positioned in the center.

Rinse and drain the rice, checking it for debris. Put it aside.

Put the milk and sugar in a small saucepan and bring to a boil over medium-low heat.

When the milk is nearly boiling, grease a 4-quart, ovenproof, lidded pot with the 1 tablespoon oil. Place it over medium heat, and when the oil is hot, add the rice. Turn the rice in the oil for a minute or two, until it is well coated and hot to the touch. Be sure it doesn't scorch.

Stir in the boiling milk, salt, cinnamon, and a few grindings of black pepper. When the milk returns to a boil, cover the pot and place it in the oven. Bake for 18 to 22 minutes, until the rice is cooked al dente and is still a bit wet.

Pour the contents of the pot into a shallow bowl, smooth the top, and cover with a dishcloth. Cool the pilaf to room temperature.

To form the patties, first cover a work surface or sheet pan with a length of waxed paper. Gently roll a small amount of the rice between your hands to form a 1¾-inch ball. Flatten it into an oval, ½ inch thick. Place it on the waxed paper.

When all the patties are formed, pour the ½ cup oil into a heavy 9-inch skillet over medium heat. When the oil is hot, fry the patties, in two batches, for about 1½ minutes on each side, until barely golden on the surface. Drain on brown paper or paper towels, and serve hot.

'Nsalata 'i Caroti

## Cooked Carrot Salad

The humble carrot takes on new sparkle in the flavor of this simple salad. The carrots are cooked in water infused with extra-virgin olive oil and a hint of garlic, then cooled in the liquid to further absorb the flavor. Afterwards, their sweetness is complemented by the addition of lemon juice and capers.

Serve this as part of an antipasto or as an accompaniment to grilled meat or fish.

*For 6 servings*

2   cups water
¼   cup extra-virgin olive oil
1   small clove garlic, peeled and halved
⅛   teaspoon salt
1¼ pounds large carrots
2   tablespoons lemon juice
2   tablespoons capers, rinsed

Put the water, olive oil, garlic, and salt in a medium-sized saucepan, cover, and bring to a boil over medium-high heat.

Scrape the carrots and cut them at a 45° angle, slightly thicker than ⅛ inch. Cook them in the boiling water, covered, for 8 to 10 minutes, until tender but still quite firm. Remove the pot from the heat, partially uncover it, and let the carrots cool in the liquid for at least 3 hours.

Using a slotted spoon, transfer the carrots to a serving platter, discarding the garlic. Toss with the lemon juice and then the capers. Serve at room temperature or slightly chilled.

# Ciuri 'i Cucuzzeddi Chinu 'i Braciamella
## Zucchini Flowers Stuffed with Béchamel

Béchamel sauce was conceived by Louis de Béchamel, Marquis of Nointel, a wealthy financier who was granted the honorary appointment of *maître d'hôtel* for Louis XIV. Over the centuries, the simple sauce of butter, flour, and milk found its way to the Sicilian kitchen. The Sicilian version, however, differs somewhat from the classic French. In Sicily, the flour is added to the butter off the heat, the milk is added cold, and the sauce is generally thicker. In this recipe the sauce is flavored with mushrooms.

Zucchini flowers are plentiful in the kitchen gardens of Polizzi throughout the late spring and summer. The larger male flowers (those without zucchini) are used for stuffing. Removing them from the plants actually increases productivity. When picked at first light, they will remain open, making them easier to stuff.

In this country, zucchini flowers have become popular at farmers' markets and in specialty produce markets.

*For about 30 stuffed flowers*

Sea salt
33 zucchini flowers (about 6 ounces total)
½ cup all-purpose flour
6 tablespoons (¾ stick) unsalted butter
2 cups whole milk
Black pepper
4 scrapes of nutmeg
1 small yellow onion, peeled
1½ ounces cremini mushrooms
Extra-virgin olive oil for greasing and drizzling

Fill a medium-sized bowl with lightly salted water. Cut the stems from the flowers. Discard any flowers that are torn all the way down to the base. Clean the flowers by putting them in the bowl of water and soaking them until needed. The salt will cause any critters inside to come out.

Sift the flour. Put the butter in a medium-sized heavy-bottomed saucepan over the lowest heat possible. When the butter has melted, remove the pan from the heat and whisk in the flour to form a smooth paste. Return the pan to the stove and whisk in the milk, a little at a time to avoid lumps.

Turn up the heat a bit and keep whisking until the mixture comes to a boil. Season with salt, and add a few grindings of pepper and the nutmeg. Add the whole onion. Continue to let it boil very gently, stirring constantly to make sure the milk doesn't scorch at the bottom, until the sauce is quite thick and velvety, about 12 minutes.

Pour the béchamel into a bowl, discard the onion, and let it cool. Stir it from time to time so a crust doesn't form on top. When it has cooled to room temperature, the béchamel will form a soft paste.

Meanwhile, wipe the mushrooms clean, using as little water as possible. Chop them very fine. Generously oil a nonreactive skillet and heat it over medium-high heat. When the oil is nearly smoking, put the mushrooms in the pan and sauté for about 1 minute. Transfer them to a plate and allow to cool to room temperature.

Preheat the oven to 350°F, with a rack positioned in the upper third.

Thoroughly drain the flowers. Shake out the excess water, and pat dry the outer surface. Line them up on a work surface. Mix together the cooled mushrooms and the béchamel. Lightly grease a sheet pan with olive oil.

Stuff each flower with a rounded teaspoonful of the sauce. Place them right next to each other on the sheet pan. Lightly drizzle with olive oil and bake for 10 minutes, until the flowers have softened.

Cool the flowers on the pan just until the stuffing has reset enough to not leak out. Using a spatula, gently place the flowers on a platter and serve warm.

# Frocia 'i Ciuri 'i Cucuzzeddi

## *Zucchini-Flower Omelet*

In several cycles throughout the summer season, there is a moment when the zucchini has formed and the flower is still intact. One way to eat these baby zucchini and their flowers is to cook them in an omelet.

If you don't have a vegetable garden of your own, these flowers with baby zucchini may be difficult to find. Sure sources to investigate are specialty produce and farmers' markets.

Serve this omelet as a lighter second course or as part of an antipasto.

*For 4 to 6 servings*

12  ounces Yukon Gold, Yellow Finn, or russet potatoes
    Sea salt
12  zucchini flowers with baby zucchini (about 2½ inches long) attached
3   tablespoons unsalted butter, softened
¼   cup heavy cream
½   cup milk
6   eggs, beaten
½   cup finely grated Italian *ricotta salata* or Greek *myzithra* cheese
4   sprigs Italian parsley, chopped
    Black pepper
¼   cup extra-virgin olive oil

Peel the potatoes and cut them into large chunks of equal size. Put them in a pot of lightly salted cold water and place it over medium-high heat. Bring to a boil, reduce the heat to medium, and simmer until tender, 35 to 40 minutes.

While the potatoes are cooking, soak the zucchini in lightly salted cold water for 20 minutes. This process will release any insects that may be inside the flowers. Gently shake the zucchini to remove excess water from the flowers, and pat them dry. Trim and discard the stem end of each zucchini.

When the potatoes are cooked, drain them thoroughly and put them in a large bowl. Add the butter and mash them into a smooth puree with a potato masher or fork. Mix in the cream and milk. When the mashed potatoes have cooled enough not to cook the eggs, mix them in well, along with the grated cheese, parsley, and black pepper to taste.

Pour the olive oil into a heavy, well-cured, 9-inch skillet. Heat it over medium-low heat until the oil is hot.

Slip the zucchini into the skillet and sauté for about 7 minutes, or until tender but firm. Turn them carefully with tongs so that they do not separate from their flowers and do not brown.

The moment the zucchini are cooked, transfer them to a plate. Leave about 2 tablespoons oil in the skillet and pour off the rest. Reheat the skillet over medium heat until the oil is nearly smoking.

Pour the potato-egg mixture into the skillet, distribute it evenly, and smooth it with a spatula. Reduce the heat to very low and cook for about 10 minutes, until the eggs have set enough so that when the zucchini are placed on top, they will sink slightly but not fall to the bottom. Carefully arrange the zucchini in a spoke pattern, with the flowers along the circumference of the pan.

Continue to cook gently for an additional 10 to 15 minutes, until the bottom is a rich golden color. (You can peek at it by gently lifting the edge with a metal spatula.) Meanwhile, preheat the broiler.

When the bottom is ready, finish the top by placing the skillet under the broiler at the greatest possible distance from the flame (with the handle sticking out if it is not flameproof). Cook in this manner for only a few minutes, until set. Check it often, as it can easily burn.

To remove the omelet from the pan, place a plate on top and turn the plate and the skillet over. Repeat with another plate so that the zucchini pattern is on top.

Cut into wedges and serve hot, warm, or at room temperature.

## Stufateddu d'Agneddu

# *Braised Lamb Chops*

Shoulder lamb chops, which are not as tender as loin chops, benefit from braising, an excellent method for tenderizing the connective tissue and bringing out the wonderfully rich, complex flavors. Onions, white wine, and cherry tomatoes enhance the taste. This is one of the ways in which Franco D'Anna prepares shoulder lamb chops at the restaurant of Donna Giovanna.

In order to avoid any unnecessary cooling of this dish, bring the pan directly to the table, and serve the chops and sauce in shallow bowls with crusty bread for dipping.

*For 4 servings*

2   medium-sized yellow onions
12  vine-ripened cherry tomatoes
3   pounds shoulder lamb chops, cut ½ inch thick
2   tablespoons extra-virgin olive oil
1   cup dry white wine
    Sea salt
    Black pepper

Peel the onions, cut them in half, and slice them into ¼-inch-thick half-circles. Rinse the tomatoes and cut them in half, keeping them separate from the onions.

If the structure of any of the chops permits them to be easily pulled in half, do so. Put 1 tablespoon of the oil in a heavy 9-inch skillet. Heat it over high heat until very hot, nearly smoking. Sear the chops in two batches, about 2 minutes for each batch. Remove all the chops from the pan.

Reduce the heat to medium and add the remaining 1 tablespoon oil. Separate the onion pieces and sauté until golden, about 6 minutes. Remove them from the pan. Put the chops back into the pan with the onions on top. Distribute the tomatoes over all.

After a minute or so, when the chops are hot, pour in the wine. Season with salt and add a few grindings of black pepper. Boil the wine for 1 minute to evaporate the alcohol. Then cover the pan, reduce the heat to low, and simmer gently for 20 to 25 minutes, until the meat is quite tender. Serve immediately.

# Brioche

In Sicily, brioche is enjoyed as a breakfast bread, but it is eaten with even more delight as part of a ubiquitous Sicilian snack—brioche and gelato sandwiches. The brioche are formed in the shape of hamburger buns, split open, and filled to overflowing with soft gelato.

*For 12 brioche*

1   envelope (2¼ teaspoons) active dry yeast
1   tablespoon sugar
½   cup warm water (105° to 115°F), plus additional if needed
1   egg, at room temperature
2   egg yolks, at room temperature
1   teaspoon honey
2½ cups all-purpose flour, plus additional as needed
¼   teaspoon sea salt
½   cup (1 stick) unsalted butter, well softened
1   egg white, at room temperature

Mix the yeast and sugar together in a tall warmed glass. Add the ½ cup warm water, and mix with a wooden spoon. Let stand for 7 to 10 minutes, until the yeast is foamy.

Meanwhile, beat together the whole egg, egg yolks, and honey. Set aside until needed.

Using an electric mixer with a paddle, or by hand, mix the flour and salt together in a large warmed bowl.

When the yeast is ready, mix it into the flour. Continue to mix, adding the butter a spoonful at a time until the flour achieves the consistency of cornmeal.

Changing the mixer tool to a dough hook, or continuing by hand, add the egg mixture. Continue mixing until a ball is formed. If the dough is too sticky, add a bit more flour; if it is too dry, add more warm water in teaspoonfuls. Knead until the dough is smooth and elastic, about 10 minutes after a ball is formed, dusting with pinches of flour as necessary.

Lightly sprinkle flour on the inside of a warmed bowl that is large enough to hold the dough when it has doubled. Put the dough in it, and cut a ½-inch-deep cross on top with a sharp knife. Cover with a dish towel and set it in a warm place for 2 to 3 hours, until the dough has doubled in bulk.

Gently punch down the dough. Re-form the ball and divide it into 12 smaller balls, 1½ inches in diameter. Place them as far apart as possible on a sheet pan. Cover with a dishcloth and let them rise and spread for 1 hour, until they are about the size of hamburger buns.

During this time, preheat the oven to 450°F, with a rack positioned in the center.

After the second rising, lightly beat the egg white, and brush each brioche with it. If they have lost their roundness while rising, use the pastry brush to gently push them back into shape.

Bake for 12 to 15 minutes, until a deep golden brown. Cool in the pan for 5 minutes, then transfer to a rack to cool to room temperature.

## Torta 'i Crema 'i Nuciddi

### *Hazelnut-Cream Torte*

This is a smaller version of the birthday cake Pino made for Andrea. The sponge cake layers are brushed with Strega, an Italian liqueur flavored with herbs and flowers.

Removing the torte from the freezer an hour before serving allows the whipped-cream frosting to soften, while the hazelnut-cream filling remains frozen and maintains a delightful "crack."

It is best to prepare this torte the day before it is to be served.

*For one 10-inch cake, about 16 servings*

| | |
|---|---|
| 10 | ounces (about 2 cups) shelled whole raw hazelnuts (filberts) |
| 3 | cups heavy cream |
| ½ | cup plus 1 tablespoon confectioners' sugar |
| 1 | sponge cake (see page 124, thoroughly cooled to room temperature |
| ⅓ | cup Strega liqueur |
| 2 | ounces bittersweet chocolate, shaved |

**Prepare the nut topping, whipped cream, and hazelnut cream:** Preheat the oven to 400°F, with a rack positioned in the center.

Toast the hazelnuts on a baking sheet in the oven for about 10 minutes. Take care that they do not burn. Remove the pan from the oven, wrap the nuts in a dishcloth, and let them steam for a couple of minutes; then rub them together to remove as much of the brown skin as possible. Return the nuts to the oven and toast for an additional 4 minutes.

Coarsely chop ⅔ cup of the whole nuts to be used as topping; set aside. Grind the remaining nuts in a food processor into a very fine paste. Cool to room temperature.

Using an electric mixer or by hand with a wire whisk, beat 2 cups of the cream and 6 tablespoons of the confectioners' sugar into a thick whipped cream. Refrigerate, uncovered, for about 1 hour to set.

In a separate bowl, beat the remaining 1 cup cream and the remaining 3 tablespoons sugar into a thick whipped cream. While continuing to beat, add the hazelnut paste. Let this also set in the refrigerator, uncovered.

**Assemble the torte:** Cut the sponge cake in half horizontally, making sure the layers are equal. (This is easily accomplished with a large serrated knife: Cut around the edge first to maintain the center line, and then cut the cake through. An alternative is to use an adjustable cake cutter. These methods will make a straight cut and keep the cake from crumbing excessively.)

Place the bottom half, cut side up, on a cake platter. Using a pastry brush, sprinkle it evenly with half the Strega. Do not, however, moisten the cake to the point that the liqueur leaks through. Spread the top of this half with all of the hazelnut cream in an even layer.

Fit the other cake layer in place, and sprinkle with the remaining Strega. Using a flat metal spatula, "plaster" the side of the torte with as much whipped cream as will easily hold to the surface. Cover the top with the remaining whipped cream in a flat, even layer. Cover this with an even layer of the chopped nuts.

Place the torte in the freezer for at least 3 hours. Remove it 1 hour before serving. Just before serving, sprinkle with the shaved chocolate.

# Eleven

# Wintertime

*T*he car I was driving corkscrewed up the mountain to Polizzi, the air growing colder and colder. The sky became iced steel, sluicing out freezing rain. Polizzi itself was wrapped in a dense, bone-chilling fog, whipped together with the smell of burning wood-stove smoke and sodden earth. It was winter. I had never visited Polizzi in wintertime and I wanted to know what it's like.

The coldness of the season could never cool the warm hearts of the generous Polizzani, but the people had become contemplative and rather philosophical. They did not express the carefree ease of warmer days.

One evening I huddled with a group of friends in Bar Cristallo. Although not yet dinnertime, it was long after what little light the short day offered had been spent. The glass front, wide open in summer, was now closed; access was through a narrow door only. We sat around a small table in our coats, drinking cups of tea laced with rum against the chill. We carefully blew on and slurped the beverage, trying to drink it down as hot as possible. The various pitches and harmonies we made while concentrating on not burning our mouths made us sound like a herd of slurping sheep.

Gasparinu, his dancing cocktail shaker retired for the season, was behind the bar scrupulously examining two small, empty soft drink bottles. They were oddly shaped and it was questionable as to whether or not they held exactly the same capacity. He had lined up a row of small plastic cups, filled one of the bottles with water, and then poured an equal amount in each cup. He noted the quantity, spilled it out, and repeated the experiment with the other bottle.

Had it been summer, he simply would have drunk the soda, caring not about the bottle's capacity but rather about its ability to quench his thirst. But in the wintertime, priorities derive from a more considered motive—to make the time pass.

Gasparinu's experiment reminded me of another Sicilian, a native of the ancient Greek city of Siracusa. Surely it must have been in winter that Archimedes conceived the principle of specific gravity. In the hot summer, he would have been interested only in dropping himself in water, and stopped there. Perhaps all aspects of ancient Mediterranean culture were conceived in winter.

Moffu Schimenti burst through the door, bringing with him a blast of cold, wet air. We inside lamented with a sigh, our efforts at staying warm compromised. Quickly, though, we got back on track with another round, Moffu joining us, slurping along with the rest of the herd.

A man of the 1960s, Moffu is now in middle age. A composer of traditional-style songs and the singer with a folk music group, he remains active in political and cultural matters. Out of absolutely nowhere, he asked, "Who was Federico II's father?" After a moment's thought, someone said, "Ruggerio II."

One of our company was quick to say no: that Ruggerio was Norman and had lived centuries earlier.

Another tried a historical review. "Let's see. Federico I, Barbarossa, was the grandfather. If I remember correctly, the father was king for only seven years. The poor man died, I think in a crusade." All took a moment's pause in mourning the tragic death of the king whose name we couldn't remember.

A grumpy man who chose to take his coffee alone at the end of the bar piped in. "Federico II, Federico II," he said repeatedly, as if he were mouthing curses. "He's the root of all our problems! Because of him, we are part of Europe, but we should still be part of Africa. He's the real reason for all Sicily's economic problems!" The fact that Federico has been dead for almost eight hundred years mattered little to either his anger or his argument.

My companions and I exchanged glances, not knowing quite how to respond. A wise older gentleman at a nearby table settled the issue with the only response possible—a non sequitur. "During the war," he said, "the American army traveled on the road just below Polizzi. The soldiers seemed like good men. It was in late summer and the cacti were filled with ripe prickly pears. Some of them picked the fruit as they passed, eating them whole, spines and all. They didn't know. We felt so bad for them and wanted to say, 'Stop! Let us peel them for you,' but we didn't know if it was permissible to speak. From time to time, I think of how ill they must have become. I still feel bad for them."

After nodding at his story, we returned to our studies. Beginning with the ancient Greeks, we listed every ruler of Sicily we could remember, but the father of Federico II remained elusive. While we were thus engaged, a man walked in and nodded a greeting. We nodded back. He stood at the bar, ordered a grappa, shot it down, and without hesitation, moved back toward the door. As his hand reached the knob, with casual confidence and in a clear voice he sang out, "Enrico VI." Before we could agree, he was gone.

The question of Federico II's lineage well settled, we then considered dinner. Some went home, but Santo, Nino, Moffu, and I decided to go to the Pioneer Pizzeria, more for the warmth of the wood-burning oven than anything else. We settled at a table as close to it as possible.

We all made the same selection: a tomato-mozzarella pizza, topped after it is baked with very thinly sliced prosciutto, a crop of arugula, and a scattering of shaved pecorino. A bottle of plain extra-virgin olive oil and one flavored with hot red pepper were placed on the table, offering two choices to drizzle on top.

The pizza was perfect, as always. The crust, thin and crunchy, was perfumed by the wood fire. The aromatic flavor of the arugula reminded us all of warmer seasons and the fertile earth. We ate our individual twelve-inch pizzas with a knife and fork. The sawing motion needed to cut through the crust, the hot food, and the piquant olive oil warmed us enough to let us remove our coats.

During dinner, we talked about heating methods. There is no central heating in Polizzi. The city has never been piped with natural gas, and to use any other fuel would be extremely costly. Also, there would be the problem of outfitting old stone houses with radiators or ducts. In some homes there are propane or electric space heaters, but these are turned off at night for safety reasons. The room where I was staying above DA . . . DA . . . CI . . . CCIO had a propane heater. By morning, I could see my breath.

About eighty percent of the homes are still heated by wood-burning stoves. These little metal stoves, about fourteen inches square and three feet tall, are lined with ceramic tiles. The wood is put in on end. The stoves stay quite hot through the night, long after the fire has gone out. The living areas of homes heated by wood are the warmest. The bedrooms, however, stay quite icy. Thick down comforters, and sometimes a warm brick in the bed, do provide some relief.

After dinner, Moffu took us to his godmother's house for her family's nightly warming activity. Zà Momó (Aunt Gandolfa) still used an ancient heating device called *'a bbrascera.* As we were welcomed into the house, I saw a dozen people sitting close together in a circle. They each held the edge of a large blanket that covered their legs. Under the center of the blanket, on the tiled floor, was the *bbrascera:* a 2½-foot-diameter hardwood wheel, *'a ruota,* with a brass brazier filled with charcoal on top. Covering the brazier is a dome-shaped olivewood grid, *'a cuba,* which protects the blanket from burning if it should fall onto the hot coals.

Potatoes and eggs in their shells were being roasted in the coals, and chunks of *caciocavallo* cheese wrapped in oiled paper were being melted on the *cuba.* Moffu's cousin bade us all sit down, moving over to make a place for me next to her mother, Zà Momó. A small glass of wild strawberry liqueur was placed in my hand; I clutched my edge of the blanket with the other. The instant warmth that the *bbrascera* sent to my legs and feet, numb from the winter cold, was indescribable.

Zà Momó, ninety years old if a day, turned to me with a coquettish smile. Waving a scolding finger, she sweetly admonished me in Sicilian, "Remember, your hands must stay on top of the blanket." Her daughter shrieked with embarrassment, but quickly joined the rest of us, laughing. Everyone, it seemed, had blushing memories of youthful explorations under blankets around the *bbrascera*.

As time passed, we happily grew warmer and warmer. At one point I said to Zà Momó, in total earnestness, "I'm just reaching under to check on the eggs." Giddy from the heat, this sent everyone over the edge. We composed ourselves to enjoy the smoky flavor of the eggs and the hot roasted potatoes dipped in olive oil and salt. We bit into the creamy, scalding cheese right off the paper. Wild-strawberry liqueur added to the contentment.

The *bbrascera* experience, special to me but a nightly wintertime activity for Zà Momó and her family, kept me warm on the walk home. All through the night, and even in the chill morning, I still felt the warmth of the coals and the laughter.

As the cold, dreary days passed, I developed a system for forecasting the weather. Each morning, upon rising, I would open the shutters, look at the sky, and put my hand on the windowpane. I would then know how many layers I would need to get through the day.

One morning, as I threw open the shutters, the room filled with bright sunlight. What a surprise! People on the streets breathed more easily, and that evening many even took the traditional stroll from the main piazza to the overlook. Wearing down-filled parkas or loden coats, the Polizzani looked like an odd race of Sicilian-Alpine-Eskimos. But all were not cheered by a day of sun. At the overlook, many strollers paused to stare at the mountains. There was no snow. People shook their heads. "If the snow doesn't come," one man said to me, "there will be drought this summer. And then what will we do?" Polizzi is a watershed area, even providing part of the supply for Palermo. A poor snowfall in the Madonie Mountains impacts the water supply of the whole island.

That sunny day, however, was a tease. By the next evening, we were locked in a stronger grip of ghastly weather. A few flurries fell in the mountains, but nothing worth noting. Snow became the obsessive topic of conversation throughout the city. Words, even prayers, seemed fruitless. There was still no snow.

Winter life in Polizzi wore on. Days turned into weeks. Shoes didn't completely dry out, ever. Noses sniffled and chests grew sore with coughing. One evening in Gasparinu's, I was introduced to Ninettu (Little Nino). Noticing the miserable condition of his old friends Santo and Moffu, he invited all of us to dinner at his home the next night.

Ninettu's house is deep in the forest above Polizzi. We drove up winding dirt roads through sleeping fields. Turning down a driveway that seemed more like a wash, we honked as we parked, and Ninettu and his wife, Tina, came to the door.

Ninettu is a diminutive man with a round belly. His ruddy face is adorned with a well-trimmed beard, patched in gray. When he smiles, his small, cheery eyes turn to slits. His wife, Tina, is slightly shorter, but trim and clean shaven. Standing in the normal-sized doorway of their cottage, they looked like a pair of gnomes. Ninettu and Tina, still very much in love after thirty years of marriage, stood with arms around each other's waist as they welcomed us into their home.

We entered the sparsely furnished living room where Moffu, Nino, and the other guests were waiting. A great fire snarled and crackled inside an enormous hearth, taller than the proprietors. The mantel was decorated with objects Ninettu had found in the forest: A briar gnarl that looked exactly like a human foot stood at one end; a piece of tree branch that could have been a pitcher with a handle rested at the other end; and at the center was perched a colossal piece of insect-scarred tree trunk that was the image of an eagle in flight.

As Ninettu pointed to each object, he proudly confirmed that he had not enhanced them in any way. Aside from cleaning them up, they were exactly as he had found them. "There is a life in the forest," he said, "that we will never fully understand."

Tina invited us into another room, twice the size of the first, for dinner. Along the wall on one side was a large stove, a deep sink with a step stool in front of it, and a modest refrigerator. A huge butcher block divided the kitchen area from the rest of the room. The height of this work surface was lower than usual, about thirty inches, scaled for the host and hostess.

Another fire, nearly the size of the one in the front room, roared. The walls of smooth unpainted plaster had grown nutty brown with years of fire smoke. Bare lightbulbs hung from the corrugated metal roof, giving a fluttering, yellowish light. Perpendicular to the fireplace, under a row of high windows, a large (but shorter than usual), sturdy refectory table with benches was laid with a white cloth and dishes.

As we entered, Tina had just finished ladling chickpea soup into the bowls at each place. Steam rose steadily from the bowls, fogging the windows and beckoning us to table. Ninettu settled in his place at the head, offering me the place next to his. I stowed my long legs as best I could under the low table and we began to eat.

The soup was thick and hearty. It was flavored only with salt, black pepper, and wild fennel. Ninettu's unfiltered extra-virgin olive oil was passed around to spiral on top. The only way to hold the large-handled soupspoons was to grab them in our fists, rustic-style. We alternated the delicious soup with bites of just-baked semolina bread and morsels of home-cured prosciutto and salami. Golden, fruity homemade wine was the beverage.

Next, Tina set down a large bowl of pork rinds cooked in tomato sauce. Ninettu had slaughtered one of his pigs two days earlier, and fresh rinds were one of the delights. They were meltingly rich and sweet. To accompany these, Tina had prepared an assortment of wild vegetables that Ninettu had foraged that day.

The vegetables were blanched, then sautéed, and mixed with just enough eggs and pecorino to form them into "pies," called *frittatedda*. The wild rapini was deep green, intensely flavored but not bitter; the wild cardoons were concentrated with the tang of artichoke; and the wild spinach tasted to me more earthy than spinach ever had before. That night, the forest of Polizzi Generosa truly came to the table.

For dessert, a tall pyramid of *taroccu* oranges from the lower slopes of Mount Etna adorned the center of the table. Their vibrant color, punctuated with their bright green leaves, reminded everyone of summer sunshine. The *taroccu* season comes just before that of Sicily's most famous fruit, *sanguneddu*, the sweet blood orange. *Tarocci* are nearly as non-acidic and are streaked with deep red. We peeled and ate them in silence, recalling with each juicy bite the feeling of the hot sun on our skin. Afterward, Tina collected the rinds and threw them into the fire, filling the room with their perfume and extending the joyful remembrance of summertime.

Ninettu noticed that Santo had a wart on his index finger. While the host carefully examined it, Santo explained that Ninettu was a *cermu*, a folk-healer.

The word *cermu* derives from the ancient Greek *harmon,* the same root as "harmony," meaning agreement or accord.

Although on the decline, folk-healing still holds an important position in Polizzani daily life. Children with pinworms are more likely to be taken to a *cermu* for treatment than to a doctor. Adults find relief from chronic headache or general malaise from the herbs and incantations of these traditional care-givers.

When a child has been deeply frightened, say by a fierce dog or a near-miss car accident, he or she might exhibit ongoing skittish behavior. Taking notice, the mother might say to the father, "This child has *u scantu* (the fear). We must do something about it." The mother knows that "the fear" will prevent the child from having a good life. This phobia might prevent him from marrying and raising a family, or keep her from a successful career.

The mother will take the child to a *cermu* whose specialty is *u scantu.* The practitioner will massage the child's belly with warm olive oil while saying secret prayers. After a few visits, the child's fear disappears. In modern terms, it is like treating phobia with massage therapy. But in Polizzi, the practice of this science has deeper, more ancient resonance.

Ninettu's specialty is warts. An old woman, noticing that he had the gift, taught him the secret knowledge. He must pass the art to a woman, and then she to a man, as prescribed by the ancient tradition.

He said to Santo, "I can cure that wart for you." Santo agreed, and Ninettu gave Tina a nod. She left the table and returned with a length of string. Ninettu took his folding knife out of his pocket, opened it, and set it on the table. He put one end of the string in his mouth and the knife in his left hand. As Santo held out his finger, Ninettu mumbled an incantation while making a cross with the knife blade over the wart, barely touching it. He then tied a knot in the string hanging out of his mouth, using only his left hand. The ritual was repeated seven times.

*Cermu* Ninettu went to the fire and tossed in the piece of string. Turning to the table while refolding his knife, he announced, "That wart will fall off within two weeks." Ninettu noticed that I saw a wart on his own left index finger. Nodding with sad resignation, he explained, "You see, Vicenzu, I can do the healing only with my left hand, so I can do nothing about my own wart."

· · ·

Changing the subject, Ninettu invited me to see his *cantina*. Every country house in Polizzi has an outbuilding or shed that is used as a storehouse. With flashlight in hand, he led the way through the cold night down a muddy path. We entered a building and he turned on the master electrical switch. A workshop filled with tools in organized disarray presented itself in the light. Through a doorway I could see a room hung with curing salamis and prosciuttos. Adjacent was another with aging pecorino cheese. Yet another held wine barrels and stored wine-making equipment. Within this maze of ad hoc partitions was a small room with a still for grappa, and a larger one with shelving filled with jars and bottles of home-canned tomatoes, jams, and other fruits and vegetables. Throughout, lush bunches of wild oregano and bay leaves hung drying. Ninettu filled with the pride of this wealth gained by his hard work, and seemed to grow in stature.

As we walked back to the house, he stopped in front of a row of large flowerpots near the front door. "Now it is the dead of winter, but here, around *my* house . . . look!" He aimed the flashlight at the flowerpots and dramatically trained its beam up the plants, revealing a garden of roses in full bloom.

The first thing Tina said when we walked in was "Did you show him?" He smiled at her so broadly that his eyes nearly slitted shut. She smiled back, so sweetly, that I smiled with them. By this time all of the other guests had moved back to the living room, and to the fire, and were lounging about like contented house cats. There wasn't a cough or a sniffle to be heard.

Ninettu sat down in a special rocking chair he had made out of the slats of an old wine barrel. It was scaled exactly for his size. In front, between the rockers, was a platform for his feet to rest upon. Tina sat upright on the edge of a sofa close by. They held hands and closed their eyes as the rocking reached sustained speed. It was as if they were spinning the enchantment that surrounded their cottage and their lives, giving joy and peace to all present.

The next morning it snowed. It fell from the sky like a storm of goose down, landing in pillows on all the church towers, rooftops, and streets of Polizzi. It snowed many days during the next two months. Between snowfalls, the air stayed cold enough to maintain the mountains in full mantle. Everyone smiled. What a glorious summer it would be!

Capunata 'i Cucuzza 'i Miernu

# Pumpkin Caponata

Although pumpkin is indigenous to America, our cuisine does not include many recipes for the savory use of this delicious gourd. (The gourd family also includes muskmelon, watermelon, and squash.) In Italy and Sicily, however, small pumpkins and pieces of larger ones are marketed throughout the autumn and winter for use in a variety of savory dishes.

In this unique caponata of "winter squash," *cucuzza 'i miernu*, as the Polizzani call pumpkins, thinly sliced crescents of sautéed pumpkin are tossed with a sweet-and-sour dressing of vinegar, sugar, and olives.

Small pumpkins yield slices of just the right thickness for this dish. They are available in most produce markets between Halloween and Thanksgiving, and at specialty stores throughout the winter.

*For 8 servings*

Two 2¼-pound pumpkins (about 3 pounds total when cleaned and peeled)
⅔ cup extra-virgin olive oil
Sea salt
35 (about 5½ ounces) calamata olives
½ cup red wine vinegar
2 tablespoons sugar
Black pepper

Snap off the stems and cut the pumpkins in half. Using a large soup-spoon, remove the seeds and scrape away all of the fibrous strings. Cut each cleaned piece in half lengthwise.

Using a sharp paring knife, peel the pumpkin. Work slowly and cautiously, as the knife can easily slip against the hard skin.

Slice the pumpkin pieces into long, thin crescents, about ⅛ inch thick.

Pour the olive oil into a 10- or 12-inch skillet. Heat it over medium-high heat until the oil is very hot but not smoking. Slip in half the pumpkin slices, turn them in the oil, and then slip in the other half and turn them all together. Season with salt and sauté for 15 to 18 minutes, until the pumpkin is cooked yet firm and has gained some color.

Meanwhile, squeeze the pits out of the olives and tear them in half. Set aside. Mix the vinegar and sugar together in a small bowl.

When the pumpkin is ready, transfer the slices to a serving platter with a large slotted spoon or tongs. Put the olives in the same skillet and sauté them for about 1 minute to release their flavor. Add the vinegar mixture and let it bubble for a minute, until a strong vinegar aroma rises from the pan. Pour the liquid and the olives over the pumpkin. Toss.

When the dish has cooled to room temperature, toss it again, sprinkle with several coarse grindings of black pepper, and serve.

## Favi e Castagni Vugghiuti

# Dried Fava Bean and Chestnut Soup

The most ancient staple of the rustic Sicilian diet is dried fava bean porridge, called *màccu*. Because of Polizzi's mountain location, this version contains dried chestnuts, which give the soup a wonderful smoky flavor.

Both dried fava beans and chestnuts are available at Italian specialty stores.

*For 6 servings*

1  **pound dried peeled (yellow) fava beans**
4  **ounces dried chestnuts**
8  **cups spring water**
   **Sea salt**
   **Extra-virgin olive oil, for drizzling**
   **Black pepper**

The evening before the dish is to be served, put the fava beans in a colander and wash them under cold running water. Check them for stones and other debris. Transfer the beans to a large bowl, cover with cold water, and allow to soak for 12 hours. Clean the chestnuts, and set them aside to soak in another bowl of cold water.

After soaking, remove any bits of brown skin from the fava beans. Drain and rinse them. Using the point of a paring knife, remove the hard brown skin from the crevices of the chestnuts. Drain and rinse them.

Put the chestnuts in a heavy 6-quart pot, and add the spring water and 1 teaspoon salt. Bring to a boil, adjust the heat, and cook, uncovered, at a tremble (barely boiling) for 20 minutes. Add the fava beans and continue cooking for about 40 minutes, until the chestnuts are tender and the favas have mostly disintegrated into a thick porridge. Stir occasionally to prevent sticking.

Check for salt, and serve directly from the cooking pot. Drizzle each bowl with a spiral of olive oil and grindings of black pepper to taste.

# Favi Spizzicati

## *"Jazzed Up" Fava Bean Soup*

The "jazz" here is the addition of green chard to this common staple. It thins and lightens the porridge-like soup while maintaining its deeply rustic character.

Choose green chard with crisp, crinkly, deep green leaves and tender white stalks.

*For 6 servings*

1   pound dried peeled (yellow) fava beans
10  cups spring water
    Sea salt
1   or 2 bunches (about 1½ pounds total) green Swiss chard
    Extra-virgin olive oil, for drizzling
    Black pepper
    Crushed red pepper

The evening before this dish is to be served, put the fava beans in a colander and wash them under cold running water. Check them for stones and other debris. Transfer the beans to a large bowl, cover with cold water, and allow to soak for 12 hours.

After soaking, remove any bits of brown skin from the fava beans. Drain the beans and put them in a heavy 6-quart pot with 8 cups of the spring water and 1 teaspoon salt. Bring to a boil, adjust the heat, and cook, uncovered, at a simmer for 1 hour. Stir occasionally to prevent sticking.

Clean the chard and trim the ends. Cut both white and green parts into pieces about 1¼ inches long. Drain the chard in a colander until needed.

When the beans have cooked for an hour, add the remaining 2 cups spring water to the pot. Raise the heat and bring it to a boil. Add the chard and salt to taste, and stir. Adjust the heat and cook at a tremble (barely boiling), partially covered, for about 10 minutes, until the chard is quite soft and the beans have mostly disintegrated into a porridge. Check for salt, adding more if needed.

To keep the soup hot, serve directly from the pot. Drizzle each bowl with a spiral of olive oil and both cracked black pepper and crushed red pepper to taste.

Ciciri Vugghiuti chi Purpetti e Britt

## Chickpea Soup with Meatballs and Chard

The disarmingly simple nature of this recipe gives little indication of the hearty complexity of its flavor. The consistency is more like a soupy stew, and it is best eaten from the bowl with a large soupspoon.

In the original recipe *dui carduna* (two cardoons) are used to subtly enhance the flavors. The cardoon resembles a wide, flat celery stalk and has a flavor similar to an artichoke. Any Polizziani cook can walk into her garden or out into the countryside and easily find cardoons. Unfortunately in this country they are marketed only at Christmastime and in any case are often too large and fibrous for this soup. The tender heart of an artichoke is a good substitute, enhancing the flavor in a similar way.

*For 6 servings*

1   pound (2 cups) dried chickpeas
    Sea salt
1   lemon
1   large artichoke
1   medium-sized yellow onion, finely chopped
1   bunch (about ¾ pound) green Swiss chard
8   ounces lean ground veal
    One 1½-inch-thick slice Italian bread, crust removed, soaked in milk and
    squeezed of excess liquid
1   egg
¼   cup grated imported pecorino cheese, preferably Locatelli brand
2   tablespoons chopped Italian parsley
    Black pepper
    Extra-virgin olive oil, for drizzling

The evening before the soup is to be served, put the chickpeas in a colander and wash them under cold running water. Check for small stones and other debris. Then put them in a heavy 6-quart nonreactive pot, cover with water by a generous inch, and allow to soak for 8 to 12 hours. After soaking, add more water if necessary to keep them well covered.

Add 2 teaspoons salt to the chickpeas. Cook them in the same soaking water, covered, over low heat, stirring from time to time, for 1 hour.

While the chickpeas are cooking, put 3 cups water in a bowl. Juice the lemon, and add the juice and the squeezed halves to the water. Cut ¾ inch off the top of the artichoke. Remove the outer leaves to the place where the leaves are thin and pale green. Cut the trimmed artichoke into quarters.

With a sharp paring knife, trim away the dark green base of the leaves around the heart. Peel the stem and cut off the end. Carefully remove and discard the spiny choke and the purple leaves with a paring knife or a spoon. Cut off the stem, coarsely chop it, and put it in the lemon-water. Thinly slice the heart with the leaves attached, and put these pieces in the lemon-water.

When the chickpeas have cooked for 1 hour, discard the lemon rind and thoroughly drain the artichoke pieces. Stir them into the pot. Add the onion as well. Continue to cook the chickpeas for another 1½ hours, until tender but still slightly underdone (the cooking time depends on the size and age of the chickpeas). Add more water as necessary to keep them covered.

Meanwhile, clean the chard and trim the ends. Cut both white and green parts into pieces about 1 inch long. Cut the wider leaves in half. Drain the chard in a colander until needed.

**Prepare the meatballs:** Put the veal, bread, egg, grated cheese, parsley, and a few grindings of black pepper in a bowl. Knead together by hand, squeezing the mixture through your fingers. Gently form the mixture into about 30 small round meatballs, ¾ inch in diameter. Place them on a platter in one layer until needed.

When the chickpeas have cooked for about 2½ hours, and are still slightly underdone, add the chard and cook for 20 minutes. Then gently put the meatballs in the pot, cover the pot, and cook for several minutes, until the meatballs firm up a bit, before stirring them into the other ingredients. Cook the meatballs for a total of 10 minutes.

Turn off the heat and leave the pot on the stove, covered, for 15 minutes, until the chickpeas are tender but firm. Check for salt. Serve from the cooking pot. Drizzle each bowl with olive oil and sprinkle with grindings of black pepper to taste.

## Risu chi Cùtini e Piseddi

### *Rice with Pork Rinds and Peas*

Pork rinds are the outer skin and fat layer of the pig. Throughout Italy, small amounts of prosciutto rinds are used for flavoring, mostly in bean dishes. In this recipe, however, the rinds are fresh-cooked. The addition of peas, wild fennel, and pecorino cheese makes this delicately rich rice dish burst with flavor.

*For 6 servings*

 4  ounces fresh pork rinds
    Sea salt
10  cups spring water plus additional if necessary
 2  ounces fennel (sweet anise) leaves and tender stems, wild if possible (see headnote, page 188)
 1  pound (about 2½ cups) *arborio* rice
 1  cup fresh peas (1 pound before shelling)
 ⅔  cup grated imported pecorino cheese, preferably Locatelli brand
    Coarsely ground black pepper

In a heavy 4-quart pot, blanch the pork rinds in lightly salted boiling tap water, covered, over high heat for 5 minutes. Remove the rinds, discard the water, and clean the pot. Cut the rinds into very narrow strips about 1 inch long, and put them aside.

Fill the pot with 8 cups spring water, and add 1 teaspoon salt. Cover and bring to a boil over high heat. Blanch the fennel in the boiling water, covered, for 2 minutes. Remove the fennel with tongs, and save until needed.

Put the rind strips in the boiling water. Cover, reduce the heat, and cook at a gentle boil for 30 minutes, until the rinds are soft and curled.

During this time, rinse the rice, checking it for debris, and set it aside in a colander. Finely chop the cooled fennel.

When the rinds are ready, add 2 cups spring water to the pot, return it to a boil, and stir in the rice and then the peas. Cook at a gentle boil, with the cover askew, for 10 minutes. Stir from time to time to prevent sticking. Stir in the chopped fennel and cook for another 10 minutes, until the rice is tender. Add more water if necessary to complete the cooking.

Remove the pot from the heat and stir in the grated cheese. Serve the rice in bowls directly from the cooking pot, with grindings of black pepper to taste.

## Gaddina China

### *Stewed Stuffed Chicken*

The delicate flavor of stewed chicken is enhanced by a light, simple dressing of giblets, Italian parsley, and a flavoring of pecorino cheese. In addition to the more customary aromatics of carrots, celery, and onion, saffron lends its sparkle to the broth.

Serve the chicken and vegetables in pasta bowls with a ladleful of the broth. Pass some thick slices of crusty bread to dip in the liquid.

*For 4 servings*

| | |
|---|---|
| 2 | medium-sized yellow onions |
| 3 | large carrots |
| 2 | ribs celery |
| 22 | whole black peppercorns |
| 4 | cups spring water |
| | One 4-pound free-range chicken, including the neck, liver, gizzard, and heart |
| 1½ | cups chopped Italian parsley |
| ⅓ | cup grated imported pecorino cheese, preferably Locatelli brand |
| 1 | egg, slightly beaten |
| | Black pepper |
| 1 | teaspoon coarse sea salt |
| 2 | pinches saffron threads |

Peel the onions and cut them in half. Scrape the carrots and cut them in half. Clean the celery and halve it as well. Place these ingredients and the peppercorns in a heavy 5- to 6-quart pot with a tight-fitting lid. Pour in the spring water, cover, and bring to a tumbling boil over medium heat.

While the water is heating, clean the chicken under cold running water. Clean the neck and giblets as well. Remove and discard the fat from around the opening, inside the crop, and around the giblets. Let the chicken drain, tilted, in a colander.

Mince the liver, gizzard, and heart and place in a bowl. Add the parsley, cheese, and egg. Season with salt, add a few grindings of black pepper, and mix everything into a paste.

Sew the crop end of the chicken closed with a large needle and kitchen string. Spoon the dressing into the cavity and sew it closed.

When the water boils, stir in the coarse salt and the saffron. When it returns to a tumbling boil, put the neck and the chicken, breast side down, in the pot. The chicken should be submerged as much as possible, with the vegetables around it.

Cover and cook at a gentle boil for 2 hours. (Fierce boiling will cause the chicken to fall apart; cooking too slowly will cause it to release all its flavor into the broth.)

Place the cooked chicken, breast side up, on a warmed platter. Place the broth, neck, and vegetables alongside it at the table, either in the pot or in a serving bowl. Serve very hot.

## Spitini

# Pork, Mozzarella, and Savory Pudding Skewers

*Spitini* is the Sicilian (and Italian) word for skewers. Usually *spitini* are made of thin slices of veal or beef filled with a modest bread crumb stuffing. This dish is quite different.

Lean pork meatballs made with pecorino cheese are skewered alternately with mozzarella and a thick, savory milk pudding. Each portion is then passed through egg and bread crumbs and fried. The delicious counterpoint of the meatballs, the mozzarella melted inside its breading, and the pudding creates a harmony of flavors. Eaten with an accompaniment of mixed green salad, the melody is complete.

The milk pudding is a rudimentary version of *biancumangiari (blancmange)*, an ancient dish. It was introduced into Sicily by the North Africans in the ninth century. By the Middle Ages, the dish had grown in popularity throughout Europe, its style becoming more and more elaborate. Along with a white starch for thickening, such as rice flour or blanched almonds, other ingredients might include milk, almond milk, clear meat or fish broth, capon breast, or fish.

In Europe today, only a sweet version of *biancumangiari* survives, eaten as a pudding or used as filling for pastries. *Spitini* is one of the rare recipes in which a rudimentary savory *biancumangiari* is still used.

A note about the pork: The pork for this recipe must be extremely lean. Purchase meat from the loin, and have it trimmed of fat and then ground.

*For 4 servings*

2   cups cake flour
2   cups plus 1 tablespoon milk
    Sea salt
1   pound very lean ground pork (see note above)
4   eggs
¾   cup grated imported pecorino cheese, preferably Locatelli brand

1 pound mozzarella cheese
2½ to 3 cups unflavored bread crumbs
3 cups pure olive oil, for frying

**Prepare the pudding:** Put the flour in a mixing bowl and slowly whisk in the 2 cups milk until smooth, with no lumps. Add a pinch of salt. Pour the mixture into a 1½-quart saucepan with a heavy bottom. Cook over low heat, stirring constantly, for about 4 minutes, until the mixture becomes a thick, heavy paste. This paste will start to form as lumps at the bottom of the pot; stir well to prevent scorching.

Turn the paste out onto an 8-inch plate. Flatten and smooth it with a knife, and let it cool, uncovered, to room temperature. Then roll it between sheets of waxed paper to form a rounded rectangle about 4 inches long, 3½ inches wide, and 2 inches thick, approximately the size of a 1-pound mozzarella.

**Prepare the meatballs:** Put the pork, 2 of the eggs, and the grated cheese in a bowl. Knead together by hand, squeezing the mixture through your fingers. Form the mixture into 12 round meatballs, about 2 inches in diameter. Place them on a plate until needed.

**Make ready the other ingredients:** Cut the mozzarella in half lengthwise. Slice it into 12 pieces, each about ¼ inch thick, 1¾ inches wide, and 2 inches long. Place them on a plate until needed. Unwrap the paste and cut it to the same dimensions, plating it as well.

In a shallow soup bowl at least 8 inches in diameter, beat the remaining 2 eggs with the remaining 1 tablespoon milk. Put the bread crumbs in another shallow bowl.

**Assemble and cook the *spitini:*** Stand a piece of paste on a work surface. Put a meatball next to it, followed by a piece of cheese. Gently flatten the meatball between the paste and cheese until it is the same size and all three ingredients are even at the edges. Continue assembling in this order: meatball, cheese, paste, meatball, cheese, paste. You will have used 3 of each item. Gently push the meat and paste with your hands to conform to the edges of the cheese, creating a loaf shape about 6 inches long.

Holding a hand against one end of the loaf, slowly push a thin bamboo skewer through from the other end. It should protrude at each end no more than ½ inch. Break off the excess with the aid of kitchen scissors or a knife.

Place the *spitini* in the egg wash. It will not be possible to turn it, so use a spoon to coat the top and sides, but do not let the egg wash pool on it. Transfer the loaf to the bread crumbs and coat it well.

Repeat with the remaining ingredients, creating 4 *spitini*.

Pour the oil into a 12-inch skillet, and turn on the heat to medium-high. When the oil is hot, gently place a *spitini* on a large spatula. Using a second spatula, carefully slide the *spitini* into the oil. Fry until browned, about 3 minutes. Using the two spatulas, turn the *spitini* over, taking care to avoid splattering the oil. Fry for 3 minutes, until that side is browned. Turn the *spitini* back to the first side and fry for 3 more minutes to ensure doneness. If necessary, reduce the heat a bit to keep the bread crumbs from burning. Remove the *spitini* and place it on brown paper or paper towels to drain. Repeat with the remaining *spitini*. Serve hot.

# Sosizza chi Qualazzi

## *Sausage and Rapini Stew*

This quick-to-prepare dish is hearty, rustic, and filled with flavor. Choose rapini with thin stems—mostly leaves and very few broccoli-like buds per stalk. These have a less fibrous texture and a mellower, less metallic flavor. The presence of little yellow flowers means that the rapini has gone to seed and will be too bitter.

Crusty bread is a good accompaniment here.

*For 6 servings*

2  bunches (about 2 pounds) rapini (broccoli rabe)
1¾ pounds sweet (mild) thick or thin Italian sausages, without fennel seeds
2  tablespoons extra-virgin olive oil
1  cup dry white wine
   Sea salt
   Black pepper

Clean the rapini and cut off the fibrous ends. Cook in boiling water, covered, over high heat until it is soft, about 5 minutes. Drain in a colander and cool quickly under cold running water. Cut the rapini into 1½-inch lengths and place them in a bowl until needed.

Cut thin sausage into 2-inch lengths, thick ones into 1-inch lengths. Put the oil in a heavy 9-inch skillet and heat it over medium-high heat. When it is hot, add the sausages and lightly brown them on all sides, about 8 minutes.

Pour off the grease, return the pan to the stove, and pour in the wine. Carefully turn the heat back on and let the wine bubble for 2 minutes to evaporate the alcohol. During this time, scrape the pan and turn the sausages in the wine. Cover, reduce the heat to low, and simmer until the sausage pieces are cooked, 10 to 15 minutes.

Uncover, raise the heat to medium-high, and add the rapini, mixing it well with the sausage. Season with salt and a few grindings of black pepper. Cook for 2 to 3 minutes, allowing the flavors to mingle, and serve in pasta bowls.

## Cucuzza 'i Miernu chi Patati

# *Pumpkin and Potato Stew*

Delicious and warming, this vegetarian stew has a beautiful delicate orange color. The flavor and texture are enriched with the final addition of eggs beaten with grated pecorino cheese.

Serve it in pasta bowls with crusty bread to dip in the "gravy."

*For 6 servings*

1½ pounds russet, Yukon Gold, or Yellow Finn potatoes
 One 2¼-pound pumpkin (about 1½ pounds cleaned and peeled)
1 medium-sized yellow onion
½ cup extra-virgin olive oil
 Sea salt
3 eggs
¾ cup grated imported pecorino cheese, preferably Locatelli brand
 Black pepper

Peel the potatoes and cut them into chunks 1½ inches across and 1 inch thick.

Snap off the stem and cut the pumpkin in half. Using a large soupspoon, remove the seeds and scrape away all of the fibrous strings. Cut each piece in half again. Using a sharp paring knife, peel the pumpkin. Work slowly and cautiously, as the knife can easily slip against the hard skin. Cut the pumpkin into pieces the same size as the potatoes.

Peel and finely chop the onion.

Pour the olive oil into a heavy 4-quart pot. Add the onion and sauté over medium heat until it turns pale gold, about 10 minutes. Add the pumpkin and potatoes, turn them in the pot, and lightly salt (the later addition of cheese will add saltiness). Continue to sauté for a couple of minutes for the flavors to mix together. Do not brown the pumpkin or potatoes in the slightest.

Add 2 cups water, cover, and boil gently until cooked, 30 minutes. Stir from time to time to prevent sticking, and adjust the heat to avoid violent boiling.

Beat the eggs and cheese together in a small bowl. When the stew is cooked, remove the cover, reduce the heat to very low, and stir in the beaten eggs. Stir and cook for a minute or two until the eggs have barely set.

Serve very hot, with a grinding of black pepper.

# Frittatedda 'i Qualazzi

## *"Little" Rapini Omelet*

Blanched rapini is sautéed and mixed with just enough eggs to hold it together. The result is by no means an omelet, but a way of forming the greens into an intensely flavored omel*ette*.

I ate this dish at Ninettu's house. The Polizzani also use the same method to form spinach, wild cardoons, and asparagus. The dish can be served at any temperature from hot to room temperature, as an accompaniment, or as part of an antipasto.

*For 6 servings*

    Sea salt
1    bunch (about 1 pound) rapini (broccoli rabe) with thin stems and no yellow flowers
4    eggs
¼    cup grated imported pecorino cheese, preferably Locatelli brand
⅓    cup finely chopped yellow onion
¼    cup extra-virgin olive oil
    Black pepper

Put 3 quarts water in a 4-quart pot, lightly salt, cover, and set it over high heat to boil. Meanwhile, clean the rapini, cut off the tough fibrous ends, and set it aside. In a small bowl, beat the eggs with the grated cheese and set it aside.

Place the onion and oil in a heavy 9-inch skillet. Sauté over low heat until golden.

At the same time, drop the rapini into the boiling water and cook, uncovered, for about 6 minutes, until the stems are soft. Transfer the rapini to a colander, rinse it under cold running water to stop the cooking, and chop it into 1-inch lengths.

When the onion is ready, raise the heat to high and fold in the rapini. Continue to sauté for about 3 minutes, until the water is mostly evaporated and the rapini is just beginning to crackle. Reduce the heat to medium-low and pour in the eggs. Lift the rapini with a spatula or a fork, allowing egg to pass through and cover the bottom. Continue to cook for about 7 minutes, until the bottom is golden. (Check by lifting the edge with a spatula.)

Meanwhile, preheat the broiler.

Put the skillet under the broiler (with the handle sticking out if it is not flameproof) and cook until set and golden on top, about 2 minutes.

Slide the "omelet" onto a serving dish, sprinkle it with several grindings of black pepper. Serve warm or at room temperature.

## Patati a Puviriedda

# *Poor Man's Potatoes*

The simple satisfaction of eating potatoes prepared in this humble way can be easily enjoyed by everyone, regardless of financial status.

Roasting the potatoes over the charcoals of *'a bbrascera* certainly enhances their flavor. If that luxury is not available, the next best thing is baking them in the oven.

*For each serving*

**One 8- to 10-ounce russet potato**
**Sea salt**
**Extra-virgin olive oil**
**Black pepper**

Preheat the oven to 375°F.

Scrub the potatoes with a vegetable brush. Wrap each one in aluminum foil and bake for 1 hour.

Unwrap the potatoes, cut them in half the long way, and roughly chop them inside the skin. Liberally salt, generously drizzle with olive oil, and sprinkle well with coarsely ground black pepper. Serve.

Castagni 'Ncaramilla

## *Candied Chestnuts*

Greek mythology tells us that Mount Olympus was covered with a forest of chestnut trees. This humble, versatile nut is also native to the Madonie Mountains of Sicily. Over the centuries, chestnuts have found their way into both sweet and savory regional dishes.

Although preparing fresh chestnuts is a bit arduous, the sweet simplicity of these candied chestnuts is well worth the effort. As an added bit of Olympian spectacle, the chestnuts are served with flaming rum and shaved chocolate.

*For 6 servings*

**1¾ pounds plump fresh chestnuts**
**1   cup sugar**
**⅔   cup water**
**⅔   cup dark Barbados rum**
**2   ounces bittersweet chocolate, shaved**

Preheat the oven to 375°F, with a rack positioned in the center.

Rinse the chestnuts and shake off the excess water. Using a small sharp knife, or a small hooked one designed for this purpose, incise a shallow cross into the curved side of each chestnut. (The skin must be cut or the chestnuts will explode while roasting.)

Put them in a chestnut pan or a regular baking dish that is large enough to accommodate them in one layer. Roast for 60 minutes, or until the chestnuts are cooked through but have not hardened. Shake the pan a few times during roasting to prevent the nuts from burning.

When the chestnuts are cool enough to handle, shell and skin them. Be sure to remove every bit of fuzzy skin from the surface and crevices. If this skin is impossible to remove, discard the nut. Some of the nuts may end up in pieces, but the bulk of them should be whole. Preparation to this point can be done up to 48 hours before the dessert is to be served. Store the nuts in a sealed plastic bag, refrigerated, until needed.

The candying process may be begun up to 5 hours before the dessert is to be served. Fill the sink with a few inches of cold water to serve as a water bath in which to quickly cool the pot of syrup and chestnuts.

Choose a heavy 1½-quart frying pan or saucepan with a flameproof, non-reactive surface. Put the sugar and water in it. Stir over low heat until the sugar is dissolved. Stop stirring, raise the heat to medium, and bring to a boil. Immediately add the chestnuts and turn them in the syrup. Constantly turning the chestnuts in the pan, boil for 5 minutes. Remove the pan from the heat and immerse the bottom in the water bath for a few seconds. Place the pan, uncovered, in a warm place until needed.

About 40 minutes before the dessert is to be served, put the pan over low heat and bring the syrup to a boil. Stir the chestnuts to prevent scorching. Boil for 25 to 30 minutes, until all of the syrup has been absorbed.

Remove the pan from the heat, and while letting the mixture settle for a moment, clear the area of anything flammable. Slowly (to avoid splattering) pour in the rum and mix it in. Stand back and light it with a long match. When the flame goes out, turn the contents of the pan onto a platter. Sprinkle with the chocolate, and serve immediately.

*P*olizzi Generosa, if it isn't raining, it's foggy." This sums up Polizzani weather in an old satirical saying. In the original Polizzani dialect, it even rhymes: *Polizzi Generosa, si nun chiova é nigghiusa*. Actually, the fog settles in mostly during the colder months, warming the nights with its insulation and giving the city a mysterious, romantic, almost melancholic feel.

My friend Peppe has friends who live in the lowest part of Polizzi, outside the historic walls of the city. Their home is next to the ruin of the Church of Santo Giovanni La Maddalena, known locally as *'a Commenda* (from the Latin *commendam*, meaning an ecclesiastical holding). The church was built in 1386 by the Knights Hospitalers of St. John of Jerusalem. A religious order of knights, the Hospitalers were founded in Jerusalem during the first Crusade (1096–1099). Their original mission was to establish hospitals for those wounded in battle. They also offered aid to the needy, but they themselves did not take a vow of poverty, and indeed, they lived in splendor. Their presence in Polizzi dates from 1177, when the order built the first water-powered grain mill in the area.

The Hospitalers were a secret, esoteric organization, deeply involved in mysticism and spirituality. 'A *Commenda* was established in this isolated area so the Knights could be free to engage in their rituals and meditations without intervention. Originally the *commendam* included a monastery and two nearby hospitals, at which Polizzani were treated in times of epidemic.

The church itself was beautifully appointed: marble altarpieces, exquisitely carved statues, magnificent paintings and carpets, and gold and silver monstrances, chalices, and candelabra. The compound was positioned for a grand view of the entire valley as well as every bell tower in Polizzi. In ages past, during troubled times, smoke and fire signals were sent up from *'a Commenda* to alert the population. It is rumored that a secret tunnel once ran from under the church to the center of town.

For more than five hundred years, the Hospitalers, who later evolved into the Knights of Malta—a lay fraternity still in existence around the world—aided in the spiritual and physical well-being of the Polizzani. But by 1889, the church was in little use and the hospitals and monastery had been abandoned. All were scheduled for demolition to make way for the state road then under construction. In July of that year, the sacred and precious objects were removed by the Church and all the buildings were destroyed, except the bell tower and the apse, today in ruins. Under its floor, close to where the main altar stood, a marble slab still marks the final resting place of a fourteenth-century Grand Knight.

To this day, even in its ruined state, the majestic power of the place evokes an uneasy, almost dizzy feeling. I am not the only person among the Polizzani who finds *'a Commenda* to be haunted and a little frightening.

On one of Polizzi's foggy, foggy nights, Peppe went to visit his friends. As he parked his car close to *'a Commenda*, he heard the distant sound of many voices singing. At first he thought his radio was playing on low volume, but it had been turned off. As he moved away from the car the voices grew louder, and Peppe realized that the sound was coming from *'a Commenda*.

With cautious curiosity, he approached. Through the billowing fog he could see more than thirty modern-day Knights of Malta in full regalia. Their plumed helmets rippled in the breeze, and what little moonlight filtered through glinted off their bright swords. The Knights were standing in salute around the grave of their long-fallen, but not forgotten, leader. Their voices, in solemn unison, raised an ancient Latin chant in prayer and remembrance.

Peppe was transfixed. The Knights noticed him standing there but did not further acknowledge his presence. He stood by for about an hour, and then quietly left to visit his friends, knowing he had witnessed something very special. When Peppe returned to his car near dawn, the Knights had vanished as discreetly as they had arrived, leaving behind only a bouquet of roses on the grave of their ancient leader.

•   •   •

Polizzi's glorious past is taught to every schoolchild, reflected on every street, and commemorated on each traditional holiday. Less publicized events, like the one with the Knights of Malta, relive that past, if only for a moment. Although steeped in history and tradition, modern Polizzi's destiny is at a crossroads. The city is faced with its most serious dilemma: how to survive.

The relatively recent eclipse of Polizzi's 2,500-year-old agricultural-pastoral-based economy has been truly difficult, leaving few opportunities for the unskilled worker. For those with a profession or a trade, livelihood is more assured. Some commute daily to Cefalù, or Termini Imerese, or even the seventy miles to Palermo, finding a way to live in Polizzi. For many, however, the chance of good jobs in the cities of northern Italy or other European countries calls them away. Families would like to stay, but at the moment Polizzi provides them little prospect for prosperity beyond sustenance. Each year the population dwindles. Things change.

During the summer of 1997, renovation was begun on the Chiesa Madre, the main church of Polizzi. A serious structural fault was discovered in its foundation, rendering the building unsafe for the congregation. Whether or not effective repair is possible remains a question. The closing of this church, a holy place in which generations and generations of Polizzani have been baptized, married, and sent to their final resting places, presents the Polizzani with a serious break in the continuity of time.

In September 2001, an event occurred, which, for the Polizzani, has been of significant portent: DA . . . DA . . . CI . . . CCIO closed its doors. Earlier that year, Zà Rosa had broken her hip. Recovery has been long and slow, making it obvious to her family and to all that she will not be returning to the café to cook her magnificent food. Don Ciccio, himself a man of advanced years, saw no point in continuing the business.

Late one evening, Mayor Lo Verde, alone in his great office, took pen in hand to write an open letter to Don Ciccio and Zà Rosa, expressing the whole community's feeling of loss at the closing of this important Polizzani establishment.

*Polizzi Generosa, 20 September 2001*

*To: Signor and Signora Ficile and to the City*

*As every morning, while on my way to the City Hall, I raised my eyes to greet you, but you were not there. Your daily activity at Bar Da . . . Da . . . Ci . . . Ccio has come to an end.*

*Something is missing now in our city: a piece of its own recent history. We have come to miss the tone of your voice, your outspoken opinions, your pride at having been a member of the old Liberal Party, always trying to better the life of the people.*

*Now, we find you in retirement, along with your wife, Signora Rosa.*

*How can we ever forget her wonderful cuisine, appreciated over the years by all of us Polizzani, as well as by so many prestigious visitors?*

*How could we pretend it didn't matter?*

*I, myself, feel an emptiness inside which will be not easily filled.*

*For all that you and your wife are, and for all that you have done, I thank you in the name of the whole city for your "service" and for the good example you have set for all generations of Polizzani.*

*Warmest regards,*
*The Mayor,*
*Giuseppe Lo Verde*

Although a new place will be opening close to where Don Ciccio's was, and although Francesco has made a deal with the new owner so that the famous granita will continue to be made by the Ficile family, for the people all is not quite settled.

Like many other ancient small cities and towns of Sicily and Italy, the future of Polizzi is obscured in the fog of transition. When it clears, some of these places will have perished. But the city Polizzi Generosa and its people stand as a benchmark of history, art, and culture. As they say, "Before Rome, there was Polizzi."

A perspective on the life of Polizzi can be gained from the yeast starter that is used there to leaven bread. The starter is called *criscenti*, "the growing thing." I have tried to learn how to make it, asking many home cooks and all the professional chefs of Polizzi for a recipe. Everyone said the same thing: "How to *make criscenti*? I don't know, but I could lend you some."

I would explain that I wasn't going to make bread right then, but wished to have only the starter recipe. "We never make *criscenti*. It's always been here. If ours runs out for some reason, we borrow from someone else."

They would then carefully explain the method by which they, their grandparents, and generations of ancestors back to antiquity have fed and handled the starter when active or dormant, keeping it alive. Surely the mother of this yeast is at least as old as that first grain mill of the Knights Hospitalers, and even that thousand years is far less than half as old as Polizzi.

For me, and for many others, time has proved that Polizzi, like the yeast, will keep on growing and changing forever. The generous, independent, resourceful Polizzani will make it so.

The mayor, Giuseppe Lo Verde, and his family visited Los Angeles on unofficial business a few years ago. I showed them the sights, and afterwards he said to me, "It's nice here, a beautiful, big city. But you know, Vicenzu, you should come and stay with us in Polizzi." Every time I see him, he replants the idea, one on which I do not need any convincing.

On another foggy, foggy night, I met the mayor as he was leaving City Hall. He said with more than his usual excitement, "Come with me. I want to show you something."

We got into his car and went into the mountains via the winding road that begins under the Roman aqueduct. During the ride, the mayor talked nonstop on his cell phone, loudly and excitedly. He held the phone in one hand while gesturing emphatically with the other. We took the hairpin turns at great speed with no hands on the wheel. I was terrified.

The pavement ended abruptly, and the road's surface turned to dirt and deep ruts. The mayor mercifully ended his phone business, for a miscalculated turn now could have sent us off the mountain. A four-wheel-drive or a donkey cart would have been a more appropriate vehicle, but we continued on in his midsize sedan. When he noticed my white-knuckled grip on the dashboard, he burst into his mighty laugh, adding with assurance, "*Nun ti preoccupi* (There's nothing to worry yourself about)." We were, by now, high in the mountains, without a house in sight. I wondered what on earth we had come up here to see.

We turned another curve and came to a stop. Centered in the vista above, on a hill, stood Polizzi. Orienting myself in the darkness, I realized that we were in *u manicu 'a padedda*, the panhandle where the "mountain of gold" is, looking back at the city. Outlines of familiar buildings and churches took new form in this dreamlike view. The fog gave bright halos to the city's lights, making Polizzi look like a star come down to earth from the heavens.

The mayor turned to me. He had dropped his usual jovial manner. In a soft, slow voice pushed out over the lump in his throat, he said, "Isn't it the most beautiful thing you've ever seen?"

### Polizzi's Liqueurs

In Polizzi Generosa, one way in which the fresh fruit flavors of summer are made available throughout the bleak snowy winter is by the making of liqueurs. In these bottles can live the essence of a cherry, for example, long after the fruit has fallen from the tree. They shield the body against winter's chill, and they brighten the soul during the darkness of that season.

For those of us who live in great cities, if we wish to eat something out of season or exotic, we need only to go to a supermarket or specialty shop to choose from a veritable cornucopia of produce and other foodstuffs. This has not been the case for much of history, and is still not the case in Polizzi. Perhaps the intense flavors and vibrant colors of these homemade liqueurs can provide us modern city-dwellers with an old-fashioned agrarian sense of well-being.

Liqueur-making became popular throughout Europe during the Middle Ages. Monks concocted the earliest ones, ostensibly as tonics. As toasters of good health throughout the millennium can attest, the effects can be much more spirituous than medicinal.

The process of making liqueur is straightforward. It involves the soaking of the flavoring substance in pure neutral spirits, and the balancing of flavor and alcoholic content with sugar and water.

When sitting down to sample these homemade liqueurs, perhaps you will raise a small glass to the magical city of Polizzi Generosa and to the Polizzani.

# Master Recipe for Making Liqueurs

**Ingredients:** Only the ripest fruits, at the height of their season, should be used. It is best to use organic, homegrown, or wild fruit because systemic pesticides could impact the flavor of the liqueur. Be sure the fruits have not been waxed. (This is often the case even with organically grown citrus fruits and cherries.)

Use spring water to avoid the unpleasant taste of chlorine or fluoride, which is often found in municipal water supplies.

Only sugar that is packaged under the brand names of major producers should be used. This will indicate that the sugar has not been repackaged, thereby ensuring its purity.

The syrup is made with 2 parts sugar to 3 parts water. It is less sweet than simple syrup. Also, the water and sugar are not boiled together, as this would cause the liqueur to turn cloudy.

Alcohol is by nature a dehydrant. This means it will draw out the water content and the water-soluble flavor and color from anything soaked in it. However, alcohol does not emulsify fat, and these substances remain in the nut, fruit, or peel.

In order to properly macerate the flavoring, high-grade pure neutral spirits, rated at 190 proof (95% by volume), are required. Everclear is a common national brand of corn spirits. (The company does make alcohol at a lower proof, but it is not suitable for this purpose.)

Unfortunately, pure neutral spirits are not legal in all states. Although state alcoholic beverage control laws change constantly, at this time the product is not sold in California, New York, Florida, and parts of Illinois and Nevada. *Do not experiment with alcohols not intended for human consumption, which could cause serious, or even fatal, illness.*

Pure neutral spirits are extremely flammable. Store it tightly closed in a cool place. Never pour it while smoking or near an open flame. When discarding anything that has come in contact with this alcohol, rinse it thoroughly to avoid placing a fire hazard in the trash.

Never drink or even taste pure neutral spirits. Aside from being extremely unpleasant, it can cause illness. Taste the liqueur for strength and sweetness only after it has been diluted with the recommended minimum amount of syrup.

*These beverages are alcoholic in content. Sensible consumption is advised.*

**Determining alcoholic strength:** In this country, "proof" is the term used to designate alcoholic content. It is equal to exactly twice the percentage of alcohol. For example, 86-proof whiskey is 43% alcohol by volume.

The most accurate method for determining proof or alcohol percentage is by chemical analysis. Obviously this is impractical for someone who is making a few bottles of liqueur at home. An alternative is to use the following mathematical equation:

$$\text{volume of alcohol} \times \text{its proof} \div \text{total volume} = \text{proof of liqueur}$$

For example, if the alcohol is 190 proof and the recipe calls for 5 cups, first multiply 190 times 5, which equals 950. If 7.5 cups of syrup are added, the total volume will be 12.5 cups. Divide 950 by 12.5, which equals 76, meaning that the liqueur is 76 proof or 38% alcohol by volume.

**Essential equipment:** Most of the equipment needed to make liqueurs is readily available:

Canning jars, 2 quarts and larger, are the best containers for macerating.

Glass or stainless steel are the only materials acceptable for funnels and bowls. The strength of the alcohol will discolor or melt plastic, and the alcohol will take on the flavor of reactive metals.

A "gold" type coffee filter that has never been used to make coffee is excellent for filtering. Bear in mind that it is difficult to remove the coffee flavor from one that has been used for that purpose. Natural (unbleached) paper coffee filters or a glass dropper is needed to blot or remove residue.

Wine bottles, new or recycled, are the best containers for bottling the finished liqueur. Clear ones are better than green or brown ones for showing off the colors.

New corks and a basic, inexpensive corker will be needed to stop the bottles. These items are available at wine- and beer-making shops. Labels can also be purchased at these shops, but homemade ones, hand-written on good-quality paper in India ink, add an old-fashioned touch. White glue is needed to attach the labels.

**Method:** The preparation method for most liqueurs is basically the same. All of the recipes that follow this one may be multiplied or divided in exact proportion.

After the flavoring has been cleaned and cut according to the individual recipe, proceed as follows:

1. Place the flavoring in an appropriately sized canning jar.
2. Pour in the alcohol.
3. Close the lid so the jar is airtight, and macerate for the time indicated in the recipe.
4. The day before maceration is complete, prepare the syrup: Place the water in a covered saucepan and heat it to boiling. Remove the pan from the heat, remove the cover, and let the water cool for 2 minutes. Stir in the sugar, letting it fall in a slow, constant stream. Return the pan to very, very low heat and stir just until the sugar has dissolved and the liquid has turned clear. Transfer the syrup to a clean jar to cool.
5. The day maceration is completed, sterilize the bottles: Place them in a sink and fill them with boiling water. After a few minutes, drain the bottles and let them cool. (Because the alcohol content is a great deal higher than in wine, the rigorous sterilization process required for that purpose is not necessary.)
6. Filter the alcohol through a clean "gold" type coffee filter into a clean jar or bowl.
7. Measure, and add the minimum prescribed amount of syrup. Taste the liqueur. If more syrup is needed, add it ¼ cup or less at a time, mixing it in well and taking a small taste after each addition. Keep an accurate account of the total volume to determine proof.
8. Bottle the liqueur. Let the air bubbles escape before corking. If any cloudy fruit or nut residue has risen to the top, blot it with a corner of a paper coffee filter or remove it with a glass dropper.

9. Prepare the corks by boiling them in water for 5 minutes. Cork the bottles.

10. Write out the labels. When the ink has dried, glue them to the bottles with white glue. Place a sheet of scrap paper on a smooth work surface, and roll the labeled bottle on it to make sure the label is well sealed.

Limuncinu

# Lemon Liqueur

The Italian name for this liqueur is *limoncello*. Lately it has become quite fashionable and is found in fine restaurants throughout Italy. *Limuncinu* is best served cold from the freezer, which heightens the intense lemon flavor. Freezing also gives its green-yellow color an exquisite opalescence.

The zest only from yellow and green lemons is used for this liqueur. It is essential that the fruit not be waxed. Use homegrown or organic lemons (sometimes these, too, are waxed). To test, scrape the skin with the back stroke of a knife. If a white, waxy substance appears on the blade, the fruit has been waxed.

*For approximately 5½ bottles, 750 ml each*

12  unwaxed bright yellow lemons
3   unwaxed green (unripe) lemons
2   bottles (1.5 liters) 190-proof alcohol
11  cups spring water
7⅓ cups sugar

Wash and dry the lemons. Using a zester or a very sharp paring knife, peel off the thin layer of colored zest. Leave behind the white pith beneath (it would cause the liqueur to become cloudy and interfere with the lemon flavor).

Proceed with Master Recipe steps 1 through 10 (pages 249–50), macerating for 4 days. The minimum amount of syrup to be added in step 7 is 11½ cups to produce a liqueur at about 68 proof (34% by volume).

Freeze overnight before serving. Return the bottle to the freezer for storage.

# Fraguledda

## *Strawberry Liqueur*

It is better to use wild or garden strawberries for this liqueur rather than commercially produced ones. If store-bought ones are used, choose strawberries that are small, very red and ripe, and as tart in flavor as possible.

*For approximately 5 bottles, 750 ml each*

4   pounds organically grown strawberries, without blemish
2   bottles (1½ liters) 190-proof alcohol
7½ cups spring water
5   cups sugar

Wash and hull the strawberries. Proceed with Master Recipe steps 1 through 10 (pages 249–50), macerating for 16 days.

Add all of the syrup to produce liqueur at about 74 proof (36.5% by volume).

Rasoliu 'i Girasi

## *Cherry Liqueur*

The best cherries to use for this liqueur are the small, hard, bitter ones found on backyard trees. Commercially produced cherries can also be used, provided that they have not been waxed.

The Sicilian word for liqueur, *rasoliu,* comes from the name of a once-popular rose-petal liqueur.

*For approximately 3½ bottles, 750 ml each*

2½ pounds cherries, unwaxed and without blemish
4¼ cups (1 liter) 190-proof alcohol
5  cups spring water
3⅓ cups sugar

Wash the cherries, and pit them with the aid of a cherry pitter. Proceed with Master Recipe steps 1 through 10 (page pages 249–50), macerating for 16 days.

Add all of the syrup to produce liqueur at about 73 proof (36.5% by volume).

Rasoliu 'i Cieusi

# Mulberry Liqueur

Mulberries are not commercially produced in this country. If, however, you have a mulberry tree in your garden, try this liqueur. It has a flavor that is not to be missed.

There are three varieties of mulberry trees: *Morus rubra*, bearing a dark purple fruit; *Morus nigra*, bearing an almost black fruit; and *Morus alba*, bearing an almost white fruit. The leaves of *Morus alba* are used as food for silkworms.

In Polizzi, white or black mulberries are used for making this liqueur.

*For approximately 3 bottles, 750 ml each*

2   pounds white or black mulberries
4¼ cups (1 liter) 190-proof alcohol
4¾ cups spring water
3   cups sugar

Wash the mulberries. Proceed with Master Recipe steps 1 through 10 (pages 249–50), macerating for 16 days.

Add all the syrup to produce liqueur at about 78 proof (39% by volume).

# Finucchiedda

## *Wild Fennel Liqueur*

Wild fennel is a fernlike plant with bright green leaves that resemble dill weed, but with an aroma and flavor reminiscent of licorice. It is classified as a Zone 4 plant. In the warmer regions of this country, fennel grows wild in back-yards, in vacant lots, on hillsides—just about anywhere there is a patch of earth. It is extremely tenacious. Its season is usually from February to July. Wild fennel grows like a weed in and around Polizzi.

For this liqueur, the fennel is picked in late July, when the plant has begun to go to seed but the stalks still have leaves, flowers, and seeds. If you are certain what this plant looks like, forage it.

This refreshing liqueur is served cold from the freezer.

*For approximately 2½ bottles, 750 ml each*

2   stalks wild fennel, about 6 feet each, with leaves, flowers, and seeds
4¼ cups (1 liter) 190-proof alcohol
4¾ cups spring water
3   cups sugar

Wash the fennel and shake off the excess water. Cut it into 6-inch lengths.

Proceed with Master Recipe steps 1 through 10 (pages 249–50), macerating for 3 days.

The minimum amount of syrup to be added in step 7 is 3⅔ cups to produce liqueur at about 100 proof (50% alcohol by volume).

Freeze overnight before serving. Return the bottle to the freezer for storage.

## Nucina Virda

# *Green-Walnut Liqueur*

In early summer, walnuts on the tree have a green skin and resemble limes. Beneath the skin is a whitish pith, and at the center is the still-soft walnut shell, surrounding the nut itself. By late summer, when the walnuts are ready for harvest, this green skin and the pith beneath have begun to dry. After harvest, the outer casing is removed and the nuts are left to dry for a couple of months before being brought to market.

Green walnuts are inedible, but their rich perfume makes an excellent flavor for a liqueur. The long maceration period first causes the alcohol to absorb this perfume and the deep green-black color. Then it dries the nut, adding the familiar walnut flavor.

Unfortunately, green walnuts are not commercially available. However, they can be procured by arrangement with walnut growers at farmers' markets or by investigating sources through the growers' associations in your area. Only the common variety, called English walnuts, should be used. Do not use black walnuts. The walnuts should be picked at the exact moment they reach full size and are still soft. In Polizzi, this date is June 24, the feast day of St. John the Baptist. In an area with a longer winter, the date could be a bit later.

**Please note:** Green walnut stains are extremely difficult to remove from skin, clothing, or wooden surfaces. When cutting green walnuts, wear gloves and cover the cutting board first with plastic and then with many layers of paper. An alternative method would be to cut the nuts on thick cardboard or on a piece of wood that can then be discarded.

*For approximately 2½ bottles, 750 ml each*

30  green English walnuts
4¼ cups (1 liter) 190-proof alcohol
2½ cups sugar
1    bottle (750 ml) Sicilian or Italian white wine
1    cinnamon stick, 2½ inches long

Wearing gloves, wash and dry the walnuts. Working on a covered cutting board, cut the walnuts in half with a large sharp knife. This sometimes requires a bit of force, so for safety's sake be sure to keep your free hand on top of the knife, not under the blade, near the nut, or anywhere on the cutting board.

Put the halved nuts, together with all the other ingredients, in an appropriate-sized canning jar. Secure the lid and macerate for 2 months. Proceed with Master Recipe steps 5 and 6, and 8 to 10 (pages 249 and 250). This liqueur is about 92 proof (46% alcohol by volume).

## *Walnut Liqueur*

This liqueur is made from regular English walnuts. The addition of cinnamon gives this strong drink a somewhat spicy flavor.

*For approximately 2½ bottles, 750 ml each*

1   pound shelled raw English walnuts, in halves and pieces
2   cinnamon sticks, each 2½ inches long
4¼ cups (1 liter) 190-proof alcohol
1   bottle (750 ml) Sicilian or Italian white wine
2   cups sugar

Using the walnuts and cinnamon sticks, proceed with Master Recipe steps 1 to 3 (pages 249–50). Macerate for 15 days.

When the maceration is complete, filter the liquid into a larger jar using the method described in step 6. Add the white wine and sugar. Secure the lid. Turn the jar from time to time over the next 24 hours to dissolve the sugar.

Do not jostle the bottle for about a week, until the frothy residue stops rising to the top. Skim off this residue and proceed with steps 5 and 6, and 8 through 10.

This liqueur is about 92 proof (46% alcohol by volume).

# Rasoliu 'i Nuciddi

## Hazelnut Liqueur

Polizzi Generosa is known throughout the region for its magnificent hazelnut groves. Each August there is a Hazelnut Harvest Festival, *'a Sagra 'i Nuciddi*. For several days, the city's piazzas are filled with music, dancing, and open-air theatrical productions. The grand event of the festival is a parade led by the beautiful girls of Polizzi in traditional costume. They prance through the streets carrying baskets of hazelnuts, which they toss before them to the admiration of the crowd.

Hazelnut liqueur is most certainly a Polizzani specialty. A unique part of the process is its two-month maceration with unshelled nuts. This gives the liqueur a mellow flavor, as if it had been aged in wood.

*For approximately 2½ bottles, 750 ml each*

1 pound shelled raw whole hazelnuts (filberts), plus 30 nuts in their shells
4¼ cups (1 liter) 190-proof alcohol
2 cups sugar
1 bottle (750 ml) Sicilian or Italian white wine
½ vanilla bean

Preheat the oven to 400°F, with a rack positioned in the center.

Toast the shelled hazelnuts on a sheetpan in the oven for about 10 minutes. Take care that they do not burn. Wrap the nuts in a dishcloth, let them steam for a couple of minutes, and then rub them together to remove as much of the brown skin as possible.

When they have cooled to room temperature, put the nuts in a jar and proceed with Master Recipe steps 1 to 3 (page 249). Macerate for 15 days.

When the maceration is complete, filter the liquid into a larger jar, using the method described in step 6.

Wash the unshelled hazelnuts and place them in the jar. Add the sugar, white wine, and vanilla bean. Secure the lid. Turn the jar from time to time over the next 24 hours to dissolve the sugar. Without jostling the jar any further, macerate for 2 months.

When this time has elapsed, skim the residue off the top of the liqueur and proceed with steps 5 and 6, and 8 through 10.

This liqueur is approximately 92 proof (46% alcohol by volume).

## Rasoliu 'i Cafè

## *Coffee Liqueur*

Polizzani are dedicated coffee drinkers—they prefer their espresso short, thick, and sweet. This coffee liqueur embodies these qualities. The addition of cream floated on top turns the drink into dessert.

*For approximately 2½ bottles, 750 ml each*

3   cups (10 ounces) ground espresso coffee beans, regular or decaf
2   cups plus 2 tablespoons 190-proof alcohol
6   cups spring water
1½ cups sugar
    Heavy cream, to float on top

Place all the ingredients except the cream in an appropriate-sized canning jar. Secure the lid and macerate for 6 days.

Then proceed with Master Recipe steps 5 and 6, and 8 through 10 (pages 249 and 250). When filtering, be sure to use a filter normally used for brewing coffee, so as not to taint the one used for other liqueur flavors.

Serve in cordial glasses, with a small layer of heavy cream floated on top.

This liqueur is approximately 42 proof (21% by volume).

# Rasoliu 'i Canedda

## *Cinnamon Liqueur*

Ceylon cinnamon (*Cinnamomum zeylanicum*) and its cousin cassia (*Cinnamomum cassia*) are well documented as being the oldest spices in use, primary to the original motive behind world trade. It is quite logical that this spice would be used in Polizzi to flavor a strong and spicy liqueur.

Since a quantity of cinnamon sticks are needed for this recipe, investigate Middle Eastern or East Indian markets for better prices on cinnamon sticks in bulk.

*For about 2½ bottles, 750 ml each*

9   ounces cinnamon sticks
4¼ cups (1 liter) 190-proof alcohol
4¾ cups spring water
3   cups sugar
    Pinch of ground cinnamon for each bottle

Break the cinnamon sticks, and proceed with Master Recipe steps 1 through 8 (page 249). Macerate for 30 days.

The minimum amount of syrup to be added in step 7 is 3⅔ cups to produce a liqueur at about 100 proof (50% alcohol by volume).

Put a pinch of ground cinnamon in each bottle, and proceed with steps 9 and 10.

Turn the bottle upside down a couple of times, to distribute the ground cinnamon, before serving.

# Metric Equivalents

## Liquid and Dry Measure Equivalents

| CUSTOMARY | METRIC |
|---|---|
| ¹/₄ teaspoon | 1.25 milliliters |
| ¹/₂ teaspoon | 2.5 milliliters |
| 1 teaspoon | 5 milliliters |
| 1 tablespoon | 15 milliliters |
| 1 fluid ounce | 30 milliliters |
| ¹/₄ cup | 60 milliliters |
| ¹/₃ cup | 80 milliliters |
| ¹/₂ cup | 120 milliliters |
| 1 cup | 240 milliliters |
| 1 pint (2 *cups*) | 480 milliliters |
| 1 quart (4 *cups, 32 ounces*) | 960 milliliters (.96 *liter*) |
| 1 gallon (4 *quarts*) | 3.84 liters |
| 1 ounce (*by weight*) | 28.35 grams |
| ¹/₄ pound (4 *ounces*) | 114 grams |
| 1 pound (16 *ounces*) | 454 grams |
| 2.2 pounds | 1 kilogram (1,000 *grams*) |

# The Recipes by Category

## SECOND COURSES (*SECUNNI PIATTI*)

## ONE-COURSE MEALS (*PASTI COMPLETI*)

**Agata and Valentina,** 1505 First Avenue, New York, NY 10021. Tel. 212-452-0690. *A large Italian market with fresh local and imported Sicilian cheeses, produce, meats, and sausages.*

**Alleva Dairy,** 188 Grand Street, New York, NY 10013. Tel. 212-226-7990. *Artisanal ricotta and mozzarella, fine imported Sicilian cheeses.*

**Caseificio Gioia,** 9469 Slauson Avenue, Pico Rivera, CA 90660. Tel. 562-942-2663. *Artisanal ricotta, mozzarella, and other fresh cheeses.*

**Domingo's Italian Grocery,** 17548 Ventura Boulevard, Encino, CA 91316. Tel. 818-981-4466. *Durum wheat flour and fine imported products.*

**Giovanni D'Angelo,** via Garibaldi, 114, 90028 Polizzi Generosa (PA), Italia, Tel. 011-39-0921-649-173. The Website is accessible through www.polizzigenerosa.it. *Artisanal majolica pottery, decorated with traditional Polizzani patterns.*

**Iavarone Brothers,** 75-12 Metropolitan Avenue, Middle Village, NY 11379. Tel. 718-326-0510. *Fine imported Sicilian products; meats and sausages.*

**More Than Gourmet,** 115 W. Bartges Street, Akron, OH 44311. Tel. 800-860-9385. *Concentrated demi-glace and other sauce bases and stocks.*

**Sur La Table,** for catalog and store locations, tel. 800-243-0852.

Web: www.surlatable.com. *Quality cookware, cutlery, and tabletop items.*

**Thyme Garden,** 20546 Alsea Highway, Alsea, OR 97324. Tel. 541-487-8671. Web: www. thymegarden.com. *For fennel and other garden seeds.*

**White Lily Mills,** 218 E Depot Street, Knoxville, TN 37917. Tel. 800-264-5459. Web: www.whitelily. com. *Fine winter wheat, cake flour (marketed as "all purpose").*

# Traveling to Polizzi Generosa

**Visit Polizzi Generosa
online at
www.polizzigenerosa.it.
or
www.comune.polizzi.pa.it**

### How to Get There

**From Palermo:** Ask at the airport or at your hotel for directions to the *autostrada*. Initially the A-19 (Palermo–Catania) and the A-20 (Palermo–Messina) run together. Just past Termini Imerese, the A-19 splits off going south. Take it to the Scillato exit. Turn onto State Road (SS) 643. Follow it about 18 km to Polizzi.

There is also a comfortable bus that makes several round-trips daily. The schedule changes seasonally. Inquire at the airport or at your hotel for specific details.

**From Catania:** Autostrada A-19 (Catania–Palermo) is easily accessible from the airport. (It is not necessary to traverse the city, as it is from Palermo.) Take it to the Tre Monzelli exit. Following the signs to Polizzi, turn on to SS 120 and drive about 10 km, then on to SS 643; it's about 4 km to Polizzi.

Travel time from Palermo is 1¼ hours for the experienced Sicilian driver. The trip from Catania takes a bit longer. For a driver less experienced in the rules of the Sicilian road, I strongly recommend traveling (especially for the Palermo trek from airport to *autostrada*) between 1:00 p.m. and 2:30 p.m. Most of the population is home eating lunch at that time.

## WHERE TO STAY

There are a number of inns in the countryside that offer full or partial board. The town also offers places to stay. Currently the rates are between €20 and €50 (about $20 to $50) a night per person, including a simple breakfast. Country houses are also available. A partial list follows.

**Agriturismo Santa Venera,** 3 via Gagliardo. Tel. +39-0921-649-546. A new full-service hotel in the countryside, complete with swimming pool.

**Donna Giovanna,** Contrada da Donna Giovanna. Tel. + 39-0921-649-184. The owners are Franca and Franco D'Anna. Franca speaks English.

**Giardino Donna Lavia,** Contrada da Donna Lavia. Tel. +39-0921-551-037. Luigi, the manager, and his wife both speak English.

**La Sorgento di Iside,** Contrada da Chiaretta. Tel. +39-0921-688-277.

**The Gianfisco Family Country House.** For tourists who wish to have a true Sicilian mountain experience, the Gianfisco family country house may be rented. Usually only lodging is provided, but as Nino told me, "If someone came all the way from America, maybe we could have a dinner." For further information, e-mail Nino Gianfisco (he speaks some English) at gianfisco@tiscalinet.it or telephone him at +39-0921-688-128.

**Paese Albergo Facile,** Via D. Pagano 5. Tel. +39-0921-688-061. Run by Francesco Ficile. Two adjoining rooms with one bath are for rent.

**Paese Albergo Itria,** Via Itria 17. Tel. +39-0921-649-130. This small hotel in town has two rooms with bath for rent.

**Ai Templari,** Piazza Castello 3. Tel. +39-0921-649-478, fax +39-0921-551-009. This exquisite in-town hotel is situated in the garden of the Palazzo Notarbartolo. It is owned and operated by Doctor Cannata and his wife, Maria Angela Marramaldo.

**Villa Cariddi,** mentioned in Chapter One, is closed.

For further information about places to stay, including other country houses and short-term leases on houses in town, contact the Polizzani Tourist Office at +39-0921-649-691.

Bear in mind when phoning any of these places that the time there is six to nine hours ahead of the United States.

## WHERE TO EAT

All of the country inns have restaurants, great for lunch or dinner. Most authentic is Donna Giovanna, but all are good. The fare is determined by the seasons and what the chef chooses to prepare. There are no printed menus, but in any case it is always best to leave oneself at the "mercy" of the chef.

In town there are many good restaurants. A partial list follows.

**Orto dei Cappuccini,** Via dei Cappuccini. Tel. +39-0921-688-535. Santo Lipani's exquisite restaurant in a fourteenth-century monastic kitchen garden.

**U Bagghiu,** Via Gagliardo 3. Tel. +39-0921-649-546. This excellent restaurant is located in several large rooms that once were the stables of a grand palazzo.

**Il Poiniere Pizzeria,** Largo Zingari 1. Tel. +39-0921-649-872. The best pizzeria in town.

**Ristorante Onorato,** SS 120. Tel. +39-0921-649-370. Old-style eatery in which the menu changes daily.

**Pasticceria Onorato,** via G. Borgese. Excellent sandwiches on home-made *focaccia*.

**Ristorante Itria,** via B. Gnoffi 8. Tel. +39-0921-688-790. Great for traditional dishes and pizza.

Walking around Polizzi Generosa will reveal a number of pastry shops and cafés. My favorites are **Pasticceria al Castello,** Pino's pastry shop; **Bar Cristallo,** Gasparinu and Alfredo's place, for cocktails and for gelato-and-brioche sandwiches. Some of the other great pastry shops and coffee bars are

**Pasticceria Illarda,** via Garibaldi

**Pasticceria l'Orlando,** via Rampolla

**Pasticceria Tumasella,** piazza Gramsci

**Pasticceria Vinci,** via Garibaldi

## SIGHTSEEING

One of the many great works of art to be seen in Polizzi is a Flemish triptych of Madonna and Child that hangs in the Chiesa Madre. Several years ago, local photographer Luciano Schimmenti began the monumental task of photographing it. In August 2001, a comprehensive, beautiful book on the subject was published.

While in the process of shooting the hundreds of photos needed for the book, Luciano deduced from the painting's layout and style that it was surely painted by Rogier van der Weyden (c. 1399–1464), a renowned Flemish master. Great debate ensued at the highest levels of the fine arts community over this theory, until Luciano found the signature. On September 14, 2002, the Italian post office issued a stamp commemorating this important discovery.

For further information on churches, palazzi, and works of art, stop into the Tourist Office or the library. Both are located in the City Hall, Via Garibaldi 13.

For excursions into the Parco della Madonie, contact the main office, Corso Paolo Agliata 16, 90027 Petrolia Sottana (PA), Italia. Tel. +39-0921-680-201, fax +39-0921-680-478.

For excursions on horseback, contact the Equestrian Center *(Centri di Equitazione)* of Polizzi Generosa. Tel. +39-330-831-441.

For skiing information, contact the Italian Alpine Club of Polizzi Generosa. Tel. +39-0921-649-087.

*When making hotel reservations or while visiting Polizzi, please make a point of sending my best regards to all.*

# Acknowledgments

I extend my most profound thanks to Santo Lipani for his wonderful illustrations, which truly capture the essence of Polizzani life; for his friendship, and for sharing with me his vast knowledge of food and culture.

My sincerest thanks to my friend and literary agent, Martha Casselman, who truly has my voice in her head, and with just one, well-placed question mark in a manuscript's margin can lead me back to it.

Many heartfelt thanks to my editor, Sydny Miner, who has moved mountains in championing this work.

A very special thank-you to Greg Gorman, for having once again created an extraordinary author portrait.

To Mayor Giuseppe Lo Verde for making me see his special vision of Polizzi, and to the city council for their faith and support, I extend my deepest thanks.

To Flo Braker, Carol Field, Nick Malgieri, Russ Parsons, Ruth Reichl,

Don Silvers, Faith Willinger, and all my other colleagues on this side of the Atlantic who offered me their good counsel, I offer my grateful appreciation.

To the other Polizzani who generously shared their kitchen secrets with me, especially to Nino's mother, Stefana Russo Alesi; to Pino Agliata, who gives me correct recipes; to Franco D'Anna, for his refined rustic cuisine; to Ninettu and Tina Lo Verde whose magic is food; to Rosa Di Martino whose food is magic; to Maria Angela Marramaldo and Daniela Sammarco, editors of *Polizzi, Generosa Anche a Tavola*; and to Dr. Alfino Zafarana and the Associazione Culturale Naftolia for having published it.

I thank, with certain sadness at his passing, Mastru Stefanu Gugliuzza, shepherd, for the delicious living history of his work.

Countless thanks to *paisani* who eagerly shared their knowledge of history, culture, and lore, especially to Polizzi's librarian, Graziella Ortolano, and to Professor Celestina Salamone Cristodaro; to Alfredo D'Angelo, Pino David, Sarafinu di Bella, Pietro Di Gangi, Angela D'Ippolito, Enza Dolce, Enzo Ficile, Francesco Ficile, Cecè Galiardotto, Turiddu Gianfisco, Gandolfa Gianfisco, Gasparinu Iovino, Sebastiano Lipuma, Peppe Muzzo, Enzo Polizzotto, Ida Rampolla, Moffu Schmenti, Vincenzo "Cinqui Favi" Termini, my cousins the Vilardo family.

To Nino Gianfisco, whose friendship and generosity of spirit has catalyzed many of the events described in this book, there aren't enough thanks.

I most appreciatively thank the people of Polizzi Generosa for who they are, and for showing me a deeper appreciation of my own cultural roots.

# *Index*

# About the Author

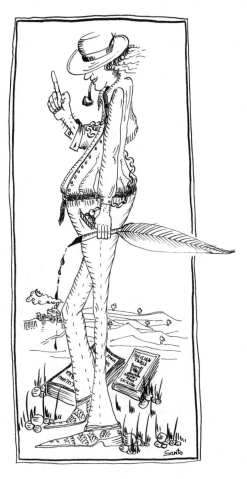

**Vincent Schiavelli** was born and raised in Brooklyn. He has written articles on Sicilian cuisine for many publications, including *Gourmet, Saveur, Arba Sicula, Copia,* and the *Los Angeles Times.* In 2001 a *Los Angeles Times* piece was awarded a prestigious James Beard Foundation Award for Excellence.

In 1999 another of his *Los Angeles Times* pieces, and in 2000 one from *Gourmet,* won first and second prize, respectively, in "A Few Words about Sicily," an international journalism competition held in Catania, Sicily.

*Bruculinu, America,* his critically acclaimed second cookbook, a Julia Child Cookbook Awards Finalist, is now in its third printing. Recently it has been published in Italian by Sellerio editore Palermo. His first cookbook, *Papa Andrea's Sicilian Table,* received a Columbus Citizens Foundation Literary Award.

Vincent has been a guest chef at cooking schools throughout the country and has done cooking demonstrations on many television shows, including *Regis & Kathie Lee* and *Good Morning America*. He was the host of *The Chefs of Cucina Amore* for PBS. He is the coproducer and host of *La Bella Vita*, a new show that explores food, wine, and the good life at the source. The first four episodes were filmed in Polizzi Generosa.

Vincent is a member of the International Association of Culinary Professionals (IACP) and a founding member of the Hollywood Convivium (Chapter) of Slow Food.

In his other career, Vincent Schiavelli is a character actor, having made over one hundred film and television appearances. His credits include *One Flew Over the Cuckoo's Nest, Fast Times at Ridgemont High, Amadeus, Ghost, The People vs. Larry Flynt, Tomorrow Never Dies, Man on the Moon, American Saint,* and *Death to Smoochy.*

Currently Vincent is involved with the founding of Casa d'Andrea, a cooking school and guest house in Polizzi Generosa. He is also writing his first novel.